THE HISTORY

OF

VIRGIL A. STEWART

AND HIS

ADVENTURE

IN CAPTURING AND EXPOSING THE GREAT "WESTERN LAND
PIRATE" AND HIS GANG, IN CONNECTION
WITH THE EVIDENCE;

ALSO OF THE

TRIALS, CONFESSIONS, AND EXECUTION

OF

A NUMBER OF MURRELL'S ASSOCIATES IN THE STATE OF
MISSISSIPPI DURING THE SUMMER OF 1835, AND THE
EXECUTION OF FIVE PROFESSIONAL GAMBLERS
BY THE CITIZENS OF VICKSBURG,
ON THE 6TH JULY, 1835.

COMPILED BY H. R. HOWARD

Introduction To Reprint Edition
By Laura D.S. Sturdivant

THE REPRINT COMPANY, PUBLISHERS
SPARTANBURG, SOUTH CAROLINA
1976

This volume was reproduced from an 1836 edition in the
Mississippi Department of Archives and History.
Jackson, Mississippi.

Reprinted: 1976
The Reprint Company, Publishers
Spartanburg, South Carolina

ISBN 0–87152–216–0
Library of Congress Catalog Card Number: 76–92
Manufactured in the United States of America on long-life paper.

Library of Congress Cataloging in Publication Data

Howard, H   R   comp.
   The history of Virgil A. Stewart and his adventure in capturing and exposing the great "western
land pirate" and his gang with the evidence.

   Reprint of the ed. published by Harper, New York.
   1. Stewart, Virgil Adam, b. 1809. 2. Murrell,
John A. 3. Crime and criminals—Mississippi.
4. Vigilance committees—Mississippi. 5. Mississippi—History. I. Title.
F341.H696   1976   364.1′092′4   [B]   76–92
ISBN 0–87152–216–0

INTRODUCTION

The interest aroused by H. R. Howard's *The History of Virgil A. Stewart, and His Adventure in Capturing and Exposing the Great "Western Land Pirate"* . . . , John A. Murrell; the "trials," confessions, and "executions" of Murrell's alleged associates in 1835; and the "executions" of five professional gamblers by irate citizens of Vicksburg, in that same year, is evidenced by the fact that it went into three printings, 1836, 1839, and 1842.

A difference in time, circumstance, and feeling from that of the present day is reflected in this book. It is evident that in a southern state like Mississippi with a large slave population in 1835 there was an inherent fear of a slave insurrection. The slave insurrection in Haiti in 1790 and the consequent murders of planters and their families had taken place within the memory of men still living. The mass hysteria generated by the discovery of the plans of John A. Murrell's "Mystic Clan" for a slave insurrection gives proof of this fear. Howard (p. 233) quotes from the "Proceedings at Livingston":

. . . The county is settled principally in large plantations, and on many of them there is no white man but an overseer, most of the large planters being absent at the north; and on a number only the families of the absent—being at least 50 negroes to one white man in the neighbourhood

of Livingston and Beatie's Bluff, where the scene
of desolation was to commence. . . . The only prospect before them was certain destruction, should
they fail to arrest the progress of the impending
danger. Intense excitement was pervading the
whole community at this time, and was increasing
every hour. . . .

The "Committee of Safety of Livingston," then a
flourishing hamlet in Madison County, Mississippi,
was formed by a number of white citizens ". . . chosen
by the unanimous consent of their fellow-citizens, assembled on the occasion, and invested by them (however unclothed with the forms of law) with the fearful
power of life and death . . ." (p. 222).

The "Proceedings at Livingston" of this committee
and that of the "Committee at Beatie's Bluff" follow
"Stewart's Life and Adventures," printed by Howard
as reported by the members of the committees themselves.

The last portion of the book, "Gamblers at Vicksburg," gives the "proceedings of the citizens of Vicksburg, in hanging five professional gamblers, on the 6th
day of July, 1835. . . ." Recognition of the prevailing
hysteria sweeping the countryside is acknowledged by
the following statement (p. 263): "It will be seen that
the difficulty with the gamblers at that place was unconnected with the insurrection, except the high state
of excitement that pervaded the whole southern country at that time, which had led the citizens to deal more
rigorously with all offenders. . . ."

There were, however, Mississippi citizens who de-
plored the departure from due process of law and the
consequent "executions" by citizens' committees with
the self-invested power of life and death. Governor

Hiram G. Runnels received a letter from Pat Sharkey
and James B. Kilborn, dated Fleetwood, Hindes [*sic*]
Co. Miss. 7th July 1835, asking that "... energetic measures be immediately taken to put a Stop to this terable
State of things. If a Proclamation were to issue commanding all illegal tribunals to desolve—and to deliver up all their prisoners to the civil authoritys—all
unlawful bands—under the name of Regulators to dis-
purce ... we fully believe it would be efficient...."

On the next day, George Wyche, who also wrote
from Fleetwood to Governor Runnels concerning the
situation, asked for a proclamation "... exhorting to
peace & moderation, & submission to the Civil Power,"
and stated that "... danger from the slaves vanished
at the detection of the Conspiracy & another danger
has taken place more formidable than that." He ended
his letter by asking that "... if this course is adopted
that messengers be dispatched to circulate the proclamation."

On 13 July 1835, Governor Runnels did issue a
proclamation in which he took note of the reports of
"... villainous Whitemen traversing the Country en-
deavoring to get up an insurrection among our Slaves
...." He continued:

... I do therefore issue this proclamation exhorting all good Citizens and commanding the officers
both Civil and Military to use the most untiring
vigilance to suppress all such insurrectionary
movements and to apprehend all suspicious persons and deliver them over to the proper authorities that they may be brought to ... punishment—
To which end I especially call on the members of
the boards of police of each County and district
to exert the authority given them by an act of the

Legislature . . . of organising in their respective
beats active and efficient patrolls. . . .

In this proclamation Governor Runnels also promised
that, if necessary, he would order the Quarter Master
General of the state and his Assistant Quarter Masters
General to issue arms to the people for their defence.

The documents cited above, with original spelling
retained, and others of interest to the situation are
preserved in the Official Archives, Governors' Records,
Record Group 27, Box 21, Mississippi Department of
Archives and History, Jackson. It should be noted that
the governor's proclamation was issued too late to
provide a legal trial for those "tried" and "executed"
by the Committee of Safety at Livingston and at
Beatie's (Beattie's) Bluff.

Virgil A. Stewart's own account of his adventures,
which was published with the assistance of Augustus
Q. Walton in Cincinnati, Ohio, in February, 1835, was
distributed throughout the lower Mississippi Valley
by Stewart himself (Howard, pp. 203–204) and was reprinted in 183? and in 1840. After the attempted
"smear" campaign conducted by Matthew Clanton
and other Murrell associates of the "Mystic Clan,"
Stewart collected additional certificates from reputable
citizens attesting to his integrity and truthfulness which
were printed in Howard's "history."

The Mississippi Library Association and the pub-
lisher of this reprint, Thomas E. Smith of The Reprint
Company of Spartanburg, South Carolina, are to be
commended for their project to reprint a selection of
rare, out-of-print Mississippiana, in which *The History
of Virgil A. Stewart* . . . compiled by H. R. Howard is
included. The assistance of the Mississippi Department
of Archives and History and especially that of Elbert

(vii)

Hilliard, Director, and Caroline Allen, Librarian, is acknowledged with appreciation.

                              LAURA D. S. STURDIVANT
Jackson, Mississippi
December 1975

THE HISTORY

OF

VIRGIL A. STEWART,

AND HIS

ADVENTURE

IN CAPTURING AND EXPOSING THE GREAT "WESTERN LAND
PIRATE" AND HIS GANG, IN CONNEXION
WITH THE EVIDENCE;

ALSO OF THE

TRIALS, CONFESSIONS, AND EXECUTION

OF

A NUMBER OF MURRELL'S ASSOCIATES IN THE STATE OF
MISSISSIPPI DURING THE SUMMER OF 1835, AND THE
EXECUTION OF FIVE PROFESSIONAL GAMBLERS
BY THE CITIZENS OF VICKSBURG,
ON THE 6TH JULY, 1835.

" I am not willing to admit to the *world* that I believe him."—*A bitter enemy.*
" I care nothing for his jealous animosity. He may vent his poisonous spleen. I am sustained
before the *world* by evidence that shall chain his envenomed tongue."—*Stewart.*

COMPILED BY H. R. HOWARD.

NEW-YORK:

HARPER & BROTHERS, CLIFF-ST.

1836.

PREFACE.

THE public have long been expecting the final history of Virgil A. Stewart's perilous and romantic adventure in capturing " John A. Murrell," the great " Western Land Pirate." We now propose giving a full and perfect account of that strange performance, in connexion with the evidence sustaining each important fact as it is related. We make no pretensions to author-craft, or skill in working up materials so as to heighten interest; nor is it necessary. The deep interest that every Southerner and every honest man must feel in the subject matter of this history, is sufficient to invest a plain and simple statement of facts with attraction. Our only care has been to adhere strictly to the truth, and to exhibit the details in a clear and intelligible narrative.

We have commenced with a brief account of Mr. Stewart's early life to the time when he undertook the capture of Murrell and his party. We then continue with his adventure on that expedition, and conclude with a full history of the insurrectionary movements among the negroes in the southern country during the summer of 1835. In

1*

the perusal of this narrative the reader will be made acquainted with many scenes of horror and depravity.

When the " Western Land Pirate" was in course of publication, Mr. Stewart's health was such that he could pay but little attention to the task of supervision, which rendered it very imperfect in many respects, and especially in the omission of some important portions of his conversation with Murrell, and of his reasons for many proceedings that should have been explained to the reader :—but as the only object of that narrative was to arouse the people of that region to a sense of their danger, past and present, he deemed it unnecessary to delay the publication.

As an apology for the detention of this work, we would remind the public that Mr. Stewart has been compelled to travel over a vast country in collecting his evidence for the compilation. In conclusion, we would congratulate those of Mr. Stewart's friends who have nobly stood by him in the hour of danger and persecution, amid a legion of exasperated enemies. He has ably sustained himself and his cause, and proved himself worthy of the confidence reposed in him by his fellow-citizens.

In the compilation of this work the most of Murrell's profanity has been suppressed; but retaining his manner of expression in every other particular, and in all cases the substance of his conversation has been preserved.

LIFE AND ADVENTURES

OF

VIRGIL A. STEWART.

A BRIEF history of the early life of Mr. Virgil A. Stewart, whose adventures will form the subject of the following pages, may not here be out of place, not only as a gratification of public curiosity, but as an important commentary upon the facts to be disclosed in the succeeding narrative; since, in substantiating the character of Mr. Stewart as a worthy and reputable citizen, the reader will be the better enabled to reject the unfounded and malicious imputations attempted to be cast upon him by some of the more daring emissaries of the Murrell gang.

Mr. Stewart was born in Jackson county, in the State of Georgia, of highly respectable parentage. His father, Mr. Samuel Stewart, migrated to Amite county, in Mississippi, while Virgil was yet an infant, and died there a few months after his arrival. His widow, becoming dissatisfied with that part of the country, returned to the State of Georgia, where her son Virgil grew up to manhood. He was sent to school until he was fourteen years of age; but little attention was paid to his pecuniary interests, and a large portion of his slender patrimony was squandered.

His early desire was to receive a liberal education; but the income of his father's estate would not allow of the expenses attendant upon a classical course.

Soon after he left school he engaged in the printing business, as an employment best suited to improve his mind. Relinquishing this, he afterward entered into a copartnership with a manufacturer of cotton-gins, in his native place, with whom he employed his time and a small capital to great advantage.

By the time he had reached his twentieth year, he had established a character for industry, decision of character, and much moral worth, among his fellow-citizens. About this time his term of partnership expired by its own limitation, and he determined to travel, and seek a place to settle upon amid the newer regions of the western country.

He concluded upon migrating to Madison county, in Tennessee, whither he removed with his property in the fall of 1830, and settled upon a farm, with his negroes, six miles west of Jackson. Here he remained until the latter part of the year 1832, closely attending to his farm and business, when he concluded to sell off his property, remove to the Choctaw Purchase, and invest his whole property in land in that country.

Mr. Stewart had now, by industry and economy, increased the little estate left him by his father to a respectable competency for a young man just starting in life ; with this he made his arrangements for visiting the Choctaw Purchase, and furnished himself with such articles of merchandise as he expected to sell with profit to the Indians and early settlers of that region.

On the first day of June, 1833, Mr. Stewart left Jackson in high spirits, on board a boat bound for Tuscahoma, in the Choctaw Purchase, and arrived at

Odom's landing, on the Yallabusha river, twelve miles below Tuscahoma, on the third day of July, where the boat was forced to land for want of water.

He had a house prepared for the reception of his goods about one mile above the town of Tuscahoma; but, soon after his arrival, sold off his stock on credit, and began examining the country so as to be prepared to enter land as soon as opportunity should offer, in which labours he was engaged until the Chocchuma land-sales in the same fall.

The period of Mr. Stewart's life at which we have now arrived is a point where it becomes necessary to examine with the strictest scrutiny every act, no matter how trivial—and not only is it necessary to notice his acts, but to scan with severity his motives for acting. No matter how trifling the circumstances here recorded, they will be found important in the progress of the narrative.

While he was attending the land-sales at Chocchuma, and awaiting the settlement of his late affairs, a Mr. Clanton, who had established a little country store in the neighbourhood, and with whom he had formerly been slightly acquainted in Tennessee, requested him to take the agency of his business until he could go to Tennessee for his family and return, alleging, as a reason for his request, " that he had been selling goods on credit, and that many of his customers would take advantage of his absence, and leave the country without paying their arrearages, as the greater part of them were strangers of doubtful character."

At this time Mr. Stewart was very much occupied with his own affairs; but, ever ready to accommodate a

A 3

friend, even at his individual inconvenience, he consented to take charge of Mr. Clanton's books and business during his absence.

Mr. Clanton then urged him to sleep at his storehouse at night, which would not interfere with his
business, as he could ride to the land-office at Chocchuma and back very easily in the day; to this Mr.
Stewart consented, provided it would not hinder too
much his own affairs.

The small quantity of goods and liquors left by Mr.
Clanton in possession of Mr. Stewart, amounted to
about two hundred and fifty or three hundred dollars.
These articles he requested Mr. Stewart to dispose of
in any way that might offer, as he expected to be much
in want of money on his return. During the six
weeks that Mr. Stewart had charge of Mr. Clanton's
affairs, he disposed of more than one hundred dollars
worth of this property—and as he received the pay for
a pint of whiskey or a handkerchief, he deposited the
money in the drawer of Mr. Clanton's store.

In this small way he took in about ninety dollars,
while at the store mornings and evenings, which was
never entered upon any book, as there was no cash-
book used in the establishment. What few goods he
sold for credit were charged upon a day-book as delivered, and upon this book he opened but one new account, which was against himself for goods delivered
to Mr. Elijah Smith, a gentleman who lived near the
storehouse, and from whom Mr. Stewart had purchased
corn for his horse while at the store, which was generally every night. The two accounts stood open ; as
Stewart required corn, he got it from Smith; and as

Smith wanted any thing that he could find among Clanton's remnants, he procured it from Stewart, the latter accounting for it by a charge against himself on Mr. Clanton's books. He also took some things for his own use, amounting to five or six dollars, which he paid for and deposited the money in the drawer, with the proceeds of the other cash sales.

In the month of January, 1834, Mr. Clanton returned from Tennessee with his family. Upon again receiving his affairs from the hands of Mr. Stewart, he expressed the highest satisfaction at the manner in which the latter had taken charge of his business, and as a token of his gratitude presented him with a lot of land in a little town-site that he had laid off for a village where his storehouse stood.

He was extremely anxious to form a copartnership with Mr. Stewart; but the latter, wishing to invest all his capital in land, declined the proposition, but accepted the lot, and promised to build upon it as soon as he should return from a visit to Tennessee, so as to induce others to settle upon the same site; and he in turn, while absent, left his property in charge of Mr. Clanton.

Previous to his departure, Clanton requested that he would have his goods removed to the house of Mr. William Vess, as he had not the room to spare in his own, observing, at the same time, that Vess was a very clever fellow, but that he (Clanton) would see to his property himself. Accordingly, Mr. Stewart had his property removed; and leaving all his affairs in the charge of Mr. Clanton, he set out upon his journey on the 18th of January, 1834. On the 21st of the same month he reached Madison county, in Tennessee, where lived his old friend and neighbour the Reverend John Henning. Soon after his arrival he called on Mr. H., who informed him that he and his son Richard had lost, on the night of the 18th of January, two negro men; and remarked, that recent developments had attached suspicion upon one John A. Murrell, a man of doubtful and suspicious character, who resided in the neighbourhood. He stated, also, that he had learned from one of Murrell's near neighbours (whom he had desired to watch his movements), that he would leave Madison county on the 25th for Randolph, a town on the Mississippi river; and suggested that, if he had stolen the negroes, his object probably was to proceed to the place of their concealment.

Mr. H. solicited Mr. Stewart, who, as the reader has already been told, was on terms of friendship and intimacy with him and his family, to accompany his son Richard in pursuit of Murrell, hoping thereby to obtain some intelligence of the negroes, as it was probable that so soon as the excitement occasioned by their abduction, and the suspicion resting upon Murrell, had in a measure subsided, he would take some measures to remove them from the country. Mr. Stewart consented, and promised to make every exertion in his power to ferret out the thief and reclaim their property.

Although Mr. Stewart had lived within five miles of Murrell's house a part of the time while he was resident in Tennessee, he had never made his acquaintance, nor had he seen him but once: he was then pointed out to him, but at a distance too remote to enable him to obtain any definite knowledge of his features. Besides, considerable time had since elapsed, so as to leave him no hope of being able to recognise him should he be so fortunate as to overtake him. He was therefore obliged to rely on the description given of him by Mr. Henning.

Mr. Henning proposed to remunerate him for his services and loss of time; but, fired with indignation against the perpetrator of such villany, Stewart refused any recompense, and professed to desire nothing beyond the gratification of being instrumental in overtaking and bringing the offender to justice. With feelings such as these, and a desire to serve an old and valued friend, he took leave of Mr. H., and proceeded to the house of a Dr. Evans, with the promise to meet Mr. H.'s son at Denmark (a small country village about four miles distant) at as early an hour on the following morning as their convenience might permit.

As much that is set forth in the "Western Land Pirate" has been questioned, we deem it due, both to Mr. S. and the public, to accompany each material statement with a certificate of undoubted authority. As such, we offer the following certificate:—

"*State of Tennessee, Madison County.*

"I do hereby certify, to all whom it may concern, that all Virgil A. Stewart has said in the 'Western Land Pirate,' so far as it relates to me and my request, is strictly correct.

"Mr. Stewart pursued John A. Murrell by my request; and I further certify that said Stewart lived in my immediate neighbourhood two years; and that there was

2

no young man who conducted himself more honour-
ably, or who deserves the confidence of the public more
than Mr. Stewart.

"Given under my hand and seal, this 10th day of Oc
tober, 1835.

[Sealed.]   "JOHN HENNING."

On the morning of January 26th, 1834, Mr. S. was
at Denmark, according to appointment; but young
Henning failed to make his appearance. He remained several hours awaiting the young man's arrival, till
at length, becoming impatient, he concluded to prosecute his journey alone, supposing that his intended
companion had been taken ill, as he had left him somewhat indisposed when they parted on the preceding
evening.

He accordingly left Denmark about ten o'clock,
A. M., and proceeded on his way to the turnpike at
Estanaula, over the Hatchee river, about seven miles
distant (this being the only crossing-place in the win-
ter season), where he expected to obtain intelligence
of Murrell.

The weather was unusually cold, and the hard-fro-
zen road, much cut up by recent travelling and covered with sleet, considerably retarded his progress.
When he reached the toll-house at Estanaula, he
inquired of the keeper if Murrell had gone by, and
whether his gates might be passed during the night
without his knowledge? While he was yet conversing with him, the keeper turned himself about, and observed, "Yonder comes Murrell, now!" Upon looking in the direction indicated, Mr. Stewart saw him;
but he was too near to admit of farther conversation

with the keeper. Murrell rode quickly up, paid his toll, and proceeded on his way; when Stewart renewed his conversation with the keeper, and asked if he was satisfied that the individual who had passed was Murrell. The keeper assured him that he was, and added that he knew him well. Upon this Mr. Stewart paid his toll and proceeded after him. He followed close upon him for a short time, with a view to learn, if possible, to what place he was travelling, without giving Murrell any occasion to suspect his intentions. At length it occurred to him, that, by falling into his company, he might obtain a better idea of his plans and business. He accordingly rode up, and accosted him very respectfully, which was returned with equal civility and address, but with a look of inquiry and scrutiny that savoured somewhat of embarrassment.

The following dialogue ensued :—

Stewart. " We have disagreeable travelling, sir."

Murrell. " Extremely so, sir."

S. " The travelling and my business correspond very well."

M. " Pray, sir, what can be your business that you should compare it to travelling on such a road as this ?"

S. " Horse-hunting, sir."

M. " Yes, yes, disagreeable indeed : your comparison is not a bad one. Where did your horse stray from ?"

S. " From Yallabusha river, in the Choctaw Purchase."

M. " Where is he aiming for ?"

S. " I do not know ; I am told that he was owned by

a man in this country somewhere ; but it is an uncertain business—a cross-and-pile chance."

(Mr. S. had been requested by a friend in the Purchase, when he was leaving that country for Tennessee, to inquire for a horse that had strayed, and made the description then given him serve his present purpose.)

M. " How far down will you go ?"

S. " I do not know. The roads are so very bad, and the weather so extremely cold, I am becoming very tired of so uncertain a business ; and I am quite lonesome travelling by myself. How far down will you go on this road ?"

M. " About eighteen miles, to the house of a friend. I am anxious to get there to-night, but it will be very late travelling in such cold weather. Perhaps your horse is stolen."

S. " No, I guess not ; though I had much rather some clever fellow had stolen him than that he should be straying." (Mr. Stewart here observed a very perceptible change in the countenance of his companion, which showed him evidently pleased with the last remark.)

M. " Are you acquainted in this part of the country ?"

S. " I am a stranger, sir."

M. " Where are you from ?"

S. " I was born in the State of Georgia, and brought up there, but have moved to the Choctaw Purchase, and have been there about nine or ten months."

M. " How do you like that country ?"

S. " Very well indeed, sir."

M. " Is there much stealing going on in that country ?"

S. " No, not much, considering we are pretty much savages and forerunners. You know how all new countries are generally first settled."

M. " Certainly; I am well acquainted with these things."

Murrell's conversation and manner now became gradually more free and open, and he appeared to scrutinize less closely the countenance and demeanour of his companion. He had feared that he was in company with one who knew his character, which occasioned the cautious reserve that appears in the preceding dialogue. But, upon learning that Mr. S. was from Georgia, and had resided in the Choctaw nation but nine or ten months, he felt assured that he could know but little, if any thing, respecting his past doings. Hence the change in his manner. Nothing was now wanting with Mr. Stewart to ensure his success but the art of dissembling well—to demean himself so as to elude suspicion; in this (as will afterward appear) he succeeded, even beyond his own expectations. Remembering that Murrell had expressed an intention of visiting a friend, he at once determined to accompany him, though at the expense of travelling late at night, and in very cold weather: for, on many accounts, he was inclined to suspect that Mr. Henning's negroes were there awaiting the arrival of Murrell.

They continued their journey, indulging an almost unreserved interchange of sentiment and opinion on various subjects—Mr. Stewart all the while engaged in

2*

studying the disposition and character of his companion. The conversation once more turned on the subject of stealing, which appeared to be Murrell's favourite theme, on which he dwelt with peculiar
interest and satisfaction, as will be seen in the following dialogue :—

Murrell. " This country is about to be completely
overrun by a company of rogues ; they are so strong
that nothing can be done with them. They steal from
whom they please ; and, if the person they take from
accuses them, they jump on more of his property ;
and it is found that the best plan is to be friendly with
them. There are two young men who moved down
from middle Tennessee to Madison county, keen,
shrewd fellows. The eldest brother is one of the
best judges of law in the United States. He directs
the operations of the banditti ; and he so paves the
way to all his offences that the law cannot reach
him."

Stewart. " Well, sir, if they have sense enough to
evade the laws of their country, which are made by the
wisest men of the nation, let them do it. It is just as
honourable for them to gain property by their superior
powers, as it is for a long-faced hypocrite to take the
advantage of the necessities of his fellow-beings. We
are placed here, and we must act for ourselves, or we
feel the chilling blast of charity's cold region. What is
it that constitutes character, popularity, and power, in
the United States ? Sir, it is property ; strip a man of
his property in this country, and he is a ruined man indeed—you see his friends forsake him ; and he may
have been raised in the highest circles of society, yet

he is neglected and treated with contempt. Sir, my doctrine is, let the hardest fend off."

M. " You have expressed my sentiments and feelings better than I could myself ; and I am happy to fall in with company possessed of principles so congenial with my own. I have no doubt these two brothers are as honourable among their associates and clan as any men on earth, but perfect devils to their enemies : they are undaunted spirits, and can never be found when they are not armed like men of war. The citizens of Madison once attempted to arrest the elder brother for having three of a certain Mr. Long's negroes in his possession ; and they carried nearly a whole captain's company for a guard ; and if they had not taken a cowardly advantage of him, he would have backed them all—though he cared nothing for the charge. He knew they could not hurt him ; but they took him prisoner, and carried him before an old fool of a squire, who neither knew nor cared for the law or his duty, and would have committed him against positive proof; and there is no doubt Long perjured himself in endeavouring to convict him. The people thought he was good for the penitentiary, but he laughed at them, and told them they were all fools ; that it was only a finable offence, to make the worst of it. He had plenty of friends to bail him. On the day of the trial, the house was thronged to hear it. He had employed the most eminent lawyer at the bar, Andrew L. Martin ; and, during the trial, he took his lawyer aside and cursed him, and told him he paid him his money to work for him, and that he could not get him to work the way he

wanted him. He showed Martin the law, and got
him in the way; and he gave them trouble. He is
a flowery fellow, but he has not dived into the quirks
of the law, like his client. They mulcted him with
a fine and the costs of suit; and, in case his property would not make the amount, he was to become
Long's slave for five years. When the verdict was
read, he winked at Long and called him Master Billy.
He took an appeal to the Supreme Court, and there is
no doubt of his getting rid of the whole scrape at the
May term, in spite of all the prejudice that is against
him. But the matter has been attended with bad
consequences : one of his strongest friends has suffered in consequence of suspicion of being his friend.
He was the deputy sheriff, and as fine a fellow as
ever lived. After they found that they could do nothing with him at law, they formed a company, which
they called Captain Slick's company, and advertised
for all honest men to meet at a certain school-house
in the neighbourhood on a certain day. They met
and bound themselves in certain matters ; made rules
and laws for the government of the company; and in
this company he had some strong friends, who would
inform him of their movements in the shortest time.
He got several guns, and made an immense quantity
of cartridges, and prepared his house and buildings
with port-holes, ready for an engagement. On the day
they published that they would be there to slick him,
he had eighteen friends who came to his assistance.
He disposed of them in different buildings, so as to
command a fair fire to rake the door of his dwelling;
but they got a hint that it would be a dangerous under-

taking, and gave it up as a bad job: and a fine thing
for them; for if they had gone, he would have been
apt to cut them all off, situated as he was—and the
law would have protected him in the course he intended to pursue.

" But all who have had any thing to do with it have
got sick of it, and are trying to make fair weather with
him. Not that they love him, but because they dread
him as they do the very devil himself—and well they
may, for he has sworn vengeance against them, and
he will execute it. He is a fellow of such smooth and
genteel manners, that he is very imposing : and many
of the more credulous part of the community are induced to believe that he is persecuted by Long, when
he only intended friendship and kindness in catching
his negroes for him. He well knows how to excite
the sympathy of the human heart, and turn things to
his advantage. He rarely fails to captivate the feelings of those whom he undertakes ; and, what is more
astonishing, he has succeeded in many instances
where the strongest prejudice has existed ; and, where
his revenge has been excited, he never fails to effect
either the destruction of their property or character,
and frequently both. He has often been compelled
to remove prejudices of the strongest kind, for the
purpose of getting a man into his power whom he
wished to destroy. In a matter of this kind he has
never-tiring perseverance ; and many have become
wise when it was too late, and sunk under the influence of his great managing powers.

" There is an old Methodist preacher and his son,
who had two very fine negro men stolen a short

time back; and this old Parson Henning and his son were officious in procuring counsel, and expressing their sentiments about him and his brother, and saying what the country ought to do with them, and all such stuff as this: and I have no doubt but those two young men have got them. They live within about two miles of the old preacher, and he and his son are as much afraid of those two young men as if they were two ravenous beasts that were turned loose in the forest: if they were sure of finding their negroes by following them off, they would sooner lose their property than fall into the hands of those dreaded men.

"In fact, they have managed with such skill that they have become a complete terror to the country; and, when property is missing in that country, and there is any suspicion that those two young men are concerned with it, all is given up as lost, and it is considered time and money spent in vain to follow them."

S. "These two young men must possess talents and acquirements of the first order, or they could never sustain themselves in a community where there are such strong prejudices against them. And that elder brother of whom you speak must be endowed with some supernatural power, or an extraordinary capacity and practical experience; for to overcome the prejudices of a stubborn nature is considered the hardest change to effect in the human mind. I would warrant them to be devoted friends and noble spirits in the sphere in which they move, and this old preacher you speak of is no more, even if he is what he pretends to be,—and that, you know, we can doubt as we please, or rather as it best suits our convenience. He was their enemy, and treated them as such, when they had not been hostile to him, and they are his enemies now, for cause ;—and if they are what my imagination has made them, he will have cause to repent in sackcloth and ashes for his sins. But, sir, to my doctrine ; let the hardest fend off. They are enemies, and let them lock horns. Of what age is that wondrous man you speak of ?"

M. " He is about thirty, I suppose, and his brother just grown up, and as smart a fellow as the elder brother, but not half the experience. I will tell you of one of his routs on a speculation a few months past, and you can judge for yourself whether he is possessed of talents or not. There was a negro man by the name of Sam, that had been sold out of the neighbourhood of those two young men to a man by the name of Eason, near Florence, Alabama. The elder brother was passing that way on one of his scouts, and happening to see Sam, inquired of him how he liked his new home and master ? ' Bad enough,' said Sam. ' Well,' said he, ' Sam, you know me ; and you know how to leave the rascal ; run away and get back to your old range, and all things are safe.' It was not long before Sam was at his house. He harboured him until Eason advertised him as a runaway, and offered a reward for him ; that was what he wanted to see. He procured a copy of the advertisement, and put it and the negro into the hands of his brother and a fellow by the name of Forsyth, and told them to push and make hay while the sun shone : they were gone about seven weeks, and his brother returned with about fourteen hundred dollars in cash, seven hundred dollars worth of ready-made clothing, and a draught on Thomas Hudnold, of Madison county, State of Mississippi, for seven hundred dollars, which is as good as gold-dust, though he has to sue for the draught; but the recovery is sure—for they can never get the negro, and without him they can never prove that he was Eason's negro, and he will recover the amount of the draught in spite of them. Hudnold became suspicious that they got the negro again, and wrote to the house on which the draught was drawn to protest it. They did not act in that matter as the elder brother, the old fox, would have done : though, for young hands, they made a fine drag. They did not go immediately on and draw the cash, as one of them should have done; but delayed, trying to make more sales, and delayed too long before the draught was presented. That is twenty-eight hundred dollars he sold Eason's negro for, and now has the negro in Texas in the hands of a friend : they did not make the disposition of Sam which they generally do with negroes on such occasions; he is too fine a fellow : and I think they will make more money on him when things get a little still. Sam is keen and artful, and is up to any thing that was ever wrapped in that much negro hide. If Eason had got on his track and caught him, he could not have done any thing with him."

S. "I cannot see how he would have evaded the law in that instance."

M. "It is a plain case, sir, when the law is examined by a man who understands it. In the first place, the negro had run away, and had escaped from Eason's possession; and, in the second place, Eason had offered a reward for his negro to any man who would catch him. This advertisement amounts to the same, in virtue, as a power of attorney, to take his property, and act for him to a certain extent ; so you see the advertisement is a commission to take the property into possession ; now, if the holder of the property chooses to make a breach of the trust which the advertisement confides in him, and, instead of carrying the negro to the owner, converts him to his own use—this is not stealing, and the owner can only have redress in a civil action for the amount of his property : and as for a civil action, they care nothing for that, for they will not keep property. Their funds are deposited in a bank that belongs to their clan. This is the way his ingenuity perplexes them. He has sifted the criminal laws until they are no more in his hands than an old almanack, and he dreads them no more. But what is it that he cannot do with as many friends as he has, who are willing to be subject to him and his views in all things ? there lies his power : his great talent in governing his clan. He is universally beloved by his followers."

S. "Such a man as that, placed in a situation to make a display of his talents, would soon render the name and remembrance of an Alexander or a Jackson little and inconsiderable when compared with his own ; he is great from the force of his own mental powers, and they are great from their station in the world, in which fortune more than abilities has placed them."

Here, for the first time, Mr. Stewart observed his encomiums on the character of this marvellous elder brother reach the modesty of Murrell. Hitherto they

had produced no other perceptible effect than to stim-
ulate his vanity—a quality with which nature seems
liberally to have endowed him.   But when he heard
himself held in flattering comparison with characters
so distinguished, he could not suppress an involuntary
blush that momentarily mantled his countenance.

Mr. Stewart had now both discovered Murrell's accessible point, and how far it might be taken advantage
of—a very important step, indeed, towards the accomplishment of his purpose.

We copy below Thomas Hudnold's certificate regarding the deception practised upon him in the purchase
of Mr. Eason's negro alluded to above :—

"*State of Mississippi, Madison County.*

" I do hereby certify to all whom it may concern, that
that part of the narrative entitled ' The Western Land-Pirate,' which gives an account of a negro man who was
stolen from William Eason, of Alabama, and sold to me
in this county, and restolen from me within a few nights
thereafter, and whom I have never heard of since, is
strictly correct.

" Given under my hand and seal this 3d day of August, 1835.

[Sealed.]   " THOMAS HUDNOLD."

Mr. Stewart and his companion had now reached the
valley of Poplar Creek.   It was growing late in the
afternoon—the sun was just sinking behind the hills
of the west—unseen by them, except as its ruddy light
was reflected from the icy tops of the beautiful growth
of poplars that imbowered their pathway.   " This
is a beautiful scene," said Murrell, " and continues
through the valley, which, when we have passed, a

good road will conduct us on to the house of my
old friend." While they were yet in the valley, and
admiring the growth of young poplars that seemed
to wave in triumphant pride and power over a region that had been once desolated by some hurricane
of past years, the twilight of evening closed over
them.

To Mr. Stewart, all that he had heard and seen seemed now to take the air of mystery—he could scarce realize that he had been travelling with, and listening to,
the conversation of a human being like himself; and
that what had passed was not all a dream. Imagination
had wellnigh led him to fancy himself directed by a
superhuman power, and that some dread fatality hung
over his destiny. All the goblin-tales of his childhood
crowded upon his recollection, and filled him with emotions of doubt, uncertainty, apprehension. A thousand
images of terror flitted before his bewildered imagination. The house of Murrell's friend might be the
place where would be acted the tragic scene of his
immolation and robbery—and that friend might be a
co-actor. These, and many other ideas equally fearful (which can better be imagined than described),
crossed the mind of Mr. Stewart as he and his mysterious companion still pursued their journey under the
thickening shadows of approaching night. Meanwhile
they had left the valley some hundred yards behind
them, and, seeing an old log burning by the roadside,
Murrell proposed to Mr. Stewart to make a halt and
warm themselves; he consented, and they dismounted
from their horses. Mr. Stewart began now to be
awakened to the reality of his situation by the numb-

ness which enchained his limbs—he found some difficulty in walking from his horse to the fire. In a short
time he was considerably relieved. Mr. Stewart began now to revolve more fully in his mind the chances
of meeting Mr. Henning's negroes at the house of Murrell's friend—their recognition of him, and the consequent hazard of his life : reflections by no means en-
couraging. Still he determined to risk the adventure,
stimulated as he was by the almost desperate hope of
being able in such an event to reclaim the negroes and
capture the rogue.

" You appear very cold, my young friend," said
Murrell to his companion, as they were seated by
the fire ; " I fear you are frosted ; you can't stand it
like me—I have undergone enough to kill a horse.
We will remain where we are till the fair queen of
night favours us with her silver beams, which will
light us to a more hospitable lodging. Did you ever
travel much by moonlight ?"

Stewart. " Not much, sir."

Murrell. " Then you have not the same love for her
silver beams as an old veteran in mysteries. I would
suppose that you are too young to be of much experience in the practical part, though you are well skilled
in the theory ; but you will find many difficulties to
surmount in the execution of plans which you have
never thought of; you will learn to suffer privations
of all kinds to the greatest extent. These privations
and difficulties, when surmounted, are what constitute
the glory of an old veteran and prominent actor."

Murrell and his companion spent some half hour at
the old log, indulging the most free and unrestricted

interchange of sentiment and opinion. Their conversation turned chiefly on the same gloomy topics of robbery and murder. Upon these Murrell appeared to dwell with peculiar and fiendish delight ; and would exhibit an air of triumphant pride whenever an opportunity was offered to introduce and enlarge upon some exploit of successful villany.

At length the rising moon, as her placid light was beautifully reflected from the sleety tops of the neighbouring trees, broke in upon their conversation by reminding them that it was time to travel. They mounted their horses and set forward on their unfinished journey. Mr. Stewart now remembered that he had but one pistol, which occasioned him momentary uneasiness. He saw himself (single-armed) unequal to a contest he knew awaited him should Murrell prove faithless in the midst of his friends. Still, nerved by the consideration of the justness of his cause, and assured by the almost hopeless pledge of a villain's honour, he found means once more to suppress his rising fears. Besides, he reflected, that to retreat at a stage in his adventure when danger appeared for the first time seriously to threaten, would savour too much of cowardice ; more particularly as his past good management had given him so much the advantage over his antagonist.

They rode briskly on, with every appearance of good-humour and renovated spirits. Mr. Stewart managing all the while to keep somewhat in rear of his companion, determined to give him no possible advantage : for he believed

"A man may smile and murder while he smiles."

3*

" Come, sir," said Murrell, " ride up; the night is cold, and we have far to go ;—let us pass the time as pleasantly as possible :—come up, and I will tell you of another feat of this elder brother of whom I have been speaking."

Stewart. " Yes, sir, with all my heart, if it is as good as the last."

Murrell. " He is a likely fellow, tall, and well proportioned, and dresses rather in the Methodist order; and when he is off on his scouts, directing his men how to proceed (for he never carries off property himself, he always has men for that purpose), he frequently makes appointments, and preaches. He is well versed in the Scriptures, and preaches some splendid sermons. He has frequently preached at a place, and before he commenced pointed out some fine horse for his friend to steal ; and while he was preaching and praying for them, his friend would save the horse for him. He always gives his residence some other course than the correct direction. In one of those jaunts he called at the house of one Nobs, a Methodist, on Elk river, in Middle Tennessee. Nobs had heard him preach a year before that in the neighbourhood, and was much taken with him as a preacher. He had given his residence in South Alabama, and had spoken a great deal of his negroes and farm ; and of the perplexity he had in getting an overseer that would do his duty, and not abuse his slaves, and all such stuff as this, and Brother Nobs drank it all down. Supper came on, and he got them all around the table on their feet; he raised his hands in the most solemn manner, as though he was just going to open the win-

dows of heaven, and select its richest blessings for
Brother Nobs, his wife, and latest posterity. He was
lengthy in his supplications at the table; but when
he came to use the books, and go to duty, he was
eloquent. The same service was rendered the next
morning.

" When about to start, he wanted to pay Brother
Nobs; but Brother Nobs was almost hurt to think
that he would suppose he would charge him. ' Well,
Brother Nobs, will you be so good as to give me
change for a twenty-dollar bill ? I am out of change,
and I dislike to offer a bill of that size to be changed
where I stay all night, for the world will say he is a
preacher, and does not like to pay for staying all night
at a tavern—see, he has presented a twenty-dollar bill
to be changed. This is the way of the world—and I
hope God, in his mercies, will enable me to live in
such a manner as never to dishonour the cause of the
Gospel, or degrade the ministry.'

" Brother Nobs, anxious to render the preacher, and,
as he thought, a very rich man, a favour, answered
him—' Yes, brother, with pleasure.' He ran to his
wife and got the keys, took out the purse, and counted
out seventeen dollars and fifty cents, when his change
gave out. Brother Nobs was in a peck of misery.
' Stay a little; I will run over to Brother Parker's and
borrow the balance.'—' Do, if you please, and I will
stay with Sister Nobs until you return.' Brother Nobs
was not long gone, when he returned with as much
pride of being able to accommodate his preacher as
an East India merchant would show at the arrival of a
rich cargo of goods. The preacher's bill is changed,
and all is right.

"*Preacher.* "Well, Brother Nobs, you have a fine young jack—did you raise him ?'

"*Brother Nobs.* 'He was foaled mine, and I have raised him.'

"*Preacher.* 'Will you trade him, Brother Nobs ?'

"*Brother Nobs.* 'I have raised him for that purpose ; but I cannot get the worth of him in this country ; I have never been offered more than one hundred and fifty dollars for him, and he is worth two hundred and fifty.'

"*Preacher.* 'Yes, Brother Nobs, he is cheap at that price ; and, if I had the money with me, I would rid you of any farther trouble with him.'

"*Brother Nobs.* 'Well, brother, you can take him. You say that you will be at our camp-meeting.   Bring me the money then—that is as soon as I will need it.'

"*Preacher.* 'Well, Brother Nobs, I will take him— I need him very much ; I want him for my own mares ; I am a domestic fellow ; I raise my own mules for my farm.'

" The trade being completed, the preacher got ready to start ; all the family gathered around him to receive his parting blessing.

"*Preacher.* 'Brother Nobs, may the Lord bless you, and save you in heaven ; farewell.   Sister Nobs, may the grace of our Lord and Saviour Jesus Christ rest and remain upon you ; farewell.   May the Lord bless your little children : farewell, my dear babies.'

" The preacher was soon gone from Brother Nobs ; but not to South Alabama, but to the western district of Tennessee.   That day and night put the preacher a long way off, as slow as his jack travelled ; though he was an uncommon fine travelling jack. The preacher sold his jack for four hundred dollars, and passed a twenty-dollar counterfeit bill on Brother Nobs. Poor Brother Nobs can never hear of his rich young preacher since; but I have no doubt he is on a voyage of soul-saving, and will visit Brother Nobs when he returns."

S. "It would be a source of the highest pleasure to me to see and become acquainted with this wondrous man; my fancy has made him a princely fellow. Perhaps I have been too extravagant in my conceptions; but I know he must be a great man, and possessed of unrivalled mental powers."

M. "That is his character, sir."

S. "I do not wonder at his being a terror to his enemies, neither am I astonished that he should be beloved by his clan. Such a leader should be beloved and adored by his party; for talents and capability should be honoured wherever found; I must confess that what I have heard of this man, alone, of itself, has excited my admiration; but perhaps it is because we are congenial spirits."

M. "Well, sir, we are within three miles of my old friend's; ride up, and we will soon be there. Will you go as far down as Randolph? your horse may have got down in that region."

S. "It is likely that I will, sir; and, if I were not rather scarce of change, I would continue my journey over into Arkansas, as cold as it is, as long as I am so near to it. I have heard much of that country, and I think the land and people would suit my designs

B 3

and inclinations very much. The land east of the
Mississippi is nearly all entered, and is very dear."

The reader will perceive that Mr. Stewart's main
object in shaping his conversation as he did, was to
acquaint himself, if possible, with the disposition and
character of Murrell; and to learn his destination and
plans. He pretended a scarcity of funds, to anticipate
an attempt at robbing him, as he had a considerable
amount of money with him, and had no sufficient assurance that Murrell was not setting a trap for him.
He calculated also to obtain, indirectly, some clew to
Mr. Henning's negroes; for he foresaw, if the negroes
were at Murrell's old friend's, his journey would probably end at that place, and he might prepare himself
for the event. If not, he expected to be apprized of it,
by Murrell's intention to continue his journey. Hence
the great caution that marked his inquiries—his
seeming as though he cared not to observe. The occasion was a critical one, and required skilful management; in this Mr. S. appears not to have been
wanting.

Murrell. " I would be very glad if you would go over
into Arkansas with me. I am going over, and I will let
you have money if you get out; and I will show you
the country as long as you wish to stay. I have thousands of friends over there—it will not cost us a
cent, if we stay six months; and I will carry you
where you can bring away a better horse than the one
you are hunting. I will learn you a few tricks if you
will go with me. A man with as keen an eye as yours
should never spend his time hunting for a horse."

Stewart. " Sir, I am much obliged to you for your

compliment, and much more obliged to you for the kind proposition you have made—I will determine to-morrow whether I will go or not; but I think I will go. I have no doubt I should learn many things under so able a teacher as I expect you are; and I should be happy to accompany you."

M. " Here is my old friend's—I am glad to see his cabin once more. Come, alight, every thing is still—we will go into the house."

The midnight visiters knocked for admittance; the old man of the house had not retired, but, like the hour, was silent as death. A moment, and the door was opened; they walked in, and were received with much attention and respect. Mr. Stewart's eyes glanced hastily round the apartment. He might, perchance, catch a glimpse of the old parson's negroes. They were not there. He felt much jaded, and in want of rest; and, after sitting a short time before the fire, he called for lodgings, and left Murrell and his friend engaged in conversation. Mr. Stewart went to bed, but not to sleep—reflections on what had passed—his present unenviable situation—and the possible detection of his hitherto successful simulation by meeting the negroes in the morning, hung like an incubus over his wakeful and bewildered imagination. It was near morning before his wearied nature, overcome with exhaustion, sank to repose.

Thus ends the story of Mr. Stewart's first day's pilgrimage with the great " Western I and Pirate."

CHAPTER II.

Mr. Stewart rose at a very early hour the morning
of the 27th, and took advantage of the first dawn of
light to stroll over the premises in search of Mr. Henning's negroes ; intending, in the event of finding them,
to apprize them of his purpose, and instruct them not
to recognise him in presence of Murrell. Upon satis-
fying himself that they were not there, he returned to
the house, where he found Murrell prepared to ride,
and giving directions for their horses ; and by the time
Aurora had emerged from her " chamber of light" in
the east—while lingering twilight yet mantled the
prospect, they were on their horses and away. Mr.
Stewart had been careful to make particular inquiry,
meanwhile, for his stray horse in Murrell's presence—
deeming such a course important to preserve consistency. They proceeded on their journey in the direction of Wesley, a small village in the county of Hay-
wood, and State of Tennessee, distant about six miles
from their late landlord's. Conversation was renewed
with their journey. They had not ridden far when
Murrell inquired, for the first time, the name of his
companion, in the following language :—

Murrell. " Well, my young friend, I believe I have
not yet been so inquisitive as to ask your name, we
have been so engaged in other conversation."

Stewart. " No, sir, we have been quite engaged
since our short acquaintance ; I seldom ever have a
name, though you can call me Adam Hues at present."

Mr. Stewart's reason for concealing his real name will appear obvious to the reader, when it is remembered he and Murrell both resided in the same county while Mr. Stewart lived in Tennessee, and, though never personally acquainted with him, Murrell had, probably, often heard of him.

Murrell. " Well, Mr. Hues, what say you of the trip to Arkansas this morning?"

Hues. " I have not yet fairly determined on that matter; though I think I will go."

M. " Go, yes, you must go, and I will make a man of you."

H. " That is what I want, sir."

M. " There are some of the handsomest girls over there you ever saw. I am in town when I am there."

H. " Nothing to object to, sir; I am quite partial to handsome ladies."

M. " Oh! well, go with me to Arkansas, and I will put you right in town; and they are as plump as ever came over, sir."

H. " I think I will go, sir; I will determine down about Wesley, which your old friend says is five or six miles from this."

M. " We can strike a breeze worth telling over there."

H. " I do not doubt it, sir."

M. " I will tell you a story about another feat of this elder brother. His young brother was living in Tipton county, below here, and he was down to see him—and while he was in the neighbourhood he decoyed off a negro boy from his master, and appointed a place where to meet him; but, instead of going himself, he

4

sent a friend.   His friend conveyed him to the Mississippi river, where there was a skiff to receive them;
his friend conducted the boy to Natchez in the skiff,
and lodged him in the care of a second friend.

"The elder brother took a passage on a steamboat for
Natchez, after he had lurked behind until he could learn
all their movements; after he reached Natchez, he
took his negro and went on another steamboat, dressed like a lord, and had as much the appearance of a
gentleman as any man aboard the boat.   He had taken
a passage to New-Orleans; but misfortunes will hap-
pen every now and then.   There was a fellow aboard
the boat who knew him well; and this rascal went to
the captain, and told him that the negro which this fellow had was stolen; and that the fellow was a notorious negro thief—and that he had better take the
black boy into custody, and carry him back, and that
he would be very apt to find his owner's advertisements as he went back up the country.   The captain,
an old villain, in hopes of getting a reward, and the
services of the negro for some time, concluded to do
so.   The negro was not suffered to see his master, but
he had been drilled to his business before.   So the
fellow waited until the boat reached New-Orleans;
and, while the boat was landing, he made his escape
on to the guards of another boat.   He went in search
of his friends in that part of the country, who were
plenty, and made all his arrangements; and sent a
friend to learn when the captain would leave the port;
so he goes to the mayor of the city, and gets a process
against the body of the captain, for unlawfully detaining his property from his possession.   The guard took

him just as he was preparing to start his boat, and he and the negro were both taken before the mayor. He charged the captain with having detained his property from his possession by violence and force of arms; and produced a bill of sale for the negro, purporting to have been given in Tipton county, State of Tennessee, and brought in a witness (one of his friends), who swore that he was present when the negro was purchased, and saw him delivered to the plaintiff. The mayor asked the captain the cause of his detaining the negro from his master.

" *Captain.* ' Why, why,—I, I was told that this man was a negro thief, sir.'

" *Mayor.* ' Have you any evidence ?'

" *C.* ' Why,—I don't know where the man is who told me. He is gone, sir.'

" *M.* ' What were you going to do with his negro ?'

" *C.* ' Why—I, I was going to keep him, sir.'

" *M.* ' Keep him !'

" *C.* ' Yes, sir, I'd keep him safe.'

" *M.* ' Yes, sir, I will keep you safe a while.

" The negro was delivered to the plaintiff, and the captain nicked with a heavy fine, and imprisoned : and his pretty friend, who knew so much, soon had a nurse that attended him day and night, until he found his way to the bottom of the Mississippi river. This was the way he fixed these two villains for their smartness in matters that did not concern them. He waited until the captain was just ready to start ; and, by his never coming about, the captain thought he had made his escape, and that he was proud to get a chance to run ; so he had no chance to make any defence, and New-Orleans is a minute place.

" He sold his negro in New-Orleans for eight hundred dollars ; and in a few nights he stole him again, and
got a friend to conduct him up the country to a friend's
house in one of the upper parishes. Here he became a
Methodist preacher, and preached for a neighbourhood
of Methodists. He had got two fine geldings near
New-Orleans, and his friend rode one and his negro
the other ; and while he was preaching and praying for
the Methodists, he told them that he had been down to
the lower country to sell his slaves ; that he had become rather conscientious on the subject of slavery,
but that the boy he had with him appeared to be so
much opposed to being sold, that he had concluded to
carry him back home again. The negro was up to this,
and he began to pretend to love one of Higginbotham's
negro women, and he began to beg his Mossa Higginbotham to buy him. Brother Higginbotham purchased
his preacher's negro, and the preacher started home to
Kentucky, an assumed residence. Brother Higginbotham gave him seven hundred dollars for his boy. He
had a friend to convey the boy across the Mississippi
river, near the Arkansas river, where he was to meet
him at the house of another friend. Brother Higginbotham is greatly distressed ; his boy is gone, who was
sold for loving his negro woman ; and his preacher was
gone with his money. He stove about in every direction like a mad bull ; but all was in vain, his negro
was gone. The preacher was prompt to attend at the
house of his appointed friend, where he met his companion with the negro. He sold him the third time on
the Arkansas river, for five hundred dollars ; and then
stole him and delivered him into the hands of his

friend, who conducted him to a swamp, and veiled the tragic scene, and got the last gleanings and sacred pledge of secrecy, as a game of that kind will not do unless it ends in a mystery to all but the fraternity. He sold that negro for two thousand dollars, and then put him for ever out of the reach of all pursuers, and they can never graze him unless they can find the negro, and that they cannot do, for his carcass has fed many a tortoise and catfish before this time ; and the frogs have sung this many a long day to the silent repose of his skeleton ; and his remembrance is recorded in the book of mysteries. Thus ended the history of the Tipton boy, and Brother Higginbotham's parson, who vanished like a spirit to the land of mystics."

H. " Wonderful and strange man ! who can tell the worth of such a noble leader ? he is great and wise in all things !"

M. " That is his character, sir."

The following is Mr. Higginbotham's certificate on that subject :—

" *Clinton, Louisiana, Sept. 12th,* 1835.
" Mr. Virgil A. Stewart :—

" Dear Sir—Your letter of the 25th of August has just come to hand, requesting a statement of the fact of Murrell's selling a negro to Mr. Higginbotham of this parish. I have to answer, in reply, that the statement set forth in ' The Western Land-Pirate' is true with but one exception. Murrell did not call himself a preacher, but left an impression with the people where he stayed that he was a professor of religion. The negro was purchased by Mr. Willis Higginbotham for Mrs. Powers. He stayed with her from Thursday un-

4*

til Saturday, and then left her ruined, and was heard of
no more.

> "Yours respectfully,
> "JOHN B. HIGGINBOTHAM."

"*State of Louisiana, East Feliciana Parish.*

"Personally appeared before the undersigned, justice
of the peace in and for said parish, the Rev. John B.
Higginbotham, who upon oath says that the above
statement is true, and has subscribed to the same this
12th day of September, 1835.

> "L. P. M'CAULEY, J. P."

The conversation between Murrell and Hues continued as follows :—

Murrell. "Well, sir, we are within a half a mile
of Wesley, and we will have a warm when we get
there."

Hues. "Yes, sir, we need it very much ; and we
will have some good brandy and something to eat at
the tavern."

M. "We will get the brandy, but I have lots of provisions in my portmanteau."

Mr. Stewart (whom the reader must hereafter know
by the name of Hues) began to feel, as they approached Wesley, considerable embarrassment lest his acquaintances in that place should recognise him in the
presence of Murrell, and thus subvert all the plans he
had been forming for his detection, and which, till
then, had succeeded much to his wishes ; for his conversation with Murrell, from their first meeting, had
been all of a character to impress him that he (Hues)
was an entire stranger in the country through which

they were travelling. He was much puzzled to know in what manner he should meet the exigency of the occasion—(and they were already in sight of Wesley). It at length occurred to him that his character of horse-hunter might be of use in furnishing an excuse to separate a short time from his companion, by which he could make an opportunity to confer with his acquaintances, and apprize them of his business. Accordingly, as they entered the village, he drew forth a flask, and desired Murrell, he being acquainted, to ride on and have it filled, remarking that he would, meanwhile, stop at the first store, and write some advertisements for his stray horse (having concluded to accompany him to Arkansas), as such a step might be the means of obtaining some account of him by their return. Murrell assented to his proposition—took charge of the flask, and, after desiring him to arrange his business with all possible despatch, rode on to the house which he had pointed out to Hues as the Wesley Inn ; for Hues had thought it necessary to make some inquiry respecting the place, in order to appear the consistent stranger.

This arrangement suited Hues very well ; for two of his acquaintances were at the tavern. He stopped at the first store he came to till he saw Murrell enter the tavern, when he made the best of his way to a grocery kept by a third friend, with a view of putting him on his guard. Upon being told that he was absent from the village, he foresaw but one important difficulty in the way of success (that of being recognised by his friend at the tavern), which, in a very short time, was most happily removed—for he saw

Murrell leave the tavern with his flask in search of liquor. He lost no time in making his way thither, and made known his situation to his friends, and gave them the requisite instructions as to the manner in which they should treat him when in company with Murrell. Colonel Bayliss, one of these friends, put a pistol into his hands for defence, in the event of an attack by Murrell or his clan, should he be fortunate enough to overtake Henning's negroes. In a short time Murrell returned with the flask of liquor, and invited his friend Hues to join him in a glass before resuming their journey ; and in a very few moments they were once more on the road.

Colonel Bayliss' Certificate.

"I have been called upon, by Mr. Virgil A. Stewart, for a statement of the circumstances which took place in the town of Wesley at the time he passed through that place in company with Murrell. Previous to that time I had formed some acquaintance with Stewart, having seen him once or twice. In passing from my dwelling-house to my store, I saw Mr. Stewart standing in the passage of the tavern; he signed to me to come to him, and, following him back in the passage, informed me that he had sought that private mode of speaking to me to prevent Murrell from knowing that he had any acquaintances in that place, for that he passed himself upon him as an entire stranger in the country, and he wished me not to recognise him as an acquaintance in his (Murrell's) presence—that Murrell was an infamous character, and was suspected of having stolen three negroes from Madison county. And that he (Stewart) had followed him for the purpose of ascertaining the fact, and discovering where the negroes were; that he had overtaken Murrell on the road from Estanaula to Wesley, and had passed himself on him under a fictitious character, but he was afraid that Murrell might be playing a deeper game than he was, and taking him over to some place where he could more easily dispose of him. He then inquired of me if I had a pistol, and if I would lend it to him; he said he had one with him, but he wanted to be prepared to defend himself well if he was discovered and attacked; that he knew that he was risking his life, but that he was determined to discover the negroes, if possible. I lent him my pistol, and we parted immediately after. Stewart and Murrell left Wesley together, since which time I had not seen Stewart until he called upon me for this statement. I was abroad from home when they returned, but was informed by the gentleman with whom he left my pistol, and others of the citizens, that they returned together and separated there.

"These are all the circumstances with which I am personally acquainted relative to the matter; and, if they afford any satisfaction to the public, or benefit the cause of right, they are freely made.

"Given under my hand and seal at Memphis, in the State of Tennessee, this 20th day of October, 1835.

[Sealed.] "WILLIAM H. BAYLISS."

The next place to which they directed their course was Randolph. When they had proceeded about a mile from Wesley, Murrell observed,—"Come, Hues, we will ride a little from the road, eat some cold victuals, and talk a little more of the God bless us." Upon which Murrell turned his horse from the road, and Hues followed. When they had gone about fifty yards into the woods, Hues inquired of Murrell his object in leaving the road so far (for he had no idea of giving him any advantage over him). To which he replied—" That old Methodist Henning, knowing me to be a particular friend of these two young men I have been speaking of, I should not be surprised if young Henning was in pursuit of me—and if so, I much prefer his being before to behind me—if he has been fool enough to undertake the adventure. I should know better how to manage him." They had proceeded some hundred yards from the road, when Murrell reined his horse up to a log, dismounted, and made arrangements for their intended repast. He drew also from his pocket the favourite flask, and bade Hues partake with him his coarse preparation—prefacing hospitalities, however, with a pledge from the flask, which now stood full in the midst of their bread and bacon. They had been seated but a short time when was commenced the following dialogue :—

Murrell. " Well, Hues, I think I can put you in better business than trading with the Indians."

Hues. "I have no doubt of that, sir."

M. " Did you ever hear of those devils, Murrells, up in Madison county in this state ?"

H. " I am an entire stranger to them, sir."

M. " I am that elder brother whom I have been telling you of."

H. " Is it possible ! I have the pleasure of standing before the illustrious personage of whom I have heard so many noble feats, and whose dexterity and skill in performance are unrivalled by any the world has ever produced before him. Is it a dream, or is it reality? I scarce can believe that it is a man in real life who stands before me. My imagination would fancy and make you the genius of some master spirit of ancient days, who is sent as a guide to protect and defend me before all which may oppose. Sir, under the protection of so able a guide and preceptor, I have nothing to fear; but look back to the hour of our meeting as the fortunate era when my importance and victories were to commence."

M. "Sir, I pledge you my head that I will give you all the instruction which my long experience will enable me to; and I flatter myself that I shall never be ashamed of the progress of so very intelligent a pupil. Sir, I am the leader of a noble band of valiant and lordly bandits; I will give you our plans and strength hereafter, and will introduce you among my fellows, and give you their names and residence before we part; but we must not be parted longer than you can arrange your business; and I will make you a splendid fellow, and put you on the high road to fortune.

" You shall be admitted into the grand councils of our clan; for I consider you a young man of splendid abilities. Sir, these are my feelings and sentiments towards you."

When Hues and his companion had finished their repast at the log, they mounted their horses, and set forward once more on their journey. They had not ridden far when Murrell renewed conversation in the following language :—

Murrell. " I am now going to the place whither I sent that old Methodist's negroes, in charge of a friend. The time has already passed at which I promised to meet him; and I fear, being ignorant of the cause of my delay, he will become alarmed, and decline wait-

ing for me.   I shall have to insist on your consenting
to travel all night.   My delay was occasioned by the
following circumstances :   About the time I had made
arrangements for leaving Madison county, I was informed by a friend (by-the-way, a most estimable man
—and one, too, who stands before the public entirely
above suspicion), that old Henning and his son suspected me of being a participant in the abduction of
their negroes—that they had their spies to watch my
movements—and were intending to follow me.   A
keen conception of the old fellow's ; and if he had
known how to hold his tongue, and not been too anxious to let others know his thoughts, he might have
given me some trouble ; but I always have men to
manage the case of such gentry as he and his son.
Upon being thus informed of their intention to pursue
me in the event of my then leaving the country, I determined at once to write Dick Henning a letter—
which I did, from the village of Denmark ; and which
ran, in substance, as follows :—' Sir, I have been told
you accuse me of being concerned in stealing your
and your father's negroes.   If it be true—I can whip
you from the point of a dagger to the anchor of a ship.
But, sir, if I have been misinformed by malicious individuals, I wish you to receive this as a letter of friendship.   I am about leaving for Randolph, and shall be
pleased to have your company—that you may be satisfied that my business is honest.'   This letter I despatched immediately, by such a conveyance as that I
am satisfied he has received it.   And I know, too, that
he will not undertake to follow me ; for he will naturally enough conclude that I will hardly go immedi-

ately to the negroes, knowing, as I do, that suspicion is upon me: much less after penning him such a letter. But, sir, I can take Dick Henning by my side, and steal and make sale of every negro he and his father own, and receive the money for them, and he shall know nothing of the transaction."

Hues. " That would be a strange manœuvre, sure! I should be pleased to learn how you would manage it."

M. " I would have an understanding with the negroes beforehand, to meet me at a certain time and place. I would also employ a friend to meet them in my place, and conduct them off to the morass whither we are now travelling. This arrangement made, I might be at home, or, if you please, at Henning's house, at the very time this friend was carrying off his negroes. I could then dispose of my interest in his negroes to *a friend,* and have my money counted out to me before his face, and he could know nothing of the nature of the transaction. True, I would not deliver the property, but my friend would know very well where to find it. It was never my intention, Hues, to disturb my immediate neighbours, until since they have commenced their sharp-shooting at me. They may now look out for breakers. Their long prayers and Methodist coats shall be no protection against my sworn vengeance; neither will they ever again see their negroes if once they fall into my hands."

H. " Your revenge is just! I shall glory in affording you any assistance that *my* feeble powers may warrant. You have but to command, and I am with you.

C   5

But, sir, above all things, I should glory in contributing to the downfall of such mistaken beings !"

M. " Well, Hues, I am delighted with your sentiments, and hope you will find me worthy the confidence you repose in me.   But we will leave the main road before we travel far, and follow a private way through the settlements.   I am well acquainted with it, and will underwrite your safe conduct.   Besides, if (as I very much doubt) the old parson has any person to follow me, he will lose my track."

H. " In travelling, sir, as in every thing else, I will endeavour to follow my leader, and profit by his example."

The following is the certificate of Mr. Richard G. Henning :—

" *State of Tennessee, Madison County.*

"I do hereby certify, to all whom it may concern, that all Virgil A. Stewart has said in the ' Western Land Pirate,' so far as my name is concerned with the same, is strictly correct in every particular; and I further certify that Murrell did send me a letter, as described in the ' Western Land Pirate,' which Mr. Stewart described after his return with Murrell from Arkansas, before I mentioned the fact to him.

" Given under my hand and seal, this 11th day of October, 1835.

[Sealed.]   "RICHARD G. HENNING."

The conversation of Murrell now turned on his future prospects of plunder, in which he dwelt much upon his own superior powers of management and the wisdom of his plans—painted his future fortunes and success in glowing perspective to his young companion, who listened with speechless attention, not un-mixed with admiration and horror. To satisfy his young pupil that he had not been guilty of misrepresentation in detailing his feats of villany, he proposed to decoy the first negro they should meet on the road; who, curious to witness a specimen of his tact and skill, readily assented. They had travelled but little more than six miles from the log at which they had stopped to eat, when they saw an old negro man, somewhat bending under the weight and decrepitude of years, at the door of a crib which stood by the road-side, preparing to take a sack of corn to the mill; it was the only building left upon the spot, from which it seems his master had but a short time before removed his dwelling-house and other buildings, to the distance of some half mile. Murrell approached and accosted the negro as follows :—

Murrell. " Well, old man, you must have a hard master, or he would not send you to mill this cold day."

Negro. " Yes, mossa, all ub um hard in dis country."

M. " Why do you stay with the villain, then, when he treats you like a dog ?"

N. " I can't help um, mossa."

M. " Would you help it if you could ?"

N. " Oh ! yes, mossa, dat I would."

M. " What is your name, old man ?"

N. " My name Clitto, mossa."

M. " Well, Clitto, would you like to be free, and have plenty of money to buy lands, and horses, and every thing you want ?"

C 2

Clitto. " Oh! yes, mossa, dat Clitto do so want em."

M. " If I will steal you, carry you off, and sell you four or five times, give you half the money, and then leave you in a free state, will you go ?"

C. " Oh! yes, mossa, Clitto go quick."

M. " Well, Clitto, don't you want a dram this cold day ?" (taking his flask of liquor from his pocket and offering it to Clitto.)

C. " Thank you, mossa, arter you."

M. " Oh, no, Clitto, after you." (Clitto drinks and returns the flask to Murrell, who also takes a drink.)

M. " Well, Clitto, have you no boys you would like to see free ?"

C. " Oh, yes, mossa."

M. " Now, Clitto, if you hear the report of a pistol at the head of a lane some night, do you think you will be sure to come to me, and bring three or four boys with you ?"

C. " Oh, yes, mossa, Clitto come dis very night."

M. " I am in a hurry now, Clitto, and can't carry you off at this time : but you must have the boys in readiness, and you shall not be with your old task-master much longer, to be cuffed and abused like a dog. I am a great friend to black people. I have carried off a great many, and they are doing well; have homes of their own, and are making money. You must keep a bright look-out now, and when you hear the pistol fire come with the boys. I will have horses ready to take you away. Farewell ! Clitto, till I see you again."

Thus ended the dialogue between Murrell and Clitto. Hues was highly amused at the exhibition he had just witnessed, and could not forbear expressing himself much pleased with his companion's manner and style of address ; taking occasion to compliment his success in achieving so speedy a conquest—for he well knew the nearest way to his heart. It had the desired effect; for Murrell turned to him with an air of self-complacency and triumph, and said that what he had just done was but a trifling job; and continued, "fifteen minutes are all that I require to decoy the best of negroes from the best of masters."

Hitherto Murrell had communicated to Hues but a few of the less startling of the schemes and adventures of his dark and diabolical confederacy. He had not yet unfolded to him the splendour of those more extensive plans of operations which stood recorded in the journals of their mysterious grand council. He began now, in the warmth of growing confidence, and the promise, at some future day, of a powerful coadjutor and zealous compatriot in the person of his hopeful pupil, to feel an inclination to afford him a more comprehensive view of the scenes in the land of mystics. Accordingly, just as the sun had rolled far down the declivity of the heavens, and while yet his parting rays bathed in a sea of ruddy light the hills and horizon of the west, Murrell began the disclosure as follows :—

Murrell. "Hues, I will tell you a secret that belongs to my clan, which is of more importance than stealing negroes—a shorter way to an overgrown fortune, and it is not far ahead. The movements of my clan have been as brisk as I could expect in that matter ; things are moving on smooth and easy. But this is a matter that is known only by a few of our leading characters.

5*

The clan are not all of the same grit; there are two classes. The first class keep all their designs and the extent of their plans to themselves. For this reason, all who would be willing to join us are not capable of managing our designs ; and there would be danger of their making disclosures which would lead to the destruction of our designs before they were perfected. This class is what we call the grand council.

" The second class are those whom we trust with nothing except that which they are immediately concerned with. We have them to do what we are not willing to do ourselves. They always stand between us and danger. For a few dollars we can get one of them to run a negro, or a fine horse, to some place where we can go and take possession of it without any danger : and there is no danger in this fellow then : for he has become the offender, and of course he is bound to secrecy. This class are what we term the strikers. We have about four hundred of the grand council, and near six hundred and fifty strikers. This is our strength, as near as I can guess. I will give you a list of their names, as I promised you, before we part.

" The grand object that we have in contemplation is to excite a rebellion among the negroes throughout the slave-holding states. Our plan is to manage so as to have it commence everywhere at the same hour. We have set on the 25th of December, 1835, for the time to commence our operations. We design having our companies so stationed over the country, in the vicinity of the banks and large cities, that when the negroes commence their carnage and slaughter, we will have detachments to fire the towns and rob the banks while all is confusion and dismay. The rebellion taking place everywhere at the same time, every part of the country will be engaged in its own defence ; and one part of the country can afford no relief to another, until many places will be entirely overrun by the negroes, and our pockets replenished from the banks and the desks of rich merchants' houses. It is true, that in many places in the slave states the negro population is not strong, and would be easily overpowered ; but, back them with a few resolute leaders from our clan, they will murder thousands, and huddle the remainder into large bodies of stationary defence for their own preservation ; and then, in many other places, the black population is much the strongest, and, under a leader, would overrun the country before any steps could be taken to suppress them."

Hues. " I cannot see how the matter is made known to the negroes without endangering the scheme by a disclosure, as all the negroes are not disposed to see their owners murdered."

M. " That is very easily done ; we work on the proper materials ; we do not go to every negro we see, and tell him that the negroes intend to rebel on the night of the 25th of December, 1835. We find the most vicious and wickedly disposed on large farms, and poison their minds, by telling them how they are mistreated ; that they are entitled to their freedom as much as their masters, and that all the wealth of the country is the proceeds of the black people's labour : we remind them of the pomp and splendour of their masters, and then refer them to their own degraded situation, and tell them that it is power and tyranny which rivet their chains of bondage, and not their own inferiority to their masters.   We tell them that all Europe has abandoned slavery, and that the West Indies are all free, and that they got their freedom by rebelling a few times, and slaughtering the whites; and convince them that, if they will follow the example of the West India negroes, they will obtain their liberty, and become as much respected as if they were white; and that they can marry white women when they are all put on a level.   In addition to this, we get them to believe that the majority of the people are in favour of their being free, and that the free states in the United States would not interfere with the negroes if they were to butcher every white man in the slave-holding states.

"When we are convinced that we have found a blood-thirsty devil, we swear him to secrecy and disclose to him the secret, and convince him that every other state and section of country where there are any negroes, intend to rebel and slay all the whites they can on the night of the 25th December, 1835, and assure him there are thousands of white men engaged in trying to free them, who will die by their sides in battle.   We have a long ceremony for the oath, which is administered in the presence of a terrific picture painted for that purpose, representing the monster who is to deal with him should he prove unfaithful in the engagements he has entered into.   This picture is highly calculated to make a negro true to his trust, for he is disposed to be superstitious at best.   After we have sworn him, we instruct him how

to proceed, which is as follows: he is to convince
his fellow-slaves of the great injustice of their being
held in bondage, and learn the feelings of all he can on
the subject of a rebellion, by telling them how successful the West India negroes have been in gaining their
freedom by frequent rebellions.

"The plan is, to have the feelings of the negroes
harrowed up against the whites, and their minds alive
to the idea of being free ; and let none but such as
we can trust know the intention and time of rebellion
until the night it is to commence; when our black
emissaries are to have gatherings of their fellow-
slaves, and invite all in their reach to attend, with the
promise of plenty to drink, which will always call negroes together. Our emissaries will be furnished with
money to procure spirits to give them a few drams,
when they will open their secret as follows : ' Fellow-
slaves, this is the night that we are to obtain our liberty. All the negroes in America rebel this night and
murder the whites. We have been long subject to
the whips of our tyrants, and many of our backs wear
the scars : but the time has arrived when we can be
revenged.

" ' There are many good white men who are helping
us to gain our liberty. All of you who refuse to fight
will be put to death ; so come on, my brave fellows,
we will be free or die.' We will have our men whom
we intend for leaders ready to head those companies
and encourage the negroes should they appear back-
ward. Thus you see they will all be forced to engage, under the belief that the negroes have rebelled
everywhere else as in their own neighbourhood, and

by those means every gathering or assemblage of negroes will be pushed forward, even contrary to their
inclination. Those strikers will be of great use at the
pinch of the game, as many of them will do to head
companies, and there will be no danger in them when
they are to go immediately to work, and have the
prospect of wealth before them: there are many of
them who will fight like Turks.

" Our black emissaries have the promise of a share
in the spoils we may gain, and we promise to conduct
them to Texas should we be defeated, where they will
be free ; but we never talk of being defeated. We
always talk of victory and wealth to them. There is
no danger in any man, if you can ever get him once
implicated or engaged in a matter. That is the way
we employ our strikers in all things ; we have them
implicated before we trust them from our sight.*

* Murrell spoke of the advantage he expected to derive from an
English lecturer on slavery ; and gave *his* opinion as to what would
be the effect of an insurrection among the slaves of the south, as
follows :—" Could the blacks effect a general concert of action
against their tyrants, and let loose the arm of destruction among them
and their property, so that the judgments of God might be visibly
seen and felt, it would reach the flinty heart of the tyrant. We can
do much at the east by working on the sympathy of the people ; but
when we remonstrate with a southern tyrant, he counts the cost of
his slaves and his annual income, and haughtily hurls it in our teeth,
and tells us the Old and New Testaments both teach him that
slavery is right. We must reach the tyrant in another way. His
interest must be affected before he will repent. We can prepare the
feelings of most of the northern and eastern people, for the final
consummation of the great work, by lecturing. Interest is the great
cement that binds the few northerners who are friendly to southern tyrants ; and if their cities, with all the merchandise that is in
the country, were destroyed, and their banks plundered of all the
specie, thousands of eastern capitalists would suffer great loss, and

" This may seem too bold to you, Hues ; but that is
what I glory in. All the crimes I have ever committed have been of the most daring ; and I have been
successful in all my attempts as yet ; and I am confident that I will be victorious in this matter, as to the
robberies which I have in contemplation ; and I will
have the pleasure and honour of seeing and knowing
that by my management I have glutted the earth with
more human gore, and destroyed more property, than

would henceforth consider a slave country an unsafe place to make
investments ; and thousands would leave the country. This state
of affairs would naturally diminish the value of slave property, and
disgust even the tyrant with the policy of slavery ; while the country would be thus in a state of anarchy and poverty. Their banking
institutions and credit sunk into disrepute with the commercial
world, it would be an easy matter to effect the total abolition of
slavery.

" Desperate cases require desperate remedies.

" And suppose the blacks should refuse to serve their tyrants any
longer : what right would the general government have to interfere
with the internal disputes of the citizens of a state respecting her
state laws ? The blacks would not be rebelling against the general
government, neither would they be invaders : but Americans, and
citizens of a state refusing obedience to a state law and power that
are, before God, utterly null and void : being an audacious usurpation
of his divine prerogative, a daring infringement on the law of nature,
and a presumptuous transgression of the holy commandments, which
should be abrogated by the Christian world. Would not the general
government have more right to interfere in behalf of the injured
and oppressed than in that of the tyrants and oppressors ? The United States' troops would be finely employed in the southern plantations forcing obedience to the unjust laws of a few tyrants and man-
stealers.

" The southerners are great men for *state rights*, and in a case like
the above, we would give them an opportunity to exercise their
sovereign functions. Make slavery unpopular with a majority of the
people of the United States, and southern tyrants will find a poor
comforter in the general government."

any other robber who has ever lived in America, or the known world. I look on the American people as my common enemy. They have disgraced me, and they can do no more. My life is nothing to me, and it shall be spent as their devoted enemy. My clan is strong, brave, and experienced, and rapidly increasing in strength every day. I should not be surprised if we were to be two thousand strong by the 25th of December, 1835 : and, in addition to this, I have the advantage of any other leader of banditti that has ever preceded me, for at least one half of my grand council are men of high standing, and many of them in honourable and lucrative offices. Should any thing leak out by chance, these men would crush it at once, by ridiculing the idea, and the fears of the people. They would soon make it a humbug, a cock-and-bull story ; and all things would be accounted for to the satisfaction of the community in short order. These fellows make strong pillars in our mystic mansion. Hues, how do you suppose I understood your disposition so quick, and drew you out on the subject of speculation, so that I could get your sentiments in so short a time after we got in company ?"

H. " That is what I do not understand, and I can only account for it as I would many other of your unrivalled performances, by attributing it to your great knowledge and experience of the world and of mankind."

M. " I had not been in company with you more than two hours before I knew you as well as if I had made you, and could have trusted my life in your hands. A little practice is all you want, and you can look into the very heart and thoughts of a man.

"The art of learning men is nothing when you once see how it is managed. You must commence in this way: Begin to tell of some act of villany, and notice the answers and countenance of the man as you go on with your story; and if you discover him to lean a little, you advance a little; but if he recedes, you withdraw, and commence some other subject; and, if you have carried the matter a little too far before you have sounded him, by being too anxious, make a jest of it, and pass it off in that way."

H. "I cannot see how you will provide the negroes with arms to fight with."

M. "We have a considerable amount of money in the hands of our treasurers, for the purpose of purchasing arms and ammunition to fit out the companies that are to attack the cities and banks; and we will manage to get possession of different arsenals, and supply ourselves from every source that may offer. We can get from every house we enter more or less supplies of this kind, until we shall be well supplied. The negroes that scour the country settlements will not want many arms until they can get them from the houses they destroy, as an axe, a club, or knife will do to murder a family at a late hour in the night, when all are sleeping. There will be but little defence made the first night by the country people, as all will be confusion and alarm for the first day or two, until the whites can imbody."

It was now a late hour in the night, and Hues, finding himself suffering very much from the cold (for the weather was unusually bitter), and considerably jaded by fatigue, insisted on seeking lodgings. Murrell con-

6

sented, though he had never once complained, or
seemed to feel the effects of the keen cutting wind
that had been preying so uncomfortably upon the frame
of his less hardened companion. They accordingly
sought the first house on their road that exhibited any
thing like an air of comfort, and solicited quarters;
and, so soon as they had restored the circulation before a blazing fire, they were lighted to their cham-
bers; but a few moments convinced them that by far
the most comfortable quarters were in the neighbourhood of the fire they had left; all else presenting
a cold, dreary, and comfortless aspect. They however retired with a determination to *live*, though there
was but little prospect of *sleeping*, through the night.

CHAPTER III.

SCARCE had rising day scattered the shadows of
twilight from the face of nature on the following morning, ere Murrell and his companion were up and away
on their journey—glad to catch the first opportunity of
making their escape from the inhospitable accommodations of their otherwise agreeable landlord. Murrell expressed great anxiety to reach Arkansas that
night; urging, that his business was of much importance, and would suffer by his absence.

Having now disclosed his plans to his young friend,
and, as he thought, completely captivated his feelings
and delighted his imagination with bright visions of

future and inexhaustible wealth, Murrell began now to
look upon him as an undoubted proselyte to his cause,
and the willing associate of his bloody and diabolical
machinations. His new but hopeful pupil had, as if
by enchantment, in the space of two short days, ripened
into his bosom and confidential friend, the pride of his
fiendish heart, and the object of his highest admiration.
He proposed a brief narrative of his life from the age
of ten years, and upon Hues expressing a willingness
to become a hearer, proceeded after the following
manner :—

Murrell. " I was born in middle Tennessee. My
parents had not much property, but they were intelligent people ; and my father was an honest man I expect, and tried to raise me honest, but I think none the
better of him for that. My mother was of the pure
grit ; she learned me and all her children to steal as
soon as we could walk, and would hide for us whenever she could. At ten years old I was not a bad
hand. The first good haul I made was from a pedler, who lodged at my father's house one night. I
had several trunk-keys, and in the night I unlocked
one of his trunks, and took a bolt of linen and several
other things, and then locked the trunk. The pedler
went off before he discovered the trick : I thought that
was not a bad figure I had made. About this time
some pains were taken with my education. At the age
of sixteen I played a trick on a merchant in that country. I walked into his store one day, and he spoke to
me very politely, calling me by the name of a young
man who had a rich father, and invited me to trade
with him. I thanked him, and requested him to put

down a bolt of superfine cloth ; I took a suit, and had
it charged to the rich man's son.

" I began to look after larger spoils, and ran several
fine horses. By the time I was twenty I began to ac-
quire considerable character, and concluded to go off
and do my speculation where I was not known, and
go on a larger scale ; so I began to see the value of
having friends in this business. I made several associates ; I had been acquainted with some old hands for
a long time, who had given me the names of some
royal fellows between Nashville and Tuscaloosa, and
between Nashville and Savannah, in the State of
Georgia, and many other places. Myself and a fellow by the name of Crenshaw gathered four good
horses, and started for Georgia. We got in company
with a young South Carolinian just before we reached
Cumberland Mountain, and Crenshaw soon knew all
about his business. He had been to Tennessee to buy
a drove of hogs, but when he got there pork was
dearer than he had calculated, and he declined purchasing. We concluded he was a prize. Crenshaw
winked at me ; I understood his idea. Crenshaw had
travelled the road before, but I never had ; we had
travelled several miles on the mountain, when we passed near a great precipice ; just before we passed it,
Crenshaw asked me for my whip, which had a pound
of lead in the butt ; I handed it to him, and he rode up
by the side of the South Carolinian, and gave him a
blow on the side of the head, and tumbled him from
his horse ; we lit from our horses and fingered his
pockets ; we got twelve hundred and sixty-two dollars. Crenshaw said he knew of a place to hide him,

and gathered him under the arms, and I by his feet,
and conveyed him to a deep crevice in the brow of the
precipice, and tumbled him into it: he went out of
sight. We then tumbled in his saddle, and took his
horse with us, which was worth two hundred dollars.
We turned our course for South Alabama, and sold our
horses for a good price. We frolicked for a week or
more, and were the highest larks you ever saw. We
commenced sporting and gambling, and lost every cent
of our money.

"We were forced to resort to our profession for a
second raise. We stole a negro man, and pushed for
Mississippi. We had promised him that we would
conduct him to a free state if he would let us sell him
once as we went on the way; we also agreed to give
him part of the money. We sold him for six hundred
dollars; but, when we went to start, the negro seemed
to be very uneasy, and appeared to doubt our coming
back for him as we had promised. We lay in a creek
bottom, not far from the place where we had sold the
negro, all the next day, and after dark we went to the
china-tree in the lane where we were to meet Tom;
he had been waiting for some time. He mounted his
horse, and we pushed with him a second time. We
rode twenty miles that night to the house of a friendly
speculator. I had seen him in Tennessee, and had
given him several lifts. He gave me his place of residence, that I might find him when I was passing. He
is quite rich, and one of the best kind of fellows.
Our horses were fed as much as they would eat, and
two of them were foundered the next morning. We
were detained a few days, and during that time our

6*

friend went to a little village in the neighbourhood, and saw the negro advertised, with a description of the two men of whom he had been purchased, and with mention of them as suspicious personages. It was rather squally times, but any port in a storm; we took the negro that night on the bank of a creek which runs by the farm of our friend, and Crenshaw shot him through the head. We took out his entrails, and sunk him in the creek; our friend furnished us with one fine horse, and we left him our foundered horses. We made our way through the Choctaw and Chickasaw nations, and then to Williamson county, in this state. We should have made a fine trip if we had taken care of all we got.

"I had become a considerable libertine, and when I returned home I spent a few months rioting in all the luxuries of forbidden pleasures with the girls of my acquaintance.

"My stock of cash was soon gone, and I put to my shift for more. I commenced with horses, and ran several from the adjoining counties. I had got associated with a young man who had professed to be a preacher among the Methodists, and a sharper he was; he was as slick on the tongue as goose-grease. I took my first lessons in divinity from this young preacher. He was highly respected by all who knew him, and well calculated to please; he first put me in the notion of preaching, to aid me in my speculations.

"I got into difficulties about a mare that I had taken, and was imprisoned for near three years. I shifted it from court to court, but was at last found guilty, and whipped. During my confinement I read the scriptures, and became a good judge of theology. I had not neglected the criminal laws for many years before that time. When they turned me loose I was prepared for any thing; I wanted to kill all but my own grit, and one of them I will die by his side before I will desert.

" My next speculation was in the Choctaw nation. Myself and brother stole two fine horses, and made our way into the Choctaw nation. We got in with an old negro man, and his wife, and three sons, to go off with us to Texas, and promised them that, if they would work for us one year after we got there, we would let them go free, and told them many fine stories. We got into the Mississippi swamp, and were badly bothered to reach the bank of the river. We had turned our horses loose at the edge of the swamp, and let them go. After we reached the bank of the river we were in a bad condition, as we had no craft to convey us down the river, and our provisions gave out, and our only means for support were killing game and eating it. Eventually we found an Indian trail through the bottom, and we followed it to a bayou that made into the river, where we had the pleasure of finding a large canoe locked to the bank; we broke it loose and rowed it into the main river, and were soon descending for New-Orleans.

" The old negro became suspicious that we were going to sell him, and grew quite contrary. We saw it would not do to have him with us; so we landed one day by the side of an island, and I requested him to go with me round the point of the island to hunt a good place to catch some fish. After we were hidden from our company I shot him through the head, and then ripped open his belly and tumbled him into the river. I returned to my company, and told them that the negro had fallen into the river, and that he never came up after he went under. We landed fifty miles above New-Orleans, and went into the country and sold our negroes to a Frenchman for nineteen hundred dollars.

" We went from where we sold the negroes to New-Orleans, and dressed ourselves like young lords. I mixed with the loose characters at the *swamp* every night. One night, as I was returning to the tavern where I boarded, I was stopped by two armed men, who demanded my money. I handed them my pocket-book, and observed that I was very happy to meet with them, as we were all of the same profession. One of them observed, ' D—d if I ever rob a brother chip. We have had our eyes on you and the man that has generally come with you for several nights ; we saw so much rigging and glittering jewellery, that we con-cluded you must be some wealthy dandy, with a sur-plus of cash ; and had determined to rid you of the trouble of some of it ; but, if you are a robber, here is your pocketbook, and you must go with us to-night, and we will give you an introduction to several fine fellows of the block ; but stop, do you understand this motion ?' I answered it, and thanked them for their kindness, and turned with them. We went to old Mother Surgick's, and had a real frolic with her girls. That night was the commencement of my greatness in what the world calls villany. The two fellows who robbed me were named Haines and Phelps ; they

made me known to all the speculators that visited
New-Orleans, and gave me the name of every fellow
who would speculate that lived on the Mississippi
river, and many of its tributary streams, from New-
Orleans up to all the large western cities.

"I had become acquainted with a Kentuckian, who
boarded at the same tavern I did, and I suspected he
had a large sum of money; I felt an inclination to
count it for him before I left the city; so I made my
notions known to Phelps and my other new comrades,
and concerted our plan. I was to get him off to the
swamp with me on a spree, and when we were returning to our lodgings, my friends were to meet us and
rob us both. I had got very intimate with the Kentuckian, and he thought me one of the best fellows in
the world. He was very fond of wine; and I had him
well fumed with good wine before I made the proposition for a frolic. When I invited him to walk with
me he readily accepted the invitation. We cut a few
shines with the girls, and started to the tavern. We
were met by a band of robbers, and robbed of all our
money. The Kentuckian was so mad that he cursed
the whole city, and wished that it would all be deluged in a flood of water so soon as he left the place.
I went to my friends the next morning, and got my
share of the spoil money, and my pocketbook that I
had been robbed of. We got seven hundred and five
dollars of the bold Kentuckian, which was divided
among thirteen of us.

"I commenced travelling and making all the acquaintances among the speculators that I could. I went
from New-Orleans to Cincinnati, and from there I vis-

ited Lexington, in Kentucky. I found a speculator about four miles from Newport, who furnished me with a fine horse the second night after I arrived at his house. I went from Lexington to Richmond, in Virginia, and from there I visited Charleston, in the State of South Carolina : and from thence to Milledgeville, by the way of Savannah and Augusta, in the State of Georgia. I made my way from Milledgeville to Williamson county, the old stamping-ground. In all the route I only robbed eleven men ; but I preached some fine sermons, and scattered some counterfeit United States paper among my brethren."

The day was now far spent, the shadows of gathering twilight had already begun to mantle the face of nature, and Murrell had not concluded the history of his life. He proposed to discontinue it for the present, promising to resume it at such time during their journey when a better opportunity and greater leisure would enable him to enter more into particulars. Their progress had been considerably delayed by the high waters of the Mississippi, which had rendered Murrell's trace through the valley impassable ; who at length suggested to Hues that it would be better to leave the trace, and by directing their course higher up they would strike the river at the foot of the Chickasaw Bluff, above the plantation of a Mr. Shelby, and continue down the bank of the river till they should reach the private crossing-place of the clan. They did so ; and as they were passing Mr. S.'s plantation, and while yet in sight of his dwelling, Murrell attempted a display of his tact in producing disaffection with a number of Mr. S.'s negroes, who were at work on the

bank of the river. The spirit of disloyalty and rebellion was soon perceptible, and in a short time became
almost violent; finding vent, first in murmurs of dis-
content, and afterward in audible execrations and ex-
pressions of hatred against their master. He soon obtained from them the promise to accompany him to a
free state at any time when he should call for them.

When they had progressed about four miles below
Mr. Shelby's, they found their way very much embarrassed by the recent overflow ; and, after many unsuccessful attempts to proceed, they determined to
take lodgings for the night of the 28th at the house of
a Mr. John Champion, who resided on the river, and
await the return of day to encounter farther the difficulties of their journey. They had not been long in
company with Mr. Champion before Murrell, or Mer-
rill, as he now called himself, began to sound him on the
subject of speculation, as he chooses to term the pursuits of his fiendish brotherhood ; nor, had he omitted
an initial, would it have been a misnomer—except, indeed, it might have fallen short of conveying an adequate idea of their deep-toned horror and infamy.
Hues found himself now obliged to listen to a recapit-
ulation of the same feats of villany and crime that had
constituted so important a part of Murrell's conversation with him since the morning of their first acquaintance on the Estanaula turnpike. Mr. Champion, however, discovered but little of the fondness for such
topics which Hues had pretended ; nor did he become
so suddenly enamoured of the character, or dazzled
by the brilliant achievements, of the distinguished
elder brother of Madison county, as Murrell's ima-

gination had led him to believe was his young fellow-traveller. During this conversation, Hues had by no means been idle or inattentive; he had marked well the countenance of Mr. Champion, noted with scrutinizing gaze every variation of feature that might indicate the operations of his mind, and caught with devouring avidity every word that fell from his lips. For he saw before him a task to be performed of the highest importance to his future movements, and upon which, as he thought, the fate of his undertaking in no small degree depended. He foresaw the great necessity of learning the character of Mr. Champion, whom he now beheld for the first time, and of making him a friend and confidant: for the time was now near at hand when, according to a prior arrangement, he was to accompany Murrell alone beyond the Mississippi, among the gloomy haunts of a lawless banditti, whose characters he had already heard painted in the blackest colours; and where, as yet, he had no sufficient assurance that he would not be immolated upon the same altar that had already been ensanguined by the blood of many others. His object in making the friendship of Mr. Champion was to leave behind him some data, which, in the event of his murder, might lead to the detection of the assassin, and furnish to the world some idea of the circumstances of his death. It was not long before Hues saw, or thought he saw, in Mr. Champion, the very individual he so much desired, and whose services and confidence he deemed of so great importance in the hazardous and almost hopeless adventure upon which he was about to enter. Notwithstanding this fortunate discovery, how-

ever, and although he had expressed to Murrell his
willingness to accompany him to Arkansas, Hues
had not yet obtained the entire consent of his own
mind thus to jeopard his life and risk the failure of
his plans upon so uncertain a tenure as the assurance
of an individual who had already confessed himself capable of the blackest and most unprincipled
falsehoods ; and whose whole history, so far as related, appeared but a continued series of the basest deceptions, and the darkest deeds of villany and crime.
He knew not but all Murrell's fair, and apparently disinterested promises, were so many toils to insnare the
more easily his unwary steps ; and painted in the alluring and seductive colours of friendship and confidence, the more readily to practise upon his credulity.
He found great difficulty, therefore, in bringing himself at length to the belief of what he had heard.
Without some such conviction, it had never been his
intention to enter the morass.   The merely contingent
hope of finding there Mr. Henning's negroes, still less
the more doubtful prospect, in such an event, of being
able, by his own unaided efforts, to capture and reclaim
them, had comparatively little weight in shaping his
determinations ; his object was " purer, higher, no-
bler." Filled with just and patriotic indignation against
these common and insidious (the more fearful because
insidious) enemies of his country and his race ; and
viewing, as he did, the thickening clouds that hung in
unseen but threatening terror over the defenceless
heads of the fairer part of creation, charged with death,
ravishment, and prostitution, in all their hideous, torturing, and humiliating forms; and the ten thousand
D   **7**

helpless innocents, destined to open their eyes in life only to sink, welter, and agonize in unnatural death, to appease the unholy vengeance and brutal ferocity of the unsympathizing and heartless assassin—made his bosom swell with emotions " too big for utterance," and which have but imperfectly found vent in the details of his subsequent adventures. At this important crisis Hues occupied a position perhaps of all others least to be envied. The period was fast approaching when he would be called upon to meet his engagement with Murrell : to retreat might excite a most unfortunate suspicion, and possibly defeat his purposes ; to comply might induce the fearful reality of the very apprehensions that had occasioned him so much indecision. Could he have been perfectly satisfied of the truth of all he had heard, he might here have ended his journey, and consummated his plan ; captured the rogue, and exposed his villany. But another difficulty presented itself—the world might be incredulous, and he had, as yet, no evidence sufficiently positive to remove their doubts; he could speak to them of nothing that he had seen ; nothing, to the truth of which he could pledge his own oath ; all so far was hearsay, which he knew at best was allowed but little weight. Besides, an account of transactions so unusual—so much above the common order of human crime, would meet with skeptics, though supported by the strongest testimony. The struggle at length over which had been warring in the mind of Hues, he resolved to accompany Murrell to Arkansas, where he might behold with his own eyes if true, and be convinced of their falsehood if not, all the representations that had been made to him respecting the dark and sanguinary operations of the morass, the ruffian band engaged in them, and learn something of the extent and tendency of their future plans : since it was his object to make known to his fellow-citizens the result of his inquiries, as he felt unwilling to require of them to believe statements of the truth of which he had not himself, as yet, been fully convinced.

During all this time Murrell had not omitted to make inquiries respecting such of his clan as lived along the river ; mentioning among the rest the names of the Lloyds, Barneys, and others. Murrell asked Mr. C. what standing they occupied as honourable and honest men, representing himself as an utter stranger to them, and the part of the country in which they resided ; and urged as a reason for his curiosity, that he was going over among them with a view of collecting some money that was due him. He also called himself a negro-trader, and spoke of a lot of negroes that he wished to dispose of ; in all which his motive will be apparent as the reader progresses in the following pages.

It was now a late hour of the night, and Hues and his companion desired to be shown to their chamber ; for they had determined to renew their journey at a very early hour on the following morning, and were already much in want of rest. Soon after they had been ushered to their lodging-room, as they found themselves alone, and all about them still and quiet, Murrell broke in upon the silence in the following manner :—

Murrell. " Well, Hues, how do you like the way in which I managed our landlord ?"

Hues. "None could have managed him better, sir."

M. " We shall be compelled, Hues, to leave our
horses here with Mr. Champion, and work our passage
through the swamp on foot, until we can meet with a skiff
to convey us to my friends on the other side of the
river.   We shall be dependant on Mr. Champion, and
I can see he is no friend to the speculators.   For this
reason I have pretended to know nothing about the people on the other side of the river.   An acquaintance
with them, you know, would afford just grounds for
suspecting us of being after no good."

CHAPTER IV.

AFTER an early breakfast on the morning of the
29th, Murrell and Hues prepared to leave Mr. Champion's, and seek, lower down on the river, a skiff to convey them across ; but, before leaving, they inquired of
Mr. C. what the prospect was ? He informed them
that there was a probability of being accommodated at
Mr. Erwin's, who lived a little below him ; but that, in
the event of a disappointment there, there was but little doubt of their obtaining a conveyance of Parson
Hargus, who lived still lower down.   With these assurances, and leaving their horses with Mr. Champion, they set forward on their journey on foot.   They
had proceeded but a few hundred yards when Hues
paused, and remarked to his companion that he had
left his gloves at the house of their late landlord, and
that the weather was so very cold he could not conve-

niently dispense with their use. He requested Murrell to wait till he could return for them, promising to be absent but a short time. The truth was, Hues had intentionally left his gloves with a view to obtain, through their means, an interview with Mr. Champion (which he had not deemed prudent to seek while with Murrell), to disclose to him the character of Murrell, his business and plans, and to claim his friendship and assistance. Murrell seated himself on a log, and Hues made all possible haste to the house of Mr. Champion, for delay might awaken suspicion. No sooner had he reached the house than he sought an opportunity to unfold to Mr. C. the story of his situation and adventure, and make known his real name. He desired him to hold himself in readiness to afford him the aid of a guard should he return to claim it ; which he should do if he found things as they had been represented. Mr. C. furnished him with an additional pistol, assured him of his friendship, and remarked that he could command a guard of fifty men at any time when he might need them. He, moreover, spoke in high terms of Messrs. Erwin and Hargus, to whose houses Hues and his companion were going in search of a skiff, and recommended to him also the advantage of their friendship in his perilous undertaking. All this was done in much less time, perhaps, than is here employed in relating it ; for Hues had foreseen the great danger of any thing that might savour of unnecessary delay.

While Hues was engaged in disclosing the above to Mr. Champion, he exhibited evident signs of alarm, and has himself since declared, that he felt more sensibly the effects of fear at that time than he had in all his life before. The idea of trusting his life in the hands of an individual whom he had never seen till the night before, made a more fearful appeal to his moral firmness and courage than any thing that had transpired during the whole history of his adventure. It called up feelings and emotions wellnigh beyond his ability to endure. He might be disclosing himself to an associate bandit. At least, he might prove dishonest and betray him, and thus make sure that destruction which he had already sufficient reason to dread. The occasion was surely one to try the nerves of the firmest, and strike terror to the heart of the boldest. Hues requested Mr. Champion to detain Murrell's horse till he should hear from him. He instructed him further, that if Murrell should return for his horse without him, to have him arrested immediately, as that would be sufficient evidence that he (Stewart) had been assassinated, or confined by the clan. Mr. Champion promised most cheerfully to attend to all his requisitions.

Hues had now grown impatient to arrest the desolating and destructive progress of this incorrigible enemy of his country. He had listened to his tales of outrage, robbery, and assassination, till his sickened and disgusted heart, almost maddened to vengeance, could only be satisfied by the most speedy visitation of that justice which had so long been cheated of its victim. Hence his determination to peril all that was sacred and valuable to him—nay, life itself, for the accomplishment of so important an object; and upon which the welfare and safety of his country and fellow-citizens so essentially depended.

Hues was now armed with three pistols ; one which he had with him when he fell in company with Murrell, a second which he received from Col. Bayliss at Wesley, and a third just presented him by Mr. Champion. He wore a thick Bolivar overcoat, by means of which he was enabled to conceal his new supply of arms, which he deemed of no little importance to him at this critical conjuncture. Mr. Champion suggested to Hues the necessity of much caution, and urged the great uncertainty and danger of the almost desperate experiment which he was about to make. He spoke to him of the fatal consequences of miscarriage, but not without representing to him also the possibility of success, and the interesting and brilliant results that would reward his efforts. They parted, and Hues hastened to rejoin his companion at the log. They were soon again on their journey. After much difficulty and toil they succeeded in crossing the sloughs that embarrassed their way, and reached the house of Mr. Erwin, distant about three miles, as had been represented by Mr. Champion, where they learned the skiff Mr. E. had been using was a borrowed one, and had been returned to its owner, who lived still three miles lower down the river ; and between whose residence and Mr. Erwin's there was a lake of considerable size, which they had no present means of crossing. They were compelled to stop at the house of Mr. Erwin, where they concluded to linger till some trading-boat or other craft should pass, in which they might obtain a conveyance beyond the lake to the house of Mr. Hargus, at which, they had been told, they would find the skiff. While with Mr. Erwin, Hues and his companion indulged comparatively but little conversation of a private nature, as they had not the advantage of a private room. Murrell, however, was by no means idle ; he was engaged, as had been his wont on such occasions, in learning the character of Mr. Erwin, and obtaining his views in regard to a subject that, more deeply than all others, interested him and engaged his thoughts. As at Mr. Champion's, here also he spoke of himself as a negro-trader : nor did his manly address and captivating demeanour fail of finding ready access to the credulity and confidence of his landlord. Mr. Erwin proposed to contract with him for three negro men, to be delivered within three weeks, to which Murrell readily assented, offering them at the price of six hundred dollars each. The terms suiting Mr. Erwin, they proceeded to close the bargain, so far as they could, till delivery was made of the negroes. This was more than Hues could suffer to pass unnoticed : he sought, as early as practicable, a private conversation with Mr. Erwin, and acquainted him with the character of Murrell, and his own business with him ; and solicited, as he had done of Mr. Champion, his assistance, should his situation require it, which he most readily promised to afford him.

Hues carried a blank-book in his pocket, from which he tore small pieces, on which he had kept a record of Murrell's plans and confessions as he progressed in his dark narrative. His object in tearing the book into pieces so small was to avoid the suspicion of

Murrell ; for he knew that nothing could escape the
ever-vigilant glance of his keen and searching eye.
While riding, as he could not then conveniently make
use of the pieces from his blank-book, he frequently
wrote the proper names of individuals, and places, and
the more prominent incidents, on his boot-legs, saddle-
skirts, finger-nails, and portmanteau, with a needle.
This was done with a view to aid his memory, when,
on stopping to dine or call for lodgings, he proceeded
to record a more enlarged account of what he had
heard on the scraps from the blank-book, which, as
they were filled and numbered, were successively deposited with care in the crown of his cap, through a
hole which he had made with his knife for the purpose.   While at Mr. Erwin's, Hues availed himself of
the opportunity of reducing to writing all that he had
heard during their journey from Mr. Champion's, and
arranging his other memoranda in such order as to
be understood whenever he should have occasion to
use them.   In this ingenious and cautious manner
Hues succeeded in keeping a correct journal of all
that occurred during his disagreeable and dangerous
wanderings with John A. Murrell.

They were at Mr. Erwin's house until the next afternoon (30th), when a small trading-boat landed at
the wood-yard, on which they secured a passage as
low down on the river as Mr. Hargus's landing.

It was late in the afternoon when they landed at the
house of Parson Hargus, who offered them, as their
only chance, a conveyance over the river in an old
canoe, which, having long been unused, was much in
want of repair.   This circumstance, though at first

D 3

discouraging, was in the end of great advantage to
Hues ; for, while Murrell was employed in calking
the boat, he sought an interview with Mr. Hargus, and
apprized him of the character of his guest, and his
own reason for being in his company.   For he had
heard the most favourable accounts of the character
of Mr. H., both from Mr. Champion and his late landlord Mr. Erwin, and therefore felt no hesitation in in-
trusting to him so important a secret.   It was long
after nightfall before Murrell had finished his repairs
on the boat, which made it necessary to postpone
crossing the river till morning ; they accordingly
sought lodgings with Mr. Hargus.

CHAPTER V.

ON the following morning of January 31st, Murrell and Hues were early at the landing, and making
arrangements for launching their boat.   But a gathering storm timely suggested to them the prudence
of delay.   They accordingly wisely determined to
await the return of fair weather ; for the frail bark
in which they found themselves obliged to take passage (at best of doubtful safety) was poorly calculated to live amid the buffetings of wind and waves.   It
was not long ere a violent storm of wind, accompanied by a heavy fall of snow, which lasted all day and
the following night, reminded them of the danger they
had escaped.

Murrell became very impatient, and his impatience (almost amounting to irritation) appeared to increase with the storm ; for he would frequently break forth in oaths, and swear that " the devil had ceased to cut his cards for him ;" and insist that " the d——d old preacher's negroes had cost him more trouble and perplexity than any he had ever before stolen." In the midst of all his excitement, however, he never once so far forgot himself as to let fall one imprudent word in presence of his landlord. On the contrary, his conversation was studiously turned on those subjects which he deemed most consonant to his feelings. He dwelt with peculiar emphasis and animation on the great advantages of a moral and religious education, and the happy effects of a general diffusion of religious intelligence.

He often expressed to Hues much curiosity as to what steps young Henning was probably taking towards the recovery of the negroes ; as frequently wishing that he might meet him over in Arkansas ; and declared that he would give five hundred dollars for the opportunity it would afford him of punishing his officiousness ; and said that he was not satisfied with stealing his negroes ; and mentioned a plan that he had already set on foot for bringing him to feel more sensibly the consequences of the free use he had been making of his and his brother's name ; which plan consisted of an arrangement he had made with a number of his friends, headed by one of the prominent leaders of his clan (Eli Chandler), to go to Henning's house some night, take him from his bed, and " give him two hundred and fifty lashes." And as he

knew suspicion would at once attach to him, he intended to lodge at a hotel in Jackson on the night it
took place. He said he entertained no fears of the
leader he had selected for the occasion, whom he pro-
nounced "a second Cesar." The affair, as related,
was surely one (laying aside all consideration of its
consummate effrontery) of a character to appeal to the
risibles of the gravest : that an individual should
first lose his property, and afterward be punished by
the thief for complaining. A recollection of his situation, however, aided by a struggle of indignation at the
danger that threatened his friend, enabled Hues to restrain his feelings.

The day gradually wore away, and night at length
succeeded. The prospect was still dark and lower-
ing, and Murrell and his companion were once more
obliged to call for quarters with Mr. Hargus.

CHAPTER VI.

THE morning of February 1st introduced the same
gloomy prospect that had detained Hues and Murrell
the preceding day (except, indeed, the wind had meas-
urably subsided); the waves still rolled high and
threatening, and the snow continued to fall, though in
less quantities. They determined, however, to make
an effort at crossing, though at great hazard. They
had proceeded but a few hundred yards from shore
when they became convinced that their apprehensions

were by no means unfounded. Their boat very soon
began to show itself unequal to a contest with the
waves and current; and they found it necessary to
make a timely retreat from a struggle in which the
chances appeared so evidently against them. They
returned to the landing whence they had set out, resolved to seek a safer conveyance, or postpone their
visit to Arkansas till fairer weather should remove the
danger of crossing the river in the boat of which they
were already in possession.

On their return, at the solicitation of Murrell, Mr.
Hargus furnished them a safer boat, and sent his son
with them to take it back (for it was one for which
he had constant use). They landed at a point on the
western shore of the river opposite the mouth of Old
River, which joins the Mississippi at the Chickasaw
Bend.

Murrell led the way, taking a northwestern course
through the swamp, which was rendered almost impassable by a thick growth of luxuriant cane, and in-
terspersed at no distant intervals with large collections
of water, occasioned by the high tide of the Mississippi. When they had been travelling about half an
hour, Hues found himself suddenly on the borders of
an extensive lake, which, swollen by the overflowing
waters of the Mississippi, had overtopped its banks,
and stretched among the surrounding timber and cane
beyond the reach of sight, and which seemed at first
to bound the prospect; till, continuing a short distance
along the shore, they discovered on their right a considerable bayou, which made out from the Mississippi
and entered the lake above them. On the opposite

8

side of the bayou lived a friend of Murrell, who afforded them a ready conveyance across. They next
proceeded in a western direction along the borders of
what appeared to be an extensive tract of overflowed
country, but which was most probably but a continua-
tion of the lake they had just left. On their way
Hues spied a small open hut at a distance, which,
from the volumes of smoke that curled away from its
chimney, he knew to be tenanted. It suddenly occurred to him that there might be deposited Parson Henning's negroes ; and there too (betrayed by their recognition of him) he might experience the fatal consequences of his desperate experiment. Sensations of indescribable horror agitated his whole frame, as, preceded
by Murrell, he advanced with almost trembling step towards the door of the hut. He had muffled his face with
his pocket handkerchief, with a view of concealing, as
far as possible, such of his features as would most
likely betray him to the negroes, and, prepared for the
worst, had cocked the two pistols which he carried in
the pockets of his over-coat, determined, in the event
of an attack, to discharge their contents among the assailants before yielding to his fate. It had all along
been his plan to keep somewhat in rear of Murrell, in
order to take advantage of the first fire, whenever he
should discover signs of hostility. On this occasion
he deemed it of the utmost importance ; for he had
much reason to fear that the hut before him might be
the spot on which was to be decided—perhaps with
his blood—the fate of his undertaking. He accordingly entered with Murrell the fearful hovel, prepared
to sell his life as dearly as possible. He found three

white men and two negroes (but not Mr. Henning's),
eating together by the fire ; and hope, " which comes
to all," once more visited him, and the possibility of
success again dawned upon the prospect. The shan-
ty, for such it was, appears to have been constructed
for temporary use, as a shelter from the weather, till
such time as discovery, or the operations of the clan,
might make it necessary to seek, in the depth of the
morass, some more private retreat.   One of the white
men Murrell appeared to recognise, and called by the
name of Rainhart; the others he had never before
seen. He made several inquiries of Rainhart as to
the prosperity of their cause, and parted with him,
promising to meet him on the following day at the
council-house ; and proceeded on his journey, accompanied by Hues, still preserving a western course.
They at length came to a second lake of considerable
size ; and, finding a skiff, embarked in it for the opposite shore. They had been on the water near an
hour, when they descried a point of elevated land not
far distant, which gave promise of a convenient land-
ing-place. They directed their skiff thither, and were
soon again on terra firma. They now travelled in a
more northern direction (as well as can be recollected);
though, in crossing the lake, they had faced nearly
every point of the compass. They had proceeded but
a short distance when their progress was again interrupted by a large bayou ; which, making out from the
Mississippi, crossed their path and entered the lake
above them. On its bank stood a small filthy cabin,
which proved the wretched abode of a white man and
his family. They entered : Hues with feelings of re-

turning apprehension and dread, lest he should meet
the old parson's negroes. A man, his wife, and two
children, who sat in drowsy silence by the fire, were
the only inmates of this gloomy and comfortless habitation. Murrell recognised them with an air of familiarity and a carelessness of demeanour that bespoke
them old acquaintances; and in a few moments withdrew to converse in private with the man of the house,
leaving but little doubt on the mind of Hues that he was
also a member of the clan; and he prepared himself
(as from the beginning he had resolved) to shoot Murrell when he discovered any thing in his manner in-
dicative of suspicion. When they re-entered the
cabin he glanced a look of scrutiny at their countenances, but discovered in them any thing but that
which he most dreaded, and felt once more secure.

They obtained here the loan of a canoe to carry
them across the bayou that stretched before them.
Owing to the overflow, which rendered the opposite
shore impassable, they did not cross immediately, but
turned down the bayou in a western direction, and
soon found themselves entering a large body of water,
formed by some recent overflow of the Mississippi or
a neighbouring lake. They were near an hour crossing, and were at last obliged to land amid a thick
growth of cane. After toiling their tedious and diffi-
cult way for a short time among the cane, a column of
smoke rising before them indicated at length their
near approach to the habitation of the living. They
advanced to the spot whence proceeded the smoke, and
found a camp, constructed of boards, and exhibiting
any thing but the appearance of comfort. In it were

seated three negroes, alone and cheerless, in filthy attire, and with subdued and downcast countenances, bespeaking rather the melancholy pensiveness of desponding criminals than the cheerful hilarity of joyful freemen. Unfortunate beings! thought Hues, as he surveyed, with emotions of pity, their forlorn condition; how soon will your delusions vanish! how soon will be written, in letters of blood, the disappointment of all your fond visions and cherished hopes of liberty and independence! There was no white person with them. Murrell inquired what had become of their leader: they replied they had not seen him for several days.

Murrell and Hues left the camp, and continued their way among the cane. They had progressed but a few hundred yards when Murrell paused; and, pointing through the morass to a large cottonwood-tree that rose in height and magnitude above the surrounding growth, and addressing himself to Hues, said, " Do you see yon lofty cottonwood that towers so majestically over all the other trees ?" To which Hues replied he did. " That tree," continued Murrell, " stands in the Garden of Eden; and we have but a quarter of a mile to travel before we shall set foot on that happy spot, where many a noble plot has been concerted." They continued along the shore of a lake which they now found themselves approaching, till, finding a canoe that belonged to the clan, they embarked for the island that rose in its midst, and on which stood the cottonwood to which Murrell had been directing the attention of his companion. The island was covered with thick matting cane and a growth of lofty trees,

8*

which, added to a luxuriant underwood, gave it an air of peculiar solemnity and gloom. Full in the midst of it, as if proud of its empire, rose a solitary cabin. It was the grand council-house of the mystic confederacy; in which, protected by the secrecy of surrounding deserts and trackless solitudes, they originated and digested a plan of operations more alarming in its tendency, extensive in its object, and destructive in its effects, than any of which history furnishes a record in all past time.

They landed on a point of the island, and proceeded towards the council-house. The most solemn and interesting reflections occupied the mind of Hues as he followed his mysterious companion towards that dismal, and, as he feared, fated spot. The fond recollections of home, and the many cherished objects that he had left behind ; the endearments of kindred and attachment of friends, from whom he might perhaps be sundered for ever; the fertile fields and smiling scenes of his native land, destined to be deluged in the blood of his fellow-countrymen; its cities and villages laid waste by the desolating march of a lawless and murderous band of ruffians and robbers, led on by a poisonous swarm from the " great northern hive" of fanatics and incendiaries, presented to his mind a picture that strung anew his sinking energies, and nerved him to meet with dauntless front an occasion to which before he had felt wellnigh unequal. He resolved—it might be at the peril of his life—to march with determined step boldly to the throne, and learn there the decrees of the dread conspiracy ; and never was there an occasion that required more cool

and deliberate firmness.   To enter alone the camp of
the enemy, listen to their secret councils, and mingle
in their debates, with no other protection than a simple disguise, which he had no certain assurance had
not been already pierced by the keen glance of their
mysterious and veteran leader, called for an effort of
moral courage that can only be accounted for, scarcely justified, by a consideration of the dangerous and
threatening cloud that hung in such fearful proximity
over the destinies of his country.

On entering the council-house they found eleven
of their most prominent characters assembled, among
whom Hues learned the four following names : James
Haines, Perry Doddridge, Samuel Robertson, and ——
Sperlock.   After the first salutation and greeting, a
general inquiry followed as to their respective prosperity and success ; what progress they had been making in the distribution of counterfeit money ; what
new speculations had been made ; were any of the
fraternity overtaken or in prison, and needed their assistance ; how many proselytes each member had
made to the cause ; who were candidates for admis-
sion, &c.   Murrell was interrogated as to the cause
of his absence from the council-house at the time designated for meeting the striker with Henning's negroes.   He replied that his too early start, occasioned
by his great anxiety to redeem his engagement, had
brought upon him a most unfortunate suspicion, but
urged that he had been detained by the high waters
of the Mississippi.   They informed him that the negroes had arrived some days before, and were badly frosted.   And that, becoming doubtful as to the

time of his return, they had deemed it best to push them, and make sales as early as possible. The usual ceremonies past, all interrogatories answered, and accounts rendered by the members of the clan, Murrell desired the attention of the house; and, taking Hues by the hand, presented him to the fraternity in the following language: "Here, my brave counsellors, this is a counsellor of my own making, and I am not ashamed of the workmanship; let Mr. Hues be examined by whom he may." They all approached and shook hands with Hues, and gave him the two degrees, and the signs by which they were distinguished. He first received the sign of the striker, and afterward that of the grand counsellor. Hues was drilled by them in giving and receiving these signs till he could equal the most skilful.

He was next desired to give his opinion respecting the negro war; and asked what was his idea of their faith and principles. The following is taken from an address which he then proceeded to deliver before them:—

"*Gentlemen of the Mystic Conspiracy:*—

"My youth and inexperience must plead the cause of any deficiency I may betray before this worthy and enlightened congregation. I am better qualified to acquiesce in the measures and sentiments of others than to advance any thing of my own. So recently have I been honoured with the secrets of this august conspiracy, that I am unable to offer any thing original. I have received all my ideas from our honourable dictator; and I should feel myself guilty of presumption were I to offer any amendments to his present deep and

well-arranged plans and purposes. Your schemes, under the guidance of our experienced leader, appear to
me practicable and praiseworthy.

"My opinion of the faith and principles of this lord·
ly band may be expressed in few words ; and as I have
been honoured by the instruction and confidence of our
gallant leader, to be whose creature only is my highest
aspiration, I flatter myself of its correctness. I consider the members of this fraternity absolved from duty
or obligation to all men save their commander. We
find ourselves placed in the world surrounded with every thing needful for our comfort and enjoyment; and
shall we stand supinely by and see others enjoy those
things to which we have an equal right, because an established order of things, which we neither believe in
nor respect, forbids our participating in them?

"We consider every thing under the control of our
power as our right : more, we consider man, earth, and
beast, all as materials subject to the enterprise of our
power. Turn your attention to the animal world ; do
we not see the beast of the field, the fowl of the air,
and the fish of the sea, all in their turns falling victims
to each other: and, last of all, turn your attention to
man, and do we not see him falling a victim to his fel-
low-man. If there be a God, he has evidently given
his sanction to this system of violence, and impressed
it upon nature with the force of a law. But, my brave
associates, we are sworn foes to law and order, and
recognise no obligations apart from those of the fraternity. Be it our boast that we are lords of our own
wills, and while we live let us riot in all the pompous
luxuries which the spoils of our enemies can afford.

"We are told in history that Rome lost her liberty by
the conspiracy of three Romans, on an island of the
river Rhenus. And why may not the conspiracy of
four hundred Americans in this morass of the Missis-

sippi river glean the southern and western banks, destroy their cities, and slaughter our enemies? Have
we no Antony to scatter the firebrands of rebellion;
no Lepidus to open his coffers of gold; or no Augustus
to lead us to battle? Such a conclusion would be an im-
peachment of the abilities of our gallant chieftain."

We give but a small portion of Mr. Hues's speech
in the council-house, which was very long, and em-
braced many topics not here introduced. He dwelt
much upon the moral irresponsibility of mankind—the
superiority of the animal over the intellectual propen-
sities, as proved from the strength of the passions con-
trasted with the weakness of the judgment of men, &c.
But we shall not longer trespass on the reader's pa-
tience.

To return to the scene at the council-house : when
Hues had finished his speech, and all unsettled business was disposed of, the assembly rose and dispersed,
each to his own residence : for many of them owned
huts, which they had erected about on points of high
land contiguous to the morass, under pretence of keeping wood-yards to accommodate Mississippi boatmen,
though really on account of their privacy, and convenience to the operations of the clan.

Murrell having business with members of the fraternity who had not made their appearance at the
council-house, proposed to visit such of them as lived
on the river, and set forward, in company with Hues,
for the house of Jehu Barney. They found their skiff
necessary during most of the way. They passed on
their right a small hut, near which were four negroes, cutting wood. Their hut stood upon the bank
of the large bayou down which they were paddling

Murrell remarked to Hues that those negroes had been stolen and sold several times, and were still in reserve for a future market; and would be again sold so soon as the excitement in regard to them should subside. They made no halt at the hut, but continued in the direction of the river. They passed in the bayou a flat-boat of considerable size, that appeared to be undergoing repair, which Murrell called his; and said that he intended it to convey negroes to some point on the river below New-Orleans, where they could be shipped to Texas at the shortest notice, on board of a packet; remarking that he had already made arrangements for some forty or fifty with that view.

They at length arrived at the house, or rather the cabin, of Jehu Barney. It was near sunset, and there was no prospect of reaching more agreeable quarters. They were consequently compelled to remain, though Hues had resolved not to trust himself to sleep, through the night; for he felt but little fondness for such chamber-companions. During the evening conversation turned on various topics, chiefly, however, on such as were more immediately connected with the operations of the morass. Among other things, Hues learned the arrangement which Murrell made for retaking the negroes he had promised to deliver to Mr. Erwin; which were, in the first place, to deliver the negroes and secure his money, leaving with them directions to appear at a certain point on the river the following night, where Barney was instructed to meet and convey them to some other market.

Hues spent the night, not in sleep, but in preparing an excuse to part with Murrell in the morning. For he had determined not to spend another day in the morass. He had seen enough to relieve his doubts as to the representations of Murrell, and being satisfied of the removal of Mr. Henning's negroes, he saw no longer any prospect of serving him there. Besides, he had so far come off victorious, and had no sufficient assurance that he would be so fortunate upon a second trial; and hence saw no good reason for longer exposing his life, and the hope of serving his fellow-countrymen, to the uncertainties and dangers with which, in that gloomy place, he saw himself surrounded. Moreover, having learned the extent of the clan, that many of its members lived in those parts of the different states where he was known, and some of them occupying respectable standings before the community, he did not know but he might meet some acquaintance; or, if not, some one who had seen him, and who might betray his disguise; for he had been told by Murrell that the meeting at the council-house on the morrow would be much larger than the one he had witnessed. Hence this resolution.

CHAPTER VII.

EARLY on the morning of February 2d, Hues made known to Murrell his intention of leaving him. Murrell appeared much disappointed (for he had never once imagined that Hues contemplated returning so soon), and objected that he had not, as yet, been enabled to redeem his promise to show him the Arkansas ladies ; and continued, that there were several subjects of importance to be brought before the council, on which he had promised himself the pleasure of hearing his views. To which Hues replied, that, as to the Arkansas ladies, for the pleasure of seeing the fair widow at Mr. Erwin's, he could afford to dispense with them for the present : and as regarded his opinions before the council, they could be of but little importance ; as he was not prepared, for reasons already given, to advance any thing new : assuring Murrell at the same time that he had the utmost confidence in his opinions on any subject that might be agitated before the house, and should be proud to adopt them as his own. This appeal to Murrell's vanity had a most happy effect in putting an end to his importunities. He offered no farther objection, but accompanied Hues on board a skiff that lay at the shore, and saw him safely landed on the opposite bank of the river. Hues set out for Mr. Erwin's, where he promised to remain till Murrell should rejoin him ; and Murrell returned to his clan. On his arrival Hues found Mr. Erwin at home, and communicated to him all that had transpired. Upon which they determined to have a guard in readiness to arrest Murrell when he should bring the negroes which Mr. Erwin had contracted to purchase ; and accordingly made arrangements to that effect. Hues preferred such an arrangement, as it would go very far to anticipate the incredulity of the world : for although he was himself satisfied, the world was yet to be convinced, which he foresaw would be attended with much difficulty, unless he could overtake him

E   9

(Murrell) in some act of villany.   Besides, should he,
by arresting him sooner, risk his statements to the public upon his own bare assertion, unsupported by the
proof of any overt act, there were many of the clan
who stood as yet unimpeached before the community,
ready to certify to Murrell's good character, and thus
discredit his testimony, perhaps bring his motives in
question, and, it might be, defeat the very purpose
which had led him to encounter so many and great
dangers.   Nay, more ; it would have been their policy
to assassinate him, and prevent his evidence from ever
coming before the public.

On the following afternoon of February 3d, Murrell returned to the house of Mr. Erwin, where he
found Hues, according to promise, awaiting his arrival.
It was not long before he took occasion to renew
with Mr. E. the subject of the negroes, and designated the time at which they were to be delivered.
At length (for he seldom remained long in the same
place) he proposed to Hues to set out for Mr. Champion's, with whom they had left their horses six days
before, to which Hues assented ; and early in the
evening of the same day they reached Mr. Champion's house.   While there Hues had no opportunity of
conversing privately with Mr. C., and hence gave him
no account of his adventure.

Early on the morrow Murrell and his companion
once more mounted their horses and directed their
course for Madison county.

The following are the certificates of Messrs. Erwin, Champion, and Shelby :—

" *State of Tennessee, Tipton County.*

" Having been called on by Virgil A. Stewart to
state to the public whether the statements set forth in
the publication entitled ' The Western Land-Pirate'
are correct or not, I do hereby certify to the world that
all that is set forth in that publication relative to the
said Virgil A. Stewart calling at my house in this county, on the bank of the Mississippi river, in the latter
part of January, 1834, in company with the notorious
villain John A. Murrell, is strictly correct in all the
many particulars set forth in that publication. The said
Virgil A. Stewart was travelling with Murrell in disguise, and under the fictitious name of Adam Hues.
Mr. Stewart then informed me of his real name and
business, and solicited my assistance, provided he should
need it. I also informed him that he might depend on
the aid of Matthew Erwin, my neighbour, who lived
a few miles below me on the river. I have frequently
conversed with Mr. Erwin on the subject of Murrell
having agreed to bring him (Erwin) three negro men ;
of the arrangement that Mr. Stewart had made with Mr.
Erwin to have a guard to arrest the said Murrell when he
should arrive with the negroes which he had promised
to bring Mr. Erwin. I have also heard Mr. Hargus,
who lives on the river below Mr. Erwin, state that Mr.
Stewart was at his house in company with the said
Murrell, and that his son carried Mr. Stewart and Murrell over the river in a skiff ; and that the said Virgil A.
Stewart informed him (Mr. Hargus) of his real name
and business with John A. Murrell.

" Mr. Stewart requested me, before he started over
to the morass, if Murrell came back to my house after his horse, and he (Mr. Stewart) was not with him,
to have Murrell arrested immediately, as I might know

E 2

that he was murdered.   Mr. Stewart and Murrell had
left their horses at my house.

"I hope these statements will be fully satisfactory
to all who are not satisfied on the subject.

"Given under my hand and seal, this 18th day of October, 1835.

[Sealed.]   "JOHN CHAMPION.

"*State of Tennessee, Shelby County.*

"Having been called on by Virgil A. Stewart to
state to the world what I know relative to the said Virgil A. Stewart and the notorious John A. Murrell being at my house while I resided on the Mississippi
river, in Tipton county of this state, in the latter part
of January and first of February, 1834, I now certify
to the world that all that is set forth in the publication entitled the 'Western Land-Pirate' is correct so far
as my name is connected with the same ; and I will
further state, for the satisfaction of all who may wish to
know it, that John A. Murrell did engage to bring me
three negro men, and that Virgil A. Stewart concerted a
plan with me to arrest Murrell when he should bring
said negroes.

"Mr. Stewart was travelling with said Murrell in
disguise, and under the fictitious name of Adam Hues.
Mr. Stewart informed me of his real name and business.   All this transpired as mentioned in the 'Western
Land-Pirate.'

"Given under my hand and seal, this 20th day of October, 1835.

[Sealed.]   "MATTHEW ERWIN."

"*Tipton County, Tennessee, Oct. 19th,* 1835.
"MR. VIRGIL A. STEWART :—

"You have requested me to state what I know of
your trip to Arkansas in company with John A. Mur-

rell, the western land-thief, which I will do in a few
words. Early in February, 1834, I was standing on
the bank of the Mississippi river, near my dwelling,
when I perceived two men riding towards me, one of
whom I suspected of being the notorious Murrell, having seen him once previously; the other I now know
must have been you; moreover, at the time, being un-
acquainted with you, I supposed you to belong to the
same gang. After you passed I went to the house, and
observed to my wife that two suspicious-looking fellows
had just gone by. She then informed me that, during
my absence from home, two white men on horseback had
been among our negroes tampering with them, offering
to take them to a free state, &c. I got on my horse
and rode out to the place where my negroes were at
work, determining to learn from them all the particulars. They described the men so as to leave no doubt
on my mind that they were the same fellows who had
passed but a short time before. I concluded then to follow you to Randolph, whither I supposed you had gone,
and to ascertain if one was Murrell (as I was not certain of it myself), and have him well Lynched; but
nothing was to be seen of you. Next day I went down to
my neighbour's (John Champion), who was then living
four miles below me on the river, to learn from him if
he had seen them and knew them. He told me they
stayed there all night, and that one of the men was Murrell, who had stolen negroes from a Mr. Henning, a
preacher of Madison county. The other was a man by
the name of Stewart, who was following said Murrell
for the purpose of detecting his villany. And Champion then related to me the conversation that passed between you and himself; the same that was afterward
published in Stewart's life of John A. Murrell.

"A few days afterward I saw another man, Mr. Mat-

9*

thew Erwin, who confirmed what Mr. Champion had
said.   With Champion I am well acquainted, and know
him to be an honest man, and any thing he would state
is deserving of credit.   I will here inform you that I
too have had some knowledge of the Murrell clan in
Arkansas, and believe them to be villains of the deep-
est die.   Many of them were concerned in robbing a
flat-boat that grounded six miles below me, in May,
1834.   As it regards the Barneys, fellows mentioned in
your list of Murrell's accomplices, I can say, they stole
from me last fall two negroes, and kept them concealed for several days ; they soon learned they were suspected, and that I was determined, if I did not get them,
to punish the Barneys agreeably to the merits of their
crime ; therefore, in a short time, my negroes were
forthcoming.

" On the subject of G. N. Saunders, the man who
certifies and swears for Judge Clanton, I will merely
state, I know nothing of him personally ; he left this
country before I moved to it ; but, from his general
character here, I should say he was a base man ; and
whatever he might say or swear to not entitled to credit.

" Respectfully, your friend,

" ORVILLE SHELBY."

Murrell now began to speak of the bad luck he
had had with the old parson's negroes, which appeared to give him much uneasiness.   Hues, deeming
the occasion a safe one, ventured, for the first time, to
ask him a direct question respecting the negroes.   He
inquired to what market he had sent them.   Murrell
replied, " They have sent my two, with three others,
and seven horses, down the river in one of those small
trading-boats ; they intended, if they could, to go
through the Choctaw pass to the Yazoo market ; and

they have with them ten thousand dollars in counterfeit money, which I fear is to upset the whole matter.
I am not pleased with the arrangement.   The fellows
whom they have sent are only strikers, and that is too
much to put in their hands at one time.   D—d if I am
not fearful they will think themselves made when they
sell, and leave us behind in the lurch ; though Lloyd
says there is no danger in them ; that he told them to
sell and mizzel."

Once more on the road, Murrell renewed the unfinished narrative of his life, as follows :—

Murrell. " After I returned home from the first grand
circuit I made among the speculators, I remained
there but a short time, as I could not rest when my
mind was not actively engaged in some speculation.
I commenced the foundation of this mystic clan on
that tour, and suggested the plan of exciting a rebellion among the negroes, as the sure road to an inexhaustible fortune to all who would engage in the expedition.   The first mystic sign which is used by this
clan was in use among robbers before I was born ;
and the second had its origin from myself, Phelps,
Haines, Cooper, Doris, Bolton, Harris, Doddridge,
Celly, Morris, Walter, Depont, and one of my brothers,
on the second night after my acquaintance with them
in New-Orleans.   We needed a higher order to carry
on our designs, and we adopted our sign, and called it
the sign of the grand council of the mystic clan ; and
practised ourselves to give and receive the new sign
to a fraction before we parted : and, in addition to this
improvement, we invented and formed a mode of corresponding, by means of ten characters, mixed with

other matter, which has been very convenient on many
occasions, and especially when any of us get into difficulties. I was encouraged in my new undertaking,
and my heart began to beat high with the hope of being able one day to visit the pomp of the southern
and western people in my vengeance ; and of seeing
their cities and towns one common scene of devasta-
tion, smoked walls and fragments.

" I decoyed a negro man from his master in Middle
Tennessee, and sent him to Mills's Point by a young
man, and I waited to see the movements of the owner.

" He thought his negro had run off. So I started to
take possession of my prize. I got another friend at
Mills's Point to take my negro in a skiff, and convey
him to the mouth of Red river, and I took a passage on
a steamboat. I then went through the country by
land, and sold my negro for nine hundred dollars, and
the second night after I sold him I stole him again,
and my friend ran him to the Irish bayou in Texas ; I
followed on after him, and sold my negro in Texas
for five hundred dollars. I then resolved to visit
South America, and see if there was no opening in
that country for a speculation ; I had also concluded
that I could get some strong friends in that quarter to
aid me in my designs relative to a negro rebellion ;
but of all people in the world, the Spaniards are the
most treacherous and cowardly ; I never want them
concerned in any matter with me ; I had rather take the
negroes in this country to fight than a Spaniard. I
stopped in a village, and passed as a doctor, and commenced practising medicine. I could ape the doctor
firstrate, having read Ewel, and several other works

on primitive medicine. I became a great favourite of an old Catholic; he adopted me as his son in the faith, and introduced me to all the best families as a young doctor from North America. I had been with the old Catholic but a very short time before I was a great Roman Catholic, and bowed to the cross, and attended regularly to all the ceremonies of that persuasion; and, to tell you the fact, Hues, all the Catholic requires or needs to be universally received, is to be correctly represented; but you know I care nothing for religion; I had been with the old Catholic about three months, and was getting a heavy practice, when an opportunity offered for me to rob the good man's secretary of nine hundred and sixty dollars in gold, and I could have got as much more in silver if I could have carried it. I was soon on the road for home again; I stopped three weeks in New-Orleans as I came home, and had some high fun with old Mother Surgick's girls.

"I collected all my associates in New-Orleans at one of my friend's houses in that place, and we sat in council three days before we got all our plans to our notion; we then determined to undertake the rebellion at every hazard, and make as many friends as we could for that purpose. Every man's business being assigned him, I started for Natchez on foot. Having sold my horse in New-Orleans with the intention of stealing another after I started, I walked four days, and no opportunity offered for me to get a horse. The fifth day, about twelve o'clock, I had become very tired, and stopped at a creek to get some water and rest a little. While I was sitting on a log, looking down the

E 3

road the way I had come, a man came in sight riding
a good-looking horse. The very moment I saw him I
determined to have his horse if he was in the garb
of a traveller. He rode up, and I saw from his equipage
that he was a traveller. I arose from my seat and drew
an elegant rifle pistol on him, and ordered him to dismount. He did so, and I took his horse by the bridle,
and pointed down the creek, and ordered him to walk
before me. We went a few hundred yards and stopped. I hitched his horse, then made him undress
himself, all to his shirt and drawers, and ordered him
to turn his back to me. He asked me if I was going to
shoot him. I ordered him the second time to turn his
back to me. He said, 'If you are determined to kill
me, let me have time to pray before I die.' I told him
I had no time to hear him pray. He turned round,
and dropped on his knees, and I shot him through the
back of the head. I ripped open his belly, and took
out his entrails, and sunk him in the creek. I then
searched his pockets, and found four hundred and one
dollars and thirty-seven cents, and a number of papers
that I did not take time to examine. I sunk the pocketbook and papers and his hat in the creek. His boots
were bran new, and fitted me very genteelly, and I put
them on, and sunk my old shoes in the creek to atone
for them. I rolled up his clothes and put them into his
portmanteau, as they were quite new cloth of the best
quality. I mounted as fine a horse as ever I strad-
dled, and directed my course for Natchez in much
better style than I had been for the last five days.

"I reached Natchez, and spent two days with my
friends at that place and the girls under the hill to-

gether. I then left Natchez for the Choctaw nation, with the intention of giving some of them a chance for their property. As I was riding along between Benton and Rankin, planning for my designs, I was overtaken by a tall and good-looking young man, riding an elegant horse, which was splendidly rigged off; and the young gentleman's apparel was of the gayest that could be had, and his watch-chain and other jewellery were of the richest and best. I was anxious to know if he intended to travel through the Choctaw nation, and soon managed to learn. He said he had been to the lower country with a drove of negroes, and was returning home to Kentucky. We rode on, and soon got very intimate for strangers, and agreed to be company through the Indian nation. We were two fine-looking men, and, to hear us talk, we were very rich. I felt him on the subject of speculation, but he cursed the speculators, and said he was in a bad condition to fall into the hands of such villains, as he had the cash with him that twenty negroes had sold for ; and that he was very happy that he happened to get in company with me through the nation. I concluded he was a noble prize, and longed to be counting his cash. At length we came into one of those long stretches in the nation, where there was no house for twenty miles, on the third day after we had been in company with each other. The country was high, hilly, and broken, and no water; just about the time I reached the place where I intended to count my companion's cash, I became very thirsty, and insisted on turning down a deep hollow, or dale, that headed near the road, to hunt some water. We had followed down the dale for near four

hundred yards, when I drew my pistol and shot him
through. He fell dead; I commenced hunting for his
cash, and opened his large pocketbook, which was
stuffed very full; and when I began to open it I thought
it was a treasure indeed; but oh! the contents of that
book! it was richly filled with the copies of love-
songs, the forms of love-letters, and some of his own
composition,—but no cash. I began to cut off his
clothes with my knife, and examine them for his
money. I found four dollars and a half in change in
his pockets, and no more. And is this the amount for
which twenty negroes sold? thought I. I recollected
his watch and jewellery, and I gathered them; his
chain was rich and good, but it was swung to an old
brass watch. He was a puff for true, and I thought
all such fools ought to die as soon as possible. I took
his horse, and swapped him to an Indian native for four
ponies, and sold them on the way home. I reached
home, and spent a few weeks among the girls of my
acquaintance, in all the enjoyments that money could
afford.

" My next trip was through Georgia, South Carolina,
North Carolina, Virginia, and Maryland, and then back
to South Carolina, and from there round by Florida
and Alabama. I began to conduct the progress of my
operations, and establish my emissaries over the country in every direction. After I had turned for home
from Alabama, I was passing by where one of my
friends lived in company with three of my associates,
who were going home with me; we stopped to see
how our friend was doing; while we were setting out
in his portico, a large drove of sheep came up to his

blocks. He went out and examined them, and found them to be the flock of an old Baptist, who lived about six miles up the road from his house ; they had been gone from their owner for three months, and he could hear nothing of them. The old Baptist had accused my friend of having his sheep driven off to market, and abused him very much for stealing them. My friend acquainted me with all the circumstances, and I conclu-ded to play a trick on the old jockey for his suspicions ; so we gathered up all the flock, and drove them on be-fore us, and got to the old Baptist's just after dark : we called the old man out to the gate, and wanted to lodge with him all night ; but he refused to take us in, and urged as a reason that his old woman was sick, and could not accommodate us as he would wish. In an-swer to these objections, I told him that we could wait on ourselves ; that I had three active young men with me, who could do all that was wanting to be done. I told him I had moved down below in the spring of the year, when my sheep were scattered, and I concluded to leave them until fall ; and that I had been up to my old place after them, and was going home ; and com-plained of the hard drive I had made that day, as an excuse to stop with the old Baptist. I then told him I had a very fine wether that I wished to kill, as he was very unruly, and hard to drive, and what we did not use that night he was welcome to. The old man showed us a place to pen our sheep, and the corn-crib, and stables ; and told us that, if we could wait on our-selves, we were welcome to stay. We soon fed our horses, and had the mutton dressed, and a large pot-ful cooking. The old man told us where to find meal,

10

milk, and butter ; and while my associates were cooking
the sheep, I was conversing with the old Baptist on
religion ; I told him I was a Baptist preacher.   When
news came that the sheep was done, I went into the
kitchen, and we had a real feast of mutton, at the expense of the old Baptist.

"After supper we went in where the old lady
lay sick. The old man got his Bible and hymn-
book, and invited me to go to duty. I used the books,
and then prayed like hell for the recovery of the old
lady. The next morning we were up before daylight,
and had the sheep all on the road. We drove them
about a mile, and scattered them in the woods, and
left them. We left the head of the wether that we
killed lying in the lot, where the old man could see
that it was his own mark. I arrived home after a trip
of six months.

"I have been going ever since from one place to
another, directing and managing ; but I have others
now as good as myself to manage. This fellow,
Phelps, that I was telling you of before, he is a noble
chap among the negroes, and he wants them all free ;
he knows how to excite them as well as any person ;
but he will not do for a robber, as he cannot kill a
man unless he has received an injury from him first.
He is now in jail at Vicksburg, and I fear will hang.
I went to see him not long since, but he is so strictly
watched that nothing can be done. He has been in
the habit of stopping men on the highway, and robbing
them, and letting them go on ; but that will never do
for a robber : after I rob a man he will never give evidence against me, and there is but one safe plan in

the business, and that is to kill—if I could not afford
to kill a man I would not rob. I have often told
Phelps that he would be caught before he knew it. I
could raise men enough to go and tear down the jail,
and take Phelps by force ; but that would endanger
all our other plans. I have frequently had money
enough to settle myself in wealth ; but I have spent
it as freely as water in carrying on my designs. The
last five years of my life have been passed in the
same way that I have been telling you, Hues ; I have
been from home the best part of the time, and have
let but few chances escape me when I could rob that
I did not do it. It would take a week yet, Hues, to
tell over all my scrapes of that kind. You must come
and stay at my house the week before I start with
those negroes to Erwin, and I will have time to tell
over all my ups and downs for the last five years. I
want you to go that trip with me. You can arrange
your business in the nation in two weeks, and get to
my house in Madison county. You will make more
that trip than all your concerns are worth in the nation, so you had better give away what you have there
than be confined to it."

The approach of night now warned Murrell and
his companion to look out for a house of entertain-
ment, and Murrell ended his narrative.

CHAPTER VIII.

MURRELL and his companion, at an early hour of
the following morning (February 5th), were on the road
and pursuing their journey. The time was drawing
near when business of an important character, as Murrell had been assured by Hues, would make it necessary for them to separate. But the short distance of
two miles lay between them and the point (Wesley)
that was to divide them. Murrell expressed himself
averse to the separation, and urged many reasons for
continuing their journey longer together. Hues, however, inexorable, still pressed the plea of business;
and Murrell, finding his solicitations unavailing, yielded on condition that Hues would hasten his business
in the Choctaw Nation, and rejoin him at his house in
Madison county; promising himself, meanwhile, to
proceed immediately homeward, and have in readiness the negroes promised Mr. Erwin by the time
Hues should visit him. Upon this, the following
(which is the last) dialogue between Murrell and
Hues ensued :—

Murrell. "Well, Hues, we part to-day, and I am
not half done talking; but I will quit telling what I
have done, and tell what I am going to do. I have
about forty negroes now engaged that are waiting for
me to run them; and, the best of it is, they are almost
all the property of my enemies. I have a great many
friends who have got in to be overseers: they are a

strong support to my plans. I have a friend by the name of Nolin, my brother-in-law's brother, who is overseeing in Alabama for a man who is from home. Nolin has decoyed six likely negro men for me. I am to go within about ten miles with a two-horse car-ryall, and stop at an appointed place. Nolin is to raise a sham charge against the negroes, and they are to run off and come to my wagon. I will put them into the wagon, and fasten down the curtains all round, and then throw fodder over them, and have a striker to drive them to the Mississippi swamp for me, where there will be no danger. I will ride a few miles behind, but never seem to notice the wagon. Nolin is to be driving the woods for the negroes, and reporting that he has seen them every day or two, un-til I have time to get clear out of the country with them. I have eight more engaged in Alabama, at one Eason's, the fellow whom I was speaking of before. The remainder of the forty I shall get in my own county. You recollect the boat I showed you in the bayou, on the other side of the river ? that boat I intend to fill with negroes for my own benefit."

Hues. "There is a fellow by the name of Bundels, or Buns, or some such name, a negro-trader, who lives somewhere in the new part of Tennessee, who, I think, is as hard to cheat as any man I have seen in all my travels ; and, if all the Tennesseans are as sharp as I think he is, I do not want to deal with many of them."

M. "O! I know who you are thinking of ; his name is Byrn ; he does pass down through your country sometimes, and a great sharper he is ; he can cheat

10*

you to death, and make you think all the time he is
putting you on the road to a fortune ; but, in spite of
him, I handled the cash that one of *his* negroes sold
for.   He suspected me of running his negro, and offered me the chance of him for three hundred dollars,
but I thought it was a poor business to give three hundred dollars for a thing I already had.   Byrn is a hard
hand, and I would as soon fall into the hands of the
devil as into his."

Hues pretended not to remember the name of Byrn,
with a view of leaving an impression on Murrell that
his acquaintance with him was very slight.   Yet he
took care to give such an account of him as enabled
Murrell, without any difficulty, to understand to whom
he alluded.

Hues knew that Byrn had lost a negro, and his object was to ascertain whether or not Murrell had
stolen him.   Hence the above ingenious plan.

Murrell. " I can tell you another trick we have,
Hues, to get horses.   One of our friends examines the
stray-books regularly ; and, whenever there is a stray
horse of any value found on them, he goes and gets a
description of the horse, and then writes for two of his
friends, if none are near, who are strangers in the
country he lives in.   He gives his friends a minute
description of the horse ; and one will go and claim,
and the other prove the property.   I was in Arkansas
this fall, and there was a man there who had found a
fine horse standing in the edge of the Mississippi
river, which had probably got off of some boat and
swum to the shore ; but he could not get up the bank.
The man dug away the bank and saved the horse.

One of my friends heard of it, and went and examined the horse, and told me all his flesh-marks. I went and asked the man if he had found a horse of such a description, describing the horse in every particular. He said he had. I looked at the horse and claimed him. I gave the fellow five dollars for his trouble, and took the horse home, and have him yet. I have swum the Mississippi twice on that horse."

Hues. "We are not far from Wesley, where we will part: but you have not yet given me a list of the names of our friends."

M. "Oh! yes, yes. Have you any paper with you? You must have that before we part."

Hues here bethought himself of the remainder of his blank-book, which he drew from his pocket; but, upon examination, found it containing but four and a half leaves, which Murrell assured him were much too little paper to contain all the names of the clan; and proposed to postpone the list till he should visit him in Madison county, at which time he would give him a complete one, accompanied with the residence of each. But Hues, reflecting that it might become impossible or imprudent, as was his design, to visit Murrell at his residence, insisted on a list, as far as the paper would warrant it, suggesting to him to confine it chiefly to the principal characters in the different sections of the country; as he would thereby be enabled to form some tolerable idea of their strength: and that, by the time they should again meet, he would be prepared, in some degree, to advance an opinion respecting the general plan of operations. Murrell replied, that, upon the whole, he thought it best himself to

give him some idea of their strength before they parted ; and accordingly proposed to ride out a little from
the road with that view. On commencing the catalogue, he remarked to Hues that it might be well, on
account of the scarcity of paper, to omit the Christian
names ; to which Hues assented, with the reservation
of the initial, as it might prevent confusion.

Hues had observed much more particularity on this
occasion, had he not intended seeing Murrell again
before his arrest. The list obtained was not pri-
marily intended for the public eye. It had been procured merely for the gratification of his own curiosity.
Circumstances, however, which happened after, made
its publication necessary.

The following are the names of the clan, as given
by Murrell, with the several states in which they reside :—

Tennessee.—Two Murrells, S. Wethers, D. Cren-
shaw, M. Dickson, V. Chisim, K. Dickson, L. Ander-
son, P. Johnson, J. Nuckels, L. Bateman, J. Taylor,
E. Chandlor, four Maroneys, two Littlepages, J. Har-
din, Esq. Wilbern, Y. Pearson, G. Wiers, five Lathoms,
A. Smith, six Hueses, S. Spiers, two Byrdsongs, Col.
Jarot, two Nolins, Capt. Ruffin, Ja. Hosskins, W. Cren-
shaw, J. Goaldin, R. Tims, D. Ahart, two Busbeys, L.
More, J. Eas, W. Howel, B. Sims, Z. Gorid, three
Boaltons, G. Sparkes, S. Larit, R. Parew, K. Deron.

Mississippi.—G. Parker, S. Williams, R. Horton,
C. Hapes, W. Presley, G. Corkle, B. Johnson, D.
Rooker, L. Cooper, C. Barton, five Willeys, J. Hess,
two Willsons, Capt. Moris, G. Tucker, three Glenns,
two Harlins, —— Bloodworth, J. Durham, R. Forrow,

S. Cook, G. Goodman, —— Stautton, —— Clanin, C.
Hickman, W. Thomas, Wm. Nawls, D. Marlow, Capt.
Medford, three Hunters, two Gilberts, A. Brown, four
Yarbers.

Arkansas.—S. Pucket, W. Ray, J. Simmons, L.
Good, B. Norton, J. Smith, P. Billing, A. Hooper, C.
Jimerson, six Serrils, three Bunches, four Dartes, two
Barneys, G. Aker, four Tuckers, two Loyds, three
Skurlocks, three Joneses, L. Martin, S. Coulter, H.
Petit, W. Henderson, two Nowlins, three Hortons.

Kentucky.—Three Forrows, four Wards, two Fore-
sythes, D. Clayton, R. Williamson, H. Haly, H. Pot-
ter, D. Mugit, two Pattersons, S. Goin, Q. Brantley, L.
Pots, four Reeses, two Carters.

Missouri.—Four Whites, two Herins, six Milers, G.
Poap, R. Coward, D. Corkle, E. Boalin, W. Aker, two
Garlins, S. Falcon, H. Warrin, two Moaseways, three
Johnsons, Col. S. W. Foreman.

Alabama.—H. Write, J. Homes, G. Sheridon, E.
Nolin, three Parmers, two Glascocks, G. Hammons,
R. Cunagen, H. Chance, D. Belfer, W. Hickel, P.
Miles, O. More, B. Corhoon, S. Baley, four Sorils,
three Martins, M. Hancock, Capt. Boin, Esq. Malone.

Georgia.—H. Moris, D. Haris, two Rameys, four
Cullins, W. Johnson, S. Gambel, two Crenshaws, four
Peakes, two Heffils, D. Coalmon, four Reves, six
Rosses, Capt. Ashley, —— Denson, Esq., two Lenits.

South Carolina.—Three Foarts, four Williamses,
O. Russet, S. Pinkney, six Woods, H. Black, G. Hol-
ler, three Franklins, G. Gravit, B. Henry, W. Simp-
son, E. Owin, two Hookers, three Piles, W. King, N.
Parsons, F. Watters M. Ware two Robersons.

North Carolina.—A. Fentres, two Micklejohns, D. Harilson, M. Coopwood, R. Huiston, four Solomons, J. Hackney, S. Stogdon, three Perrys, four Gilferds, W. Pariners, three Hacks, J. Secel, D. Barnet, S. Bulkes, M. Johnson, B. Kelit, V. Miles, J. Haris, L. Smith, K. Farmer.

Virginia.—R. Garison, A. Beloach, J. Kerkmon, three Merits, W. Carnes, D. Hawks, J. Ferines, G. Derom, S. Walker, four Mathises, L. Wiseman, S. Washorn, P. Hume, F. Henderson, E. Cockburn, W. Milbern.

Maryland.—W. Gwins, H. Brown, F. Smith, G. Dotherd, L. Strawn, three Morgans, D. Hays, four Hobeses, H. M'Gleton, S. M'Write, J. Wilkit, two Fishers, M. Haines, C. Paron, G. M'Watters, A. Cuthbut, W. Leemon, S. Winston, D. Read, M. O'Conel, T. Goodin.

Florida.—E. Carmeter, W. Hargeret, S. Whipel, A. Sterling, B. Stafford, L. M'Guint, G. Flush, C. Winkle, two M'Gilits, E. Foskew, J. Beark, J. Preston, three Baggets.

Louisiana.—C. Depont, J. Bevley, A. Rhone, T. M'Nut, H. Pelton, W. Bryant, four Hunts, two Baleys, S. Roberson, J. Sims, G. Murry, R. Miler, C. Henderson, two Deris, J. Johnson, A. Pelkin, D. Willis, P. Read, S. M'Carty, W. Moss, D. Cotton, T. Parker, L. Ducan, M. Bluren, S. Muret, G. Pase, T. Ray.

Transient members who travel from place to place.— Two Hains, S. Coper, G. Boalton, R. Haris, P. Doddridge, H. Helley, C. Moris, three Rinens, L. Tailor, two Jones, H. Sparkes, three Levits, G. Hunter, G. Tucker, S. Skerlock, Soril Phelps.

When the above catalogue was finished, Murrell observed, " There is not paper to make a proper list; but when you come up to my house we will have time to make a complete one. This will do until then, as you will not travel any until you go with me a few trips and learn the routes. There are not near all the names on this list; but there is no more paper to write on. Hues, I want you to be with me at New-Orleans on the night that the negroes commence their ravages. I intend to head the company that attacks that city myself. I feel an ambition to demolish the city which was defended from the ravages of the British army by the great General Jackson."

Murrell and Hues arrived at Wesley, where they were to part. Hues promised Murrell that he would visit him in three weeks or sooner. They took their leave of each other and parted.

So soon as Murrell was out of sight, Hues returned to Wesley; and leaving at that place the pistol he had borrowed from Colonel Bayliss, he set out for Madison county by a route different from the one which Murrell had taken, and rode on to the house of James H. Corr, distant about seven miles from Wesley, where he spent the night.

CHAPTER IX.

AFTER an early breakfast on the following morning (February 6th), Hues continued his journey towards Madison county, and about twelve o'clock at night

reached the residence of his old friend the Rev. John
Henning, and proceeded to acquaint him with the story
of his adventure, particularly as it related to Murrell's confessions in respect to his negroes. Assisted
by Mr. H., he managed to communicate with a number of the most respectable citizens of the neighbourhood before day, who volunteered their services as a
guard to arrest Murrell. To avail himself of this silent occasion, he had travelled the last ten miles of his
journey after dark. It was not his intention to arrest
him till he should return to Mr. Erwin's with the negroes he had engaged to deliver him, as he deemed the
detection of some such overt act of his villany of no
little importance in lessening the responsibility that
would otherwise rest upon himself in his disclosures to
the public. But he found, on the following day (February 7th), much to his disappointment, that his sug-
gestions of the above prudent and cautionary measure
offered but feeble resistance to the just, though perhaps intemperate and hasty vengeance of an incensed
and injured community.

They determined never again to trust so fearful and
dangerous an enemy beyond their reach. He was
now in their power, and they were resolved to make
sure of him; and on the evening of the same day he
set out for his house, with a guard to arrest him, Hues
himself being one of the guards.

On approaching the house, Hues desired the guard
still to call him by his assumed name; and, after in-
structing them to put certain interrogatories to Murrell, remained without while they entered and proceeded to the arrest.

After they had taken Murrell into custody, the officer, as directed by Hues, asked the following questions :—

Officer. " Who went with you to Arkansas ?"

Murrell. "A young man by the name of Hues."

O. " Had you ever seen the young man before he went with you to Arkansas ?"

M. " Never, until I saw him at the bridge at Estanaula, on my way to Arkansas."

The officer then called Hues into the presence of Murrell. When he made his appearance the countenance of the arch-demon fell, and for the first time in his life his self-possession and wonted firmness forsook him. Indeed, so unexpected was the shock, that more than once he was near swooning away. The idea of having unbosomed himself, in all the confidence of fancied friendship and security, to one whom he now beheld, after the lapse of so short a time, in the attitude of an enemy—a spy—was more than he was prepared to meet ; and to see himself thus out-generalled by a mere youth, whom, but so shortly before, he had imagined captivated by the splendour of his great abilities, and charmed by the dazzling prospect of future fortune, griped to its core his obdurate and flinty heart.

The guard proceeded to conduct Murrell to the committing court at Jackson ; and while on the road he asked one of them " who this man Hues was ; and whether he had many acquaintances in the country ?" The guard, anxious to hear what he would say, replied that Hues was a stranger. " Well," continued

F 11

Murrell, " he had better remain a stranger ; I have friends. I would much rather be in my condition than his."

Guards' Certificate.

"*State of Tennessee, Madison County.*

" We, the undersigned, citizens of the county and state aforesaid, do hereby certify that we formed a part of the guard that arrested John A. Murrell in February, 1834, under the charge of having stolen Parson John Henning and his son's negroes, of this county. After Murrell was arrested he was questioned as to the young man who detected him; he then and there declared that he had never known him until he met him at the bridge at Estanaula. Virgil A. Stewart was in company with the guard, and had requested them still to call him by his assumed name, Adam Hues. Murrell was asked if he knew the name of the young man who accompanied him to Arkansas. He stated that he called his name Hues. Murrell was then desired to state when he had first seen this man Hues. He stated that he had never seen him until at the bridge at Estanaula, about eleven days before ; and that he had never heard of Hues until that time. After the guard had received Murrell, Mr. Stewart presented himself before him, and Murrell called him Hues. As the guard were going on to Jackson with Murrell, he inquired of them who this man Hues was, and whether he had any acquaintances in this country.

" We were very particular to make every discovery we could to ascertain whether Murrell could ever have known Mr. Stewart before that time. We do therefore declare to the world, that Murrell could never have had any knowledge of Mr. Stewart under any name whatever, until after Mr. Stewart practised his deception on him.

" Given under our hands, this 10th of October, 1835.

"DAVID M. HENNING,
RICHARD G. HENNING,
GEORGE HICKS,
R. H. BYRN,
WILLIAM H. LONG."

When the guard reached Jackson (February 8th), Murrell was conducted to a tavern, where he was detained in custody till a court could be called. While they were at the tavern, many persons visited Hues and the prisoner. Till then Hues had not revealed his real name. Deeming it now no longer of importance to continue his disguise, he requested his friends to call him by his proper name. When Murrell discovered that he had been mistaken also in the name of Mr. Stewart; and, instead of being, as he supposed, a stranger, that he was in the midst of his friends and old acquaintances, he betrayed much embarrassment and evident signs of despondency. His spirits, which a little before had seemed to revive, and his returning firmness at being told that Mr. Stewart (for we must hereafter call him by his proper name) was a stranger now sunk under the weight of this new discovery; and Murrell, though a mystic chief, found himself involved in a mystery he could not unfold.

In his testimony before the committing court, Mr. Stewart confined himself to such facts as related to the abduction and subsequent disposition of Mr. Henning's negroes. The deep-laid and sanguinary plot which Murrell had confessed to him was in progress against

F 2

the southern community, he deemed it both imprudent and unsafe to disclose at a period so early, and when the public mind, unschooled to deeds of such dark and desperate daring, was so little prepared to receive and credit it. He foresaw the great difficulty of bringing his fellow-citizens to believe, upon his simple assurance, a narrative, in itself so unnatural and startling; and revealing a scheme of villany so dark in its conception, so extensive in its object, and so alarming and destructive in its operations, as the one which he felt himself charged with making known to the public.

Thus circumstanced, he had much reason to fear that the cry of persecution would find but little difficulty in enlisting public sympathy in Murrell's favour, which would have defeated the very object that such a disclosure contemplated, and possibly resulted in his release. His plan was to withhold the confession of Murrell till further developments should excite public attention to the subject; for he knew that the affair had already progressed too far to be successfully crushed.

Mr. Stewart here occupied a position truly embarrassing, standing as he did between his threatened country on the one hand, and the almost inevitable destruction of himself and character on the other. Too much haste would have seriously endangered the latter; and, in an affair in which they were so intimately identified, probably the safety also of the former; and long delay would have made sure of the destruction of the one, while it held out no hope of protection to the other. At this interesting and highly important crisis, thus standing, as it were, between Scylla and Charybdis, there was but one alternative presented. That alternative, be it said to the honour and the credit of Mr. Stewart, he most wisely adopted. He determined to postpone his publication till such period before the commencement of hostilities as, while it would afford ample time for a preparation to meet the danger, would equally furnish an opportunity for the truth, in part at least, to find its way to light, through other and perhaps less questionable channels. Another reason, perhaps not less strong than the above, had its share in influencing the conduct of Mr. Stewart. He was a stranger in the country, without the aid of family influence, or the prompt and ready testimony of those who best knew his character and worth, to bear him out in his trying situation. He stood alone amid his subtle and bloodthirsty enemies, sustained only by the conscious justice of his cause; for truth, though at all times omnipotent, had not as yet sufficiently declared in his favour to afford immediate protection.

In this situation he saw before him but one dark and cheerless prospect of uncertainty and danger, perhaps of death and disgrace, unrelieved by any hope of present protection. Added to the imminent perils to which, for the public, he had already exposed himself, he now saw but little chance of escaping the sacrifice also of his life. But, like the firm mountains of his cherished country, against which the storms of centuries have raged and spent their fury, he stood unmoved, undismayed, and prepared, should it become necessary, to make this last offering upon the altar of its safety.

11*

Murrell was committed to prison, February 8th, 1834, to await his trial, which took place in July following.

CHAPTER X.

Efforts of John A. Murrell and his confederates for the destruction of the life and character of Virgil A. Stewart, with an exposition of their characters.

HAVING now secured Murrell's arrest, Mr. Stewart saw at once the importance of ferreting out other evidence than his confessions to sustain the prosecution, and vindicate his own motives at the coming trial: for, although those confessions might convict Murrell, they might fail to convince the world, which he deemed of the utmost importance to his own safety and that of the community. Murrell had told him that Mr. Henning's negroes had been sent, in charge of some of the subordinate agents of the clan, to the Yazoo country, where, if they could cross the Yazoo pass, they were to be sold. He therefore determined to proceed, accompanied by a son of Mr. Henning, immediately to that country in search of them; hoping, if they had not been conveyed to another market, to be able to overtake and reclaim them. In doing this Mr. S. found himself obliged to neglect very important business, which had already much suffered for the want of his attention; for, having a few months before made sale of his property, with a view of investing his capital in

the lands of the new purchase, he could employ no
agent who had either the leisure or the inclination to
give that attention to such business as he would have
given it himself. His time, therefore, could never
have been more dearly sacrificed than on that occasion. Could self-interest, under any circumstances,
have been a sufficient temptation to relinquish his undertaking, those were the circumstances with which
he now found himself surrounded. The public lands
had been brought into market, and were being entered
at government prices; capitalists were flocking in
from all quarters, and the chances of advantageous
speculation were rapidly passing by. But we find
such considerations weighing but little with Mr. Stewart, when put in competition with the more interesting
claims of his country's welfare, and the high and important duty which he felt himself called upon to per-
form, in contributing to avert the fearful and impending
calamity that threatened its security.

Pursuant to his determination, Mr. Stewart proposed
to young Mr. Henning to set out for Yazoo, suggesting
his reasons as given above; and, upon his assenting,
they accordingly left Madison county, in the State of
Tennessee, for Manchester, Mississippi.

On their way thither they passed through Mr. S.'s
old neighbourhood in the Choctaw Purchase. The
time was near at hand when they were to establish
courts of justice, and the day for the election of county
officers already appointed. While there, they called
at the house of Matthew Clanton and Wm. Vess, to
whom Mr. S. had intrusted the care of his property and
business during his absence. Clanton expressed him-

self much pleased to see Mr. S., and treated him with
every mark of friendship and attention.   Viewing him
in the light of a particular friend, Mr. Stewart felt no
hesitation in confiding to him the history of his recent
adventure.   He gave him also the names of several
individuals of his acquaintances whom Murrell had
numbered among his accomplices.   Clanton expressed
much astonishment at the intelligence, and manifested
much concern on the occasion ; but promised the
strictest secrecy as to the names given.

On the 12th they left Mr. Clanton, and proceeded
on their way to Manchester, at which place they arrived on the fifteenth ; but could obtain no news of
the negroes ; and were told by a boatman that, at the
time Murrell's boat was to be in the pass, boats could
not enter it ; hence they concluded that his agents had
changed their course and gone down the river.

They separated at Manchester, and young Henning
set out for Vicksburg, to make a farther search, while
Mr. S. directed his course to Madison county, Mississippi, to see Mr. Hudnold, if there was such a man, of
whom Murrell had spoken in the history of his life.
This he deemed of great importance in his intended
publication, as it would tend to corroborate some of the
statements which that publication would set forth.
Besides, his testimony would be of advantage to Mr.
Hudnold, if, as Murrell had represented to him, a suit
was pending against him, at the instance of the clan,
for the value of Eason's negro.   He was at no difficulty in finding Mr. Hudnold, a wealthy and respectable
planter of Madison county, who testified to the truth of
all Murrell had told him.   To the mind of Mr. Stewart

now, the inference was very natural, that all his other representations were equally true. He therefore returned to the Choctaw Purchase more than ever satisfied of the great importance of giving publicity to Murrell's confessions ; and resolved to do so, so soon after his trial in July as prudence might seem to dictate.

On his return to the Purchase on the 21st, he learned that it was generally known throughout that part of the country that Murrell had been arrested, and that his conspiracy had been exposed, together with the names of many of his associates ; and that many of his friends were engaged in conjuring up slanders against his (Mr. S.'s) character.

The object of these attacks upon him Mr. S. very soon discovered to be to discourage the reception of his testimony.

Among others who, as above described were attempting to cast odium upon the name of Mr. Stewart, were a certain Dr. Malone and a Mr. M'Macking, of Hendersonville. The motives of these last we refer to the judgment of the public.

Mr. Stewart remained in the Purchase ten days, during which time he became apprized of the movements of the enemy, made his arrangements accordingly, and set forward once more for Madison county, in the State of Tennessee. On his arrival there, he found the same spirit of detraction and abuse of his character prevailing among a certain class of people, that he had left behind him in the Choctaw Purchase. Some of these, whose situations enabled them to wield a more dangerous influence against him, he exposed to the

public in their true colours ; the rest—too contempti-
ble to merit the trouble—he left to sink under the
weight of their own infamy and insignificance.   While
in Madison county, where he remained until the first
of April, he had a fine opportunity to learn, and in
many instances to observe, the machinations and manœuvres of the private agents of the clan.   Much curiosity was expressed as to whether he would publish
the names of those whom Murrell had given as his
associates.   This, however, was a matter which he
deemed it prudent to say but little about, particularly
at so early a stage of affairs.   He had already seen
fearful indications of the gathering storm—already
had murmurs of threatened vengeance saluted his
ears.   He saw by no very doubtful signs how many
felt interested in his destruction ; for he knew that
the fate of too many characters depended on his testimony not to make it an object to prevent its coming
before the public, which could be accomplished in no
other way so effectually as by putting an end to his
life and destroying his papers.   This he knew would,
moreover, be of importance to them, as it might save
their leader from the penitentiary, and thus enable
them to continue their operations without any serious
interruption ; and there was but one alternative—they
must destroy Mr. Stewart, or be destroyed by him.
Thus exposed to the united vengeance of a whole
confederacy of exasperated and blood-hungry ruffians,
whose lives had presented but one black catalogue
of deeds of death, robbery, and crime, he saw the
chances for his life but too evidently against him.

Parson Henning having now given up all idea of

ever reclaiming his negroes, Mr. Stewart again returned to his business in the Choctaw Purchase, with
the promise to be at the court, which was to be held in
Madison county, in July following ; but exacted from
his friends in Madison, that, in the event any thing
should transpire during his absence that might make
it dangerous to return to court, they would transmit to
him the intelligence immediately, that he might adopt
such measures for his safety as his situation should
demand.   He found it necessary to travel with much
caution, concealing from even his best friends both his
routes and his days of travelling ; and, on all occasions, demeaning himself with almost fastidious reserve ; accessible to few, familiar with none but his
most intimate and confidential friends.

On his return to the Purchase, Mr. Stewart again
visited Messrs. Clanton and Vess, to whose care and
management, as has already been stated, he had intrusted his property and business during his adventure with Murrell.   He saw at once a change in their
conduct towards him.   Vess appeared confused whenever in his presence, and seemed disposed to shun
him.   Yet, how to account for the strange phenome-
non, he found himself entirely at fault.   It was not
long, however, before he discovered a key to the whole
mystery.   The truth was, Mr. Stewart having remained in Tennessee much longer than he had intended, and a report having reached the Purchase that
he had left Tennessee for that region in a few days
after his arrival in Madison county, Clanton and Vess
at once concluded him dead.   But whether they had
not been enlightened in relation to the danger that

threatened Mr. Stewart's life, may hereafter more fully
appear. With Vess, his death appears scarcely to
have been made a question ; for he had already taken
steps for administering on his estate (Mr. Stewart having no relations in that country), and having forged a
claim against him, equalling in amount the value of
his property, he had circulated the report that there
would be but little left to meet outstanding debts. No
wonder, forsooth, his countenance fell, when Mr. S.
made his living appearance before him ! And it can
hardly be imagined that his embarrassment was much
relieved, when, upon investigation, he was found considerably indebted to Mr. S.

Mr. Stewart had never looked upon either Vess or
his wife as worthy the character which Clanton had
given them ; who had induced them to settle near him
for the convenience of boarding with them until he
could remove his family to that country. He usually
kept Vess employed in exchange for the provisions it
required to support his family, and in this way enabled him to keep up his establishment. Vess was a
mechanic, though a very indolent and lazy man ; and
his poverty, more than any hope of being benefited by
his services, had induced Mr. Stewart to engage his
assistance in the erection of some buildings which he
had contemplated commencing on a parcel of land that
had been presented him by Clanton, in testimony of his
gratitude for his attention to his business while he was
gone to Tennessee for his family. From considerations of charity for his family, Mr. S. had taken more
notice of Vess than he otherwise would have done ;
and proffered him employ, to incite him to some efforts

for a livelihood ; and, at the suggestion of Clanton, had taken board at his house, where he continued till his visit to Tennessee, a short time before his adventure with Murrell.

On opening a chest in which he had left his books and papers, together with many articles of household convenience, a gun apparatus, and fifty dollars in specie, a part of his money, his gun apparatus, and several other articles were missing. He immediately inquired of Vess and his wife whether they had opened his chest during his absence, to which they replied they had not; but continued, that Clanton had unlocked it to get a powder-flask. This last Mr. Stewart believed was as they had represented it ; for Clanton had been frequently in the habit, before he left the Purchase, of opening his chest when he wanted any article of its contents ; but he could by no means imagine that he had also found use for his money. On the contrary, a recollection of Vess's conduct during his recent absence left but little doubt on his mind as to the manner in which that had disappeared. He was rather at a loss to conjecture how so much of it remained. He concluded, however, to say nothing about it, as Clanton, he knew, had opened his chest, and it might bring unmerited suspicion on him ; besides, the amount missing was but small, and not worth the risk of unpleasant feeling, which it might occasion, though he resolved to change his boarding-place so soon as an opportunity offered. But houses, and especially boarding-houses, were very scarce at that time in the Purchase ; and no such opportunity offering, he was obliged, for a short time, to continue with Vess.

Mr. Stewart began now to be convinced of the importance, both for his own safety and the good of the community, to adopt some measures for the punishment and expulsion from their neighbourhood of all suspicious characters, and such whose business was either unknown or disreputable, and loungers who appeared to have none. As the former were a positive nuisance, and the latter could be very conveniently dispensed with, and both might be much less harmless than appearances seemed to indicate. He accordingly proposed to a number of the better class of his neighbours the plan of organizing a regulating company, whose duty it should be to acquaint such characters with the resolutions of the neighbourhood, punishing disobedience in every instance, pursuant to the decisions of Judge Lynch, who, as a part of the arrangement, he suggested, should be clothed with unrestricted judicial authority. His proposition was readily acceded to by a number; though, to his great surprise, Clanton was found among those who refused their assent.

The first that experienced the effects of this new arrangement was a man named Tucker, from Arkansas, who, a short time before, had threatened Mr. Stewart's life. He was dealt with according to "the law," and ordered to leave the county immediately. The next was a man by the name of Glen, one of Murrell's clan, a notoriously base character. In the investigation of his case Mr. S. perceived, much to his disappointment and regret, that a little purging would by no means injure his company of associate "regulators." He found among the number some whom he had strong reasons for suspecting of being friendly to, if not positively interested in, the measures of the clan ; and through whose means Glen was finally acquitted and discharged. He saw at once that a company composed of such materials, so far from establishing order and expelling villany, would but give the appearance of order to the more secret and unsuspected, and consequently more dangerous, operations of the very individuals against whom they seemed to direct their authority ; and hence determined to abandon them.

He was now not long in discovering the great insecurity of the position he occupied, and how little confidence was to be reposed even in those who pretended most to be his friends. He had already been apprized of the disposition towards him of those who had openly avowed their hostility to him, and sworn vengeance against his life and character. He now saw himself obliged to contend with a more subtle and secret, and therefore less manageable enemy. He became also convinced, on many accounts, that Vess and his family, who had by no means been wanting in professions of friendship, were not among the least malignant of these secret enemies ; and was more than ever satisfied of the importance of procuring other accommodations so soon as an opportunity offered. Meanwhile Mr. Stewart employed himself in examining and taking the numbers of unappropriated lands in the Purchase. Returning home late one evening from one of these land-hunting excursions, he found himself obliged to sup alone. When he had swallowed a cup of coffee, and was preparing to take a second, he was taken suddenly very sick, and rose from the table vomiting most violently.   From the demeanour and general appearance of his landlord and lady during the operation, he had much reason to fear that he had been poisoned, though he had then no sufficient evidence of the truth of his conjectures to warrant him in making them public.   His vomiting, continued by repeated draughts of warm water, which his fears of poison had induced him to take, was followed by great debility, accompanied with spasmodic symptoms.   In this situation Mr. Stewart began to revolve more seriously in his mind his highly perilous condition, the ten thousand dangers that beset his path, and the great degree of cautious circumspection necessary to be observed in all his future movements; and a more careful review of Vess's recent conduct in connexion with this last strange and mysterious occurrence, left but little doubt on his mind that his life had been compassed, and that Vess had been deputed to administer the fatal dose.   On the following day he inquired of Clanton whether Vess had ever mentioned to him that he had a claim against his estate at the time it was believed he had been assassinated.   He replied that " he had, but that he was drunk, and he had attributed it all to that."   Clanton appeared much confused on the occasion; which, with his recent change of conduct towards him, Mr. Stewart found himself at fault to account for : insomuch that he did not venture, as had been his intention, to make known to him his opinion of Vess.

Returning home late in the afternoon of the same day, from the examination of a tract of land in the

neighbourhood, a man rode up from his rear and fell in
company with him, armed with a pair of holsters and
a large Buoyer knife. Mr. S., as was natural, with the
knowledge he had by this time acquired of his situation, put himself at once upon his guard ; for, unarmed
as he was, contrary to custom, should his new companion be of the Murrell tribe, he saw his only safety
in cautious and well-managed dissimulation. The
stranger rode near him, and, after the usual common-
place of travellers, inquired whether he had any acquaintances in the country about Troy ; and, among
others, whether he knew a family of Glens (a name, by-
the-way, which Mr. Stewart at once recognised among
the associates of Murrell). His suspicions, already
partially kindled by the stranger's equipments, were at
once confirmed, and he had but little doubt that he
was in the presence of a member of the clan. The
stranger continued his inquiries, as will appear in the
following dialogue :—

Stranger. " Are you acquainted with a man in this
country by the name of V. A. Stewart ?"

Mr. Stewart. " Yes, sir, just as well as I would
wish to be with all such fellows."

Stranger. " What, do you not like him, sir?"

Mr. Stewart. " I have seen people I liked as well."

Stranger. " Have you any particular objection to
this fellow, Stewart ?"

Mr. Stewart. " O ! yes, many."

Stranger. " If you are not averse to telling your objections to him, I should like to hear them, as I dislike
him very much myself."

Mr. Stewart. " O ! he is too smart.   Interferes with

12*

things which do not concern him. He had no right to take the advantage he did of a man by the name of Murrell."

Stranger. "Do you understand this?—[giving his hand a flirt. Mr. Stewart answered the sign with a flirt of his hand.] Oh! yes, you are up to it. I am glad to see you, sir; what is your name?—[shaking hands.]"

Mr. Stewart. "I have several names; but, whenever I wish to be very smart, or successful in speculation and trade, I go by the name of Tom Goodin. I see you are a master of mystic signs—what is your name, sir?"

Stranger. "My name is George Aker, sir, and I am on a mission from our council to stop the wind of Stewart. Can you give me any assistance in the matter?"

Goodin. "O! yes, sir, I am the very man to assist you in that business. I did not know there had been a meeting on the subject; but, so soon as I heard of the misfortune, and heard where Stewart lived, I was soon in his neighbourhood, waiting for a good opportunity. I have been very cautious and still. I have managed to get acquainted with Stewart, and have had some tolerably good chances; but have been waiting for a better. He thinks me a very clever fellow, and I have been waiting to get him off by ourselves."

Aker. "We collected and consulted on what plan to pursue to destroy the rascal, and restore the character of those whom he has betrayed. We have got him in a close box. He is living with his enemies, and the friends of some of the men whom he has aspersed.

We will give him hell before we quit him! Our plan is
to get Murrell out of prison, and let him go off until the
session of the court; and, after he is gone from prison,
get a charge against Stewart that will destroy his
character before the world; and when the session
comes on Murrell will appear for trial, which will convince the world that he is innocent of the charge; and,
should Stewart even appear, no person will believe
him, for we will prove him to be one of the greatest
rascals that live. Murrell will be acquitted, and the
character of those who have been defamed will be restored; but we never intend Stewart to live till the
trial; we will kill him, and disgrace him too. We
have it all fixed—the fellow with whom he lives is a
good friend to some of our clan, and we have agreed
to give him a thousand dollars to raise a charge against
Stewart; and he is a big fish—any thing he says will
be believed; you know we have some big bugs among
us. I am told he is a confidential friend of Stewart's,
and that they have frequently done business for each
other. You know it will be an easy matter for him to
make a plausible accusation; but he will not agree to
make the charge against Stewart until after he is killed, as they have always been very friendly, and he
wants no investigation by the young Tartar. We sent
one fellow before, who engaged with an old man and
his wife to poison him for a hundred dollars; but they
have not done it for some cause, and we are tired of
waiting for them, so they made up two hundred dollars for me, and sent me to despatch the traitor; and, if
I can get no chance at him this time before I leave
the Purchase, we intend to bring men from Arkansas

with an accusation against him for passing counterfeit money to them, and in this way get him in our power ; and when we get him back into the Mississippi morass we will give him hell; we will give him something else to do besides acting the spy. We will speechify him next time. But I am told Stewart has managed to get a company to take up strangers who come into the neighbourhood after his scalp."

Goodin. " Yes, but his company will not be in our way ; for I know all his habits, where he walks, and where he sleeps, just as well as he does ; and I am not in the least suspected by any person : so, you see, I can fix him."

Aker. " O ! yes, I count him mine now ; and I will give you a hundred dollars to help me get his scalp. I have no doubt the company that went on to get Murrell out have released him more than a week ago. Where do you live, Goodin ?"

Goodin. " I am a little like a stray dog, sir ; I have neither home nor master, and stay longest where there are the best speculations to be had, though I stay mostly in the neighbourhood of Commerce at present, and sometimes work, to prevent being suspected. I play off occasionally. The people think me a good sort of a fellow, only a little wild. I have still been looking out for every chance that might offer for this fellow Stewart ; I have a choice scatter gun, and one fine pistol, which I keep for the purpose of saving his scalp ; I want it very much. Have you ever been in this country before ?"

Aker. " O ! yes, frequently, though I have not been much seen. I generally come into the neighbourhood of an evening, and leave it the next morning before daylight, which you know is the usual mode of visiting among mystics. I had a chance to see Stewart some time back at an election at Troy; but there was another fellow who had undertaken to despatch him then, so I let the opportunity pass without improving it. I have never heard the Glens speak of you in this country; did you not know they were speculators?"

Goodin. " O! yes, but I never go among them. You know it is necessary to have some respectable fellows, and you know it would not do for me to be among them, as they are suspected, if I wish to play the deep game; and, to be more certain of victory, I have never made myself known to any of the Glens, or any of the speculators of this country. If you examine the list you will find my name. I have been looking out for Stewart. We have as much right to play tricks as they have: but I dislike to run too great a risk for his scalp; I would like to have a good chance, and you know there is getting away to be thought of."

Aker. " Do you think you can kill Stewart to-night, and meet me to-morrow at Glen's, to let me hear the news? You are acquainted in the settlement, and are not suspected; but I am a stranger, and had rather not be seen by any but my friends, as this company might catch me."

Goodin. " I will meet you in the morning on the path which leads from Glen's to Commerce, at a pile of house-logs. Glen can tell you how to go, but you must not let any person come with you in the morning, or say any thing to Glen, or any person else about what is going on. We are enough to know it, as it will be a very daring act. I will act for the best."

Aker. " I will be at the place soon in the morning. Here is a hundred dollars. That is not all you will get if you are successful in stopping that villain's wind. You say you have a good scatter-gun. If you can get no other chance, shoot him as he sits by the fire : you can get off without being seen, and we will make our escape to Arkansas together. We can do nothing until he is killed, as we can get no clew at his character until then."

Goodin. " That will be a daring project : but I enter into it with a determined mind ; and I am of opinion you had better not go to Glen's to-night ; but go with me to a respectable house of my acquaintance, where we will go to bed, and in the night I will get my gun and go where Stewart boards, and do what I can for him, and return to bed before day. I have a friend whom I wish to go with us to Arkansas. We can then leave his house the next morning, and I and my friend can leave the neighbourhood without being suspected of the crime."

Aker. " I have some particular business with Glen, relative to some instructions, and they must be left with him, as he will have the best opportunity of forwarding matters. You go to your acquaintance's, and do as you have said ; but I had rather not be seen by any but my friends, as a stranger would be suspected much sooner than you. I will go to Glen's ; but I will not mention your name to a living soul, as you are playing the same sort of game on him that he played on us. We will keep it to ourselves until all is over, and the villain is finished, as you have never made yourself known to the other speculators of this country. Your plan is a good one, and the best of it is to have him beat in his own way."

The parties now arriving at the place of separation, Aker continued, " Well, Goodin, I wish you great success ; we meet in the morning at the appointed place." And, shaking hands, they parted.

Mr. Stewart was now satisfied that an attempt had been made to poison him ; and revolving in his mind, as he proceeded homeward, his late extraordinary interview, he felt convinced that many of his former conjectures were by no means unfounded ; and was enabled to account for many things which, till then, had appeared mysterious. And although, at first (probably on account of favourable prejudices), it had not occurred to him that Aker's conversation had any allusion to Clanton, a very few moments' reflection taught him that much of it could apply to no other. His first impression was that Vess and family were all that were intended by the words, " *He is living with his enemies ;*" and to this he was the more inclined by a recurrence to what had happened at the supper-table only the night before, and the report of Vess's false claim against his estate ; his great suspicions against Vess had caused him to apply all of Aker's remarks to him, and prevented his using any means to define the persons alluded to. But, on reflection, he found that the words, " *He is living with his enemies,*" were equally applicable to Clanton, for Vess and Clanton were living nearly as one family, their cabins being close by each other ; and, although he

was at the time boarding with Vess, there were many
reasons that cool reflection immediately applied to
Clanton, and no other person.

The words of Aker, " *He is a big fish, and any
thing he would say would be believed*" (thereby meaning that he was a man of standing), he at once saw
were by no means descriptive of Vess. Again, the
words, " *He is a confidential friend of Stewart—they
have frequently done business for each other*," were
equally inapplicable to him. Loath still to suspect a
man that had hitherto seemed so much his friend, Mr.
Stewart would fain have suspected some acquaintance
in Tennessee with whom he was on terms of intimacy ; but he was not a resident of that state, and Aker
had conversed in the present tense. He could at
length no longer doubt that Clanton was alluded to,
though he regretted not having been more inquisitive
while with Aker. Clanton was the only man in the
Purchase for whom he had ever done any business, or
who had any claims to his confidence. In this view
of it a flood of light was at once thrown upon the
whole subject. Vess had received the hundred-dol-
lar bribe to take his life by poison ; and Clanton, at
the still higher price of a thousand, was charged with
blasting his fair fame and character. There was no
longer any difficulty in accounting for Clanton's mysterious appearance when told of Murrell's confession,
and the implication of Colonel Jarrot, of Denmark ;
his subsequent change of conduct ; his refusing to join
the company of regulators ; and his evasive behaviour
when interrogated in relation to Vess's forged claim
against the estate of Mr. Stewart.

The startling truth now rushed with tenfold force upon the mind of Stewart, that the place of his fancied security was but the " hotbed" of his enemies ; that his pretended friends were so many cherished vipers, destined, in some confiding moment, to sting him to the vitals. Should all this prove true (and that it would he had but little reason to doubt), stranger as he was in the country, he saw no longer any protector upon whom to hang his hope of safety, unless that protector, that friend, should be found in George N. Saunders, who will be better known to the reader hereafter. But he was Clanton's friend and associate, and why not a partaker also of his guilt ? But no ! his former show of friendship, and a character uniformly above suspicion, as he had been informed, could not conceal so base and black a heart. And yet he thought, " if Clanton be false, who can be depended on ?" A man in whose hands, till now, he had felt his life secure, and for whom he had never before refused its peril. He could scarce realize, even yet, that for such devoted friendship he was rewarded with such cruel treachery, such murderous and remorseless ingratitude.

But he had heard and seen too much longer to hesitate ; for the picture drawn by Aker in their recent interview, blind charity itself could nowhere find so fit an original, besides a train of circumstances. But Saunders, the slightest breath of suspicion had not as yet lit upon him ; nay, his character had always been esteemed amiable ; and his hoary locks, silvered by the bleaching winds of so many winters, and sanctified by the superaddition of the Christian name, sure-

G　　13

ly could not shelter such deep corruption—such vile
and villanous hypocrisy ! He resolved to believe him
true till time should prove him false.

Thus circumstanced, alone and undefended, amid
the desertion of friends and the threats of enemies—
beholding in every form a foe—and in every voice
recognising but the cry of vengeance ; thus exposed
to the fearful impending storm, surcharged with death
in a thousand frightful shapes, a spirit less dauntless,
less proud and determined than that of Mr. Stewart,
had shrunk from the dread encounter ; and his, but
that, already accustomed to the sight, it had grown
reckless of danger, and, from long familiarity, superior to fear.

It being late, Mr. Stewart determined not to sup at
his boarding-house, for he saw the great importance
of being ever on his guard against Vess. The more
particularly on the present occasion, as from the late-
ness of the hour he knew he would be obliged to sup
alone ; and accordingly proceeded to the house of
Saunders, distant but a few hundred yards from Vess's
and Clanton's. While reflecting on his situation, Mr.
S. was often, in the agony of excited feeling, on the
point of unbosoming himself to Saunders, and seeking
his counsel ; but the recollection that his confidence
had been so recently betrayed by those with whom he
was better acquainted, fortunately suggested the prudence of forbearance ; and how far he was indebted
for his life, the security of his character, and the subsequent important services rendered to the public
through means of his disclosures, to this single act of
prudence, will be better understood in the sequel.

When he had finished his supper with Mr. Saunders, Mr. S. walked over to his boarding-house with a view of scrutinizing more attentively the conduct of Vess and his wife. He knew Mrs. Vess would invite him to sup, and, if they wished to poison him, a period so much beyond their usual supping-hour was the one best suited to their purpose ; for they knew he would sup alone, if at all, and had doubtless made arrangements with that view. His object was to ascertain, if possible, what disposition would be made of the coffee which had been provided for his supper ; if, as he had much reason to believe, it should contain a dose, he had no doubt it would be thrown away, and resolved to make that the test.

Reaching at length the house, Mrs. Vess, as expected, invited him to sup ; and, notwithstanding the plea that he had already supped with Mr. Saunders, repeatedly insisted on his taking a cup of coffee ; but, finding him inexorable, she at length ceased her importunities, and proceeded to remove the provisions that had been served for him. Meanwhile Mr. Stewart, having concealed himself without the house, sat eying her every movement. But a few minutes had elapsed when the coffee that had been intended for his use was poured out at the door ; and, as a favourite cur came up and smelt on the ground where she had emptied the coffee, she observed, " Take care, Watch ! that was prepared for a spy. I would give you a more kind and better supper." He was now satisfied of the truth of what Aker had told him, and that Vess was the man that had been bribed to take his life.

With the earliest sunlight on the following morning,

G 2

Mr. Stewart, gun in hand, was on the road and making
the best of his way to the pile of logs, the spot designated for his appointed meeting with Aker; for he
had at length determined to meet him alone.

It was his intention, when he parted with Aker on
the preceding evening, to take a friend with him as a
pretended accomplice to witness the appointed interview, to hear Aker's account of himself, and assist in
arresting him; but subsequent reflections, as before
described, had induced him to change his plan.

Mr. Stewart awaited at the appointed place the arrival of Aker till ten o'clock, who, failing to make his
appearance, he concluded had by some means learned
his mistake; and, taking the timely warning, had made
good his escape.

If Aker had met him according to agreement, and
Clanton had proved the man alluded to in their former
interview, he had determined to shoot him and leave
the country; but his failing to appear left the subject
still involved in uncertainty, and Mr. Stewart returned
home under the influence of feelings far from agreeable; for he little doubted that Aker had been enlightened on the subject of their meeting; and if so,
he saw but too clearly the great insecurity of his
present situation.

He had commenced building, with a view to making
a permanent location in the Purchase; but the present
aspect of things pointed too evidently to the perilous
consequences that might be attendant on such a
course.

A few days of continuous and intense anxiety passed away, and Mr. Stewart remained still undecided

as to his most prudent course, but arranged his affairs for leaving the country. At length, receiving a letter from a friend in Tennessee, notifying him of Murrell's escape from prison, removed all doubts as to the wisdom of continuing longer in the Purchase. Meanwhile, he had been by no means inattentive to the manœuvres of Vess and his family, at whose house he had taken care never to eat since the supposed attempt at poisoning him. He had, however, on several occasions witnessed the same disposition made of the coffee that had been provided for him as on the evening he had supped with Mr. Saunders. He had moreover heard repeated private conversations between Vess and his wife, in which they expressed fears that they were suspected.

Having now satisfied himself that Vess was the individual alluded to by Aker, as having received a bribe to take his life; for which purpose, and to conceal his suspicions of him and Clanton, he had continued at his house as if nothing had occurred, but always making it convenient to be absent at meal-times, he made known his intention of leaving the country. All his preparations had been narrowly scanned by Clanton and Vess, who manifested much anxiety on the occasion. About this time Clanton became suddenly very much dissatisfied with the manner in which Mr. Stewart had managed his business during his visit to Tennessee, full four months before; and for which, at that time, he had expressed himself under many obligations; and in testimony thereof, as before stated, had presented him with a lot of ground in his new townsite; and moreover, in proof of his confidence, pro-

13*

posed receiving him as a partner in a mercantile establishment.

What at this late period gives birth to so important a discovery? Clanton had the same access to his books and money-drawer, and as good an opportunity to detect mismanagement, the first day or week after his return from Tennessee, as at any time during the succeeding four months. Whence, then, this new light that now so mysteriously breaks upon the conduct of Mr. Stewart? He had not before taken up arms against bandits and villains; had not " brought to light the hidden things of dishonesty," nor exposed to just infamy and disgrace the hireling hordes of incendiaries and robbers.

Clanton's dissatisfaction with his conduct, however, it is here worthy of remark, was not made known to Mr. Stewart openly and in person, but was stealthily circulated with a view to his prejudice; nor was any specific charge made that was capable of being met till after he left the Purchase. He knew that the character of Mr. S. stood too fair to be publicly attacked with any hope of success; and an investigation (for reasons that will subsequently appear) was what he little desired.

These reports having at length come to the ears of Mr. Stewart, he called on Clanton, and relinquishing his right to the lot with which a short time before he had presented him, and cautioning him against prematurity in his remarks upon his character, requested him, whenever he preferred exceptions to it, to publish them to the world. A short time after, having arranged his business and appointed Saunders his agent, Mr. S.

set out for Lexington, Kentucky, where it was his intention to prepare and publish John A. Murrell's confessions. On his way thither he passed through Madison county, Tennessee, where he spent several days with his old acquaintances. At this latter place, already much discouraged by reports of slander and the threats of destruction that everywhere beset his path, added to the intelligence of Murrell's recent escape from prison, he was wellnigh brought to the conclusion to terminate his journey. But, seeing the responsibility that rested upon him to the public, whom he saw the hapless victims of a most fatal delusion in connexion with his own almost hopeless doom, he determined to prosecute his undertaking, resolved, if his life should be the sacrifice (and he saw but too much reason to fear it would be), to offer it up freely on the altar of his threatened country. Shortly after Mr. S. left the Purchase, Clanton and his co-agents of the Murrell confederacy, growing bold at the opportunity, set on foot a report that he had stolen a quantity of goods from Clanton and eloped, intending thereby to destroy his character, and shake the confidence of the public in the exposition it was believed he was about to make of Murrell's conspiracy and plans. But, when the intelligence reached Mr. S., so far from changing his purpose, he determined to hasten his publication, which, at first, he had intended to delay till after the trial of Murrell ; but his escape from prison before his trial had made it his duty to commence the publication, as it removed all the difficulties of his pending trial. Mr. Stewart left his friends in Tennessee and proceeded on his journey, intending to take water at Randolph, and go up the river to some point in Kentucky, and thence to Lexington. The same day that Mr. S. started from Madison county, Tennessee, Parson Henning received intelligence of John A. Murrell's arrest at Florence, Alabama, and despatched his son after Mr. S. to inform him of Murrell's recapture. Mr. S. received the intelligence before he reached Randolph, having stopped on the way on business, which enabled Mr. Henning to overtake him. He being the only evidence in that part of the state, he returned to await the trial of Murrell. From this period till Murrell's trial, in July, Mr. S. found it necessary to keep himself, as much as possible, concealed; as, foiled hitherto in their attempts on his life and character, the friends and confederates of the clan became now more industrious in their efforts, since the intelligence of Murrell's recapture had made their only hope of success to depend on the most speedy destruction of the one or the other.

The following letter, found in possession of John A. Murrell by the sheriff at Florence after his recapture, of which we give an exact copy, and which was read in evidence against him, will furnish a key to Clanton's hitherto mysterious conduct, and shed some light upon other subjects which before have not been sufficiently accounted for.

Copy of John A. Murrell's Letter.

" This day *personally* appeared before us &c Jahu Barney—James Tucker Thomas Dark Joseph Dark Wm Loyd &c who being sworn in due form of law, did depose and say, that they were present and saw —————— Stewart of Yellow Busha in the evening of the first day of February last, in company with John Murrell. at the house of Jahu Barney, over the *Mississippi* River and that him the said Stewart, informed us, that he was in *pursuit* of John Murrell, for stealing two negro men from Preacher Henning and his son Richard, in Madison County, near Denmark, and that he had told Murrell his name was Hues, and he wished us to call him Hues in Murrell's hearing—we also recollect, to have heard him, the said Stewart say distinctly, that he was to get five hundred dollars for finding said negroes, & causing Murrell to be convicted for stealing them.—But he did not say, who was to give him this reward—But he held the obligation of several rich men for that amount &cc.

The above is a *copy* given to me, by one who heard him say it, in the presence of you all   You will therefore please to send me the names of all, that *will* testify these facts in writing—also send me the names of all and every man that will certify these witnesses to be men of truth &cc.

J †† MURRELL

But above all things, arrest him the said witness, for passing the six twenty dollar bills—You will have to go out in Yellow Busha, in Yellow Busha County, near the *centre*, for him, and undoubtedly, this matter will be worth your attention—for if it be one two, or three *hundred* dollars, the gentleman to whom he passed [100] it can present it before a magistrate and take a judgment for the amount; and his little provision store acc's &cc. is worth that much money,, "I shall conclude with a claim on you for your strictest attention" My distressed wife, *will* probably call on you, and if she does, you may answer all her *requests*, without reserve.

Yours &cc   J :††‡‡: MURRELL.

Dear wife, I am in tolerable health, and I hope this will find you all well; I am of opinion, that the busi-

G 3

ness, that I was endeavouring to effect, will be done, in
the course of this week — On last night there was a
man committed, which is no little PITY††.

" *State of Tennessee, Madison County.*

" I, Henry W. McCorry, Clerk of the Circuit Court of
Madison county aforesaid, certify that the foregoing is
a true and perfect copy, in word and letter, of an instrument of writing filed in my office, and read in evidence against John A. Murrell, upon his trial for negro-
stealing, at the July term of our said court, 1834.

" In testimony whereof I have hereunto subscribed
my name and affixed my private seal (there being no
public seal of office), at office in Jackson, this 29th day
of September, A. D. 1835.

[Sealed.]   " H. W. McCORRY."

In the foregoing letter, the reader will perceive a
distinct allusion to a prior meeting of the clan, in
which measures were concerted and a specific plan
relied upon for the destruction of Mr. Stewart's life
and character. This is apparent from the manner in
which it is referred to. His object seems to have
been rather to instruct his agents how to proceed in
the execution of a plan already matured, than to rec-
ommend one for their adoption. It is a most remark-
able document, and, viewed in connexion with, furnishes a key to, many of the facts contained in the
preceding narrative ; and, to enable the reader the better to comprehend its true import, we shall offer a
passing notice to each paragraph separately.

The first is nothing more than a transcript of what
Murrell wished sworn to by his friends, pursuant to
the plan alluded to, in order to discredit Mr. Stewart's

testimony against him at the coming trial. If he could have succeeded in making it appear that Mr. Stewart was hired to detect him, or was in any way interested in the issue of the trial, it would have answered the contemplated purpose in the interdiction of his testimony. It is also here worthy of remark, that Murrell takes advantage of a circumstance in naming his witnesses, which, to persons ignorant of their characters, would carry with it some plausibility. It is known to the reader that, on a former occasion, when Murrell was before the committing court, Mr. S. spoke of having made, while on his adventure with him, confidants of Col. Bayliss of Wesley, John Champion, and Matthew Erwin, on the Mississippi river; and, if them, why not these witnesses also beyond the river? for they were all equally strangers to him, and their very obscurity favoured his plan by preventing any ready acquaintance with their characters; besides, in this there would have been a further difficulty, since, residing as they did among, and being members of, the clan, nothing would have been easier than to obtain certificates of character, which, on further examination, the reader will find to have been the calculation; and the ingenuity of the manœuvre is still more clearly manifested in the omission of the names of the individuals whose obligations Mr. S. is charged with having held for the five hundred dollar reward, thus putting it out of his power to prove a negative to the testimony of his witnesses.

The second paragraph, " The above is a copy given to me by one who heard him say it in presence of you all.

You will therefore please send me the names of all that will testify these facts in writing ; also send me the names of all and every man that will certify these witnesses to be men of truth," &c., proves, as has been already asserted, that the first was a copy of what he wished sworn to by his friends from Arkansas ; and suggests, moreover, the importance of obtaining certificates to their credibility as witnesses.

The above plan was, however, only to be resorted to in the event a more desirable stratagem should fail ; that of the accusation of having passed counterfeit money, which, the reader will remember, was spoken of by Aker, in which, had they succeeded, they would have accomplished the twofold purpose of reaching both Mr. Stewart's life and character. Hence he says :—

" But, above all things, arrest him, the said witness (meaning Stewart), for passing the six twenty-dollar bills. You will have to go out on Yellow Busha, in Yellow Busha county, near the centre, for him, and undoubtedly this will be worth your attention ; for if it be *one*, *two*, or *three* hundred dollars, the gentleman to whom he *passed it* can present it before a magistrate and take a judgment for the amount ; and his little provision-store, accounts, &c., is worth that much money. I shall conclude with a claim on you for your strictest attention. My distressed wife *will* probably call on you, and if she does, you may answer *all her requests* without reserve."

It may here be remarked further, that the origination of the charge in Arkansas was also designed to

have an important bearing in the consummation of
the plan ; the intention was, doubtless, to convey him
thither, under arrest, for trial; and, when in their power, to despatch him.   Hence the remarks of Aker on
this subject :—" And if I can get no chance at him this
time before I leave the Purchase, we intend to bring
men from Arkansas, with an accusation against him
for passing counterfeit money to them, and in this
way get the d——d traitor into our power ; and when
we get him back into the Mississippi morass, we will
give him hell," &c. &c.

In the fourth paragraph, addressed to his wife, and
which reads, " Dear wife : I am in tolerable health,
and I hope this will find you all well.   I am of opinion that the business I was endeavouring to effect will
be done in the course of this week.   On last night
there was a man committed, which is no little PITY,"
it will be seen most clearly that Murrell's wife took a
conspicuous part in the above conspiracy : this is evident from her visit to his friends alluded to in the
third paragraph ; and perhaps her peculiar situation
was better adapted to forward its measures, and by
consequence made her agency of more importance to
its success than that of any one party to it ; for, being admitted into his prison apartments, she had many
opportunities of counselling with him, and communi-
cating his views unsuspected to his friends.   It is
farther evident from the above, that, when this letter was penned, the plan in contemplation was already ripe for execution.   Hence he says, " The business I was endeavouring to effect will be done in the
course of this week ;" and this letter appears to have

14

been the last step preparatory to its final consummation.

Throughout the above letter there appears to be a
constant reference to the same conspiracy spoken of
by Aker, and the same prematured plan for carrying
out its measures. And it is couched in language
which plainly proves it to have been addressed to individuals already acquainted with it.

The reader will remember that the last news from
Clanton represented him, his friend Vess, and others
of " the fraternity," industriously employed in circulating disreputable reports of Mr. Stewart's conduct
while in the Purchase; and, if he has attended to the
preceding narrative, he is doubtless by this prepared
to conjecture the object and motive of those reports.
If however, he is not yet sufficiently enlightened on
this subject—if there still remain any doubts as to the
nature of his conduct towards Mr. Stewart or his iden-
tity with his enemies and Murrell's clan, we invite his
attention to the following pages.

EXPOSITION OF THE CHARACTER OF MAT-
THEW CLANTON.

" *State of Mississippi, Holmes County.*

"The undersigned, citizens of said state and county,
having been present and heard the confessions of Capt.
Isham Medford, of Attala county, on the fifth day of
July last, do hereby certify that he stated that, although
not personally acquainted with Judge Clanton of Yallabusha county, he had understood from others engaged in
the same nefarious practices with himself that said Clanton was a friend of, and belonged to, the clan of counterfeiters and thieves with which he was associated, and

which so long had infested the country; and that the house of said Clanton, on or near Yallabusha, was about two days' ride from the section of the county in which he lived, whose house and the neighbourhood were places of rendezvous for the party.

" Given under our hands, this 8th day of August, 1835.

"JAMES C. BOLE,
ALLEN COLLINS,
EVERETT L. FORD,
JAMES S. BAINS,
A. J. PATTERSON,
JOB TAYLOR,
A. HAYS,
WILLIAM McALLISTER,
WM. JOHN O'FARRELL,
T. W. DULANY,
L. BULLOCH,
J. M. McALLISTER,
J. M. TAYLOR."

" Sworn to and subscribed before me, this 8th day of August, 1835.

[Sealed.]   "JOHN B. MURRAY, *Justice Peace.*"

Copy of a letter from Matthew Clanton to James C. Bole.

" *Yallabusha County, Miss., Aug.* 24, 1835.

"JAMES BOLE, Esq. }
  Franklin, Miss. }

" DEAR SIR—I was informed by Gov. Runnells, on Saturday last, that, as he came through your county, he saw a certificate signed by yourself and twelve others, purporting to be the confessions of Isham Medford, of Attala county, who was brought before you and tried for some charges against him, and that he impeached me in some way in his confessions. Will you be so good as to forward me a copy of the certificate you gave V. Stewart of that confession, and also state ex-

plicitly whether that confession was made under the
lash or not.   Please also to inform me where Medford
lived when he was brought before you, and where he
now lives (if you know).   I hope, my dear sir, you will
grant this favour to a man who wishes it in vindica-
tion of a character as unsullied by crime of any sort as
the mountain snow.   I am assured, by both Gov. Runnells and Col. Wyatt, that I may ask this favour of you
as a highminded gentleman who is disposed to do impartial justice to every one.

"With great respect, your obedient servant,
       "MATTHEW CLANTON."

Answer by James C. Bole to the foregoing.
       "*Franklin, Holmes County, Sept.* 14, 1835.
"MATTHEW CLANTON, }
   Pittsburg, Miss. }

"DEAR SIR—Yours of the 24th of August has been received, and I now proceed to answer the same.   You
request a copy of the certificate given to V. A. Stewart;
this I cannot give you, as I did not take a copy of that
certificate, and cannot conveniently call on any individual who did; but the certificate was given for publication,
and you will no doubt see it before long.   I will, however, give you the substance of Medford's statement, so
far as the same is connected with your name; this I
will do from memory, which serves me well on that
subject.   He stated that they (meaning the organized
band of rogues and counterfeiters) had stolen from the
citizens of this and the adjoining counties many negroes and horses, which were put under the care of a
man of the name of Hansford, but most generally known
by the name of Leiper, in Choctaw county; that this
man lived in a camp, and changed his residence as necessity required; that, so soon as the excitement produced by the loss of the property had subsided, they

would move it generally to Arkansas, Texas, or the
neighbourhood of Alexandria on Red river. He gave
the names of all the individuals at whose houses they
would call in moving this property to the aforesaid
places, and among others he gave the name of Matthew
Clanton; said that he kept a house at which they called
on their expeditions of this kind; said that he did not
know you personally, but that he knew your character
well, and that he knew you to be one of their (meaning
the rogues and counterfeiters) friends. He said that he
had never travelled the route by which the stolen property was removed, but that he had the names of their
friends on the same. I will further state explicitly for
your satisfaction, that this confession was not made
under the lash, but after he was punished; and, so far as
relates to you, was wholly voluntary on his part.

"I have now given you the substance of his confessions so far as it was calculated to implicate you.
These statements were made to a company of from
thirty to thirty-five individuals, all citizens of this county, all men of respectability. I cannot, however, dis-
miss this subject without noticing another request in
your letter, viz., that I would inform you where Medford lived when he was brought before me, and where
he now lives. After you had stated expressly, in the
outset of your letter, that he lived in Attala county, I
cannot conceive what could induce you to make such
a request. Were I disposed, I believe I could point out
other ambiguities in this letter, but do not deem it necessary. With the difficulty between yourself and
Stewart I have nothing to do. I never heard the name
of either until I saw the 'Western Land Pirate;' consequently I have no partialities for the one, nor prejudices
against the other. That V. A. Stewart has rendered
important services to his country, is a fact which no

14*

honest man will deny.   In conclusion, I will say to you,
that ' *Truth is mighty, and will prevail.*'
>   " Respectfully, your obedient servant,
>   " JAMES C. BOLE."

To the Editor of the Clinton Gazette.

" It is known to most of the community around Clinton, that some time since I had three negro fellows
stolen from me by Murrell's clan.   Being called upon
by several gentlemen, Mr. Virgil A. Stewart among others, to publish the circumstances attending their abduction and recovery, I give the following brief account.

" In December, 1833, at that time living on the Mississippi river, a few miles below Randolph, one morning
I found three of my most valuable fellows missing from
their labour.   I supposed they had got on a steamboat
with a view of reaching a free state, and probably under
the protection of some of the agents of Arthur Tappan
& Co., and had a reward for the apprehension of the
negroes published in Louisville and other places.

" About six months after this circumstance transpired, a few miles below where I had resided, in the neighbourhood of the Shawnee village, a flat-boat was robbed of most all of its load.   At this outrage the citizens
of Randolph, in a manner highly creditable to themselves, raised a company, went over the river, and
took twenty suspected persons ; whipped about half of
them, and committed some to jail.   It was from the
confessions of these that I first learned that my negroes were stolen and sold somewhere.   The Lloyds,
Bunches, Barneys, and others, names given in Stewart's publication, reside in this neighbourhood, and generally keep a great many worthless characters about
them, who have no appearance of an honest living ;

and are often taken up with counterfeit money in their possession, and generally break jail before their trial comes on.

" I made an ineffectual search for my negroes throughout the Attuckapa country, in Louisiana, and had given them over as lost; but, learning that Parson Henning's negroes had been found, in search of whom Mr. Stewart had hazarded his life, and discovered so much that is valuable to the community, I conferred with Mr. Henning, to ascertain if he had heard any thing of other negroes supposed to have been run into the country; he informed me that he had; and I went on to the parish of Avoyl, and found my negroes fifteen or twenty miles in the interior from Red river. I seized them by writ of attachment, and went over to court about three weeks since with my evidence of ownership; the defendants paid cost, and gave up the negroes without submitting the case to the court; and I now have them on my plantation, four miles north of Clinton, Mississippi. In that section of country there are now many negroes which there can be no doubt were run by Murrell's clan.

" D. O. WILLIAMS.
" *November,* 1835."

" *State of Mississippi, Holmes County.*

" The undersigned, citizens of said state and county, do hereby certify, that we were present and heard the confessions of Captain Isham Medford, of Attala county, on the 5th day of July, 1835. The said Medford did not make his confessions while under the lash, but after he was released, and was assured that he would not be farther punished. We do farther certify, that he implicated two of his own sons-in-law, as well as Judge Clanton, of Yallabusha county; and, from the consistency of his story throughout the whole matter, we are

bound to believe that he told the truth as to his own
guilt, as well as that of those whom he implicated.

" Given under our hands and seals, this 17th day of
July, 1835.

"JAMES C. BOLE,
A. J. PATTERSON,
[Sealed.]   JOB TAYLOR,
THOMAS GERREL,
A. HAYS."

There is a strong corroborative analogy between
the statements of Captain Medford, as given in James
C. Bole's letter to Clanton, and Dr. D. O. Williams's
publication as to the places of rendezvous for the clan.
We leave the reader and the public to draw their own
inferences from the evidence above.

When Clanton first began to whisper slanders
against the character of Mr. Stewart, it was done to
excite suspicion in the minds of his friends in the
Purchase, so as to enable his accusers from Arkansas
to carry him to that country to answer to their accusa-
tions. Once there, they intended to torture him to
death. Mr. Stewart had many warm friends in the
Purchase, whose confidence it was necessary to shake
before their designs could be effected.

Thus the protector of his country was to fall a victim to a false accusation, and be delivered into the
hands of his bloodthirsty enemies, even at the instance
of the laws of his venerated country, through the
agency of Clanton and his co-workers in crime ; and
thus his infamy legally sanctioned by the tribunals of
his country ; but, when they were disappointed in their
fiendish purposes, Murrell again in the iron grasp of the

law, before their bloody designs against Mr. Stewart could be accomplished, and the time of trial drawing near, all their hopes were hung on the accusation which Clanton had made against his honour; at the same time Clanton and his agents began to discover that all who were acquainted with Mr. Stewart looked on his accusation with contempt; they consequently saw the necessity of enlarging the charge, and supporting it with more substantial reasons. Mr. Stewart had been a housekeeper for several years before he moved to the Choctaw Purchase, and, when starting to move, he packed up all his table-furniture in a chest, and carried it with him, expecting to need it at some future day. Though all these articles had been used for several years, to give increased importance to his charge, Clanton accused Mr. Stewart of getting them from his store, and never accounting for them. But Providence kindly ordered it that Mr. Stewart was among his old neighbours, who knew that he had kept house, and some of whom had assisted him in packing up his furniture to move. Clanton's blunder in this particular exposed the full depth of his villany, as will be seen from the following evidence. The reader has before been informed that Mr. Stewart had furnished himself with a supply of the comforts of life necessary for exploring a wilderness country, on leaving Tennessee for the Choctaw Purchase. We offer the following for the reader's consideration:—

" *Tuscahoma, August* 15, 1835.
"Mr. V. A. Stewart:

" Dear Sir—I have been induced, since I saw Matthew Clanton's publication, to inform you of certain evidence that will remove all doubt of the baseness of the charge which he has alleged against you, which charge few of his near neighbours and friends pretend to believe and impress on others.

" Col. Duncan McIver and his family state that they saw the principal, and perhaps all the articles, stated by Clanton in hi accusation against you, in your possession while boarding at their house before you became Clanton's agent, immediately after you emigrated from Tennessee to the Purchase. Also the wagoner, Mr. Hardy, who hauled your goods from my boat, states that he saw several bolts of domestic calico, &c., in your possession, when getting medicines from you in a case of sickness. I saw several of the articles before they left my boat, particularly the ware, knives and forks, &c.

" I am quite unwell, and can hardly write.

" Respectfully yours, &c.,

" L. McLAUGHLIN.

" P. S. The people are very much exasperated against Clanton, except a few of his neighbours. They pass the severest censure and contempt on him. He cannot stand it long, for it is getting worse for him every day.

" L. McL."

" *Madisonville, Miss., Aug.* 19, 1835.

" MR. V. A. STEWART :

" DEAR SIR—I was at Vicksburg some four weeks since, and saw a card in the newspaper over your signature, requesting the people of the south to suspend their opinion concerning Matthew Clanton's pamphlet. You say you did not expect to obtain positive proof against said Clanton. I have just returned home from the Choctaw nation, and, on passing through Clanton's neighbourhood, I first met with Mr. Cobb, nine miles above Chocchuma, with whom I stayed all night. Our

evening's conversation was about the controversy between you and Clanton, having both the pamphlets in
our possession. Mr. Cobb stated that Clanton and
Saunders had stood as fair as any two men could stand;
but said that he had seen Duncan McIver a few days
before, and, conversing about the matter, he said that he
had hauled your trunk and chest from the boat when
you landed in that country from Tennessee, and that he
saw them opened, and that they then contained nearly
all the articles which Clanton now accuses you of
stealing from his store, and that he was ready to make
affidavit of the fact at any time when called on. Passing on through Coffeeville, I saw several men who
had heard Mr. McIver state the same facts. Finally,
I intended to call on Mr. McIver and get his certificate;
but, misunderstanding where he lived, I had passed him
before I knew it. I learned from a Mr. Duke, who
keeps the ferry on the Yocknepotoffa, that he had heard
Mr. McIver and sons state the same facts as above related. I left Esq. Duke's on Thursday morning last; he
promised me he would go to Mr. McIver's on Friday
and get his certificate, and send it to me by mail. I look
for it in a few days.

"I am a planter living near Canton, Madison county.
In haste, I must close, by subscribing myself your sincere friend and well-wisher,

"ROBERT G. ANDERSON."

"*State of Mississippi, Warren County :—to wit.*

"Personally appeared before me, R. J. McGinty, a
justice of the peace in and for said county, William J.
Cowan, a citizen of said county, who, being duly sworn,
on oath says, that he became acquainted with Mr. Virgil A. Stewart in July, in the year 1833, immediately
after his emigration to the Choctaw Purchase, in said
state, at the residence of Mr. Duncan McIver, about one

mile above the town of Tuskahoma. This deponent resided with Mr. Stewart about six weeks in the same house, and was present when he unpacked the goods which he brought with him to this country, and had a full knowledge of the property and household-furniture of said Stewart at that time in his possession. Said Stewart having emigrated to that section of country at a time when it was quite a wilderness, very sparsely settled by white people, brought with him a small stock of groceries suited to the demand of the early settlers; and also came better prepared for housekeeping than the majority of settlers who emigrated to the country at that time. This deponent had free access to the trunk and chest of Mr. Stewart, and every thing about the house, and was in the daily use of his furniture; among other articles, Mr. Stewart had plates, cups, saucers, spoons, knives, forks, a mattress, and bedclothing, table-cloths and towels, and small packages of coffee, tea, spice, ginger, pepper, saltpetre, medicines of various descriptions, and remnants of cotton domestic, and remnants of cloth of various descriptions. Among other articles in the house was a set of glass cup-plates, which he, this deponent, had bought at Tuskahoma, and when he, this deponent, parted with Stewart, they were left with the other table-furniture of Stewart.

"WM. J. COWAN.

"Sworn to and subscribed before me, this 18th day of July, A. D. 1835.

[Sealed.] "R. J. McGINTY, *Justice of the Peace.*"

"*State of Mississippi, Carroll County.*

"This day personally came before me, Joshua Williams, an acting justice of the peace of said county, Thomas Rhodes, who, being first duly sworn, deposeth and saith, that in the year 1833 (the summer of that year), he became acquainted with Virgil A. Stewart,

who settled on or near the Yallabusha river, near Tuscahoma, and with a Mr. William J. Cowan, then resident with the said Stewart, as he, said Rhodes, believes,
as he has seen the said Cowan and Stewart frequently
together at Stewart's own house at Tuscahoma, and at
his own (Rhodes's) house ; that he believes said Cowan
to be an honest, sober young man, and entitled to credit ;
and also that he has seen at the house of said Stewart
about the same time the most of the necessary articles
of housekeeping, such as cups and saucers, knives and
forks, plates, spoons, &c., as set forth in the affidavit
of said Cowan, and that said Stewart was as well provided for housekeeping as any or most of the new
settlers were at that time ; and that he believes the
said Stewart to be a worthy, honest, and upright young
man.

"THOS. RHODES.

" Sworn to and subscribed before me, this 20th September, 1835.

[Sealed.] " JOSHUA WILLIAMS, *Justice Peace.*"

"*State of Tennessee, Madison County.*

" Having been called on to state to the public what I
know relative to the goods and property that Virgil A.
Stewart had packed at my house, in this county, to be
shipped to the Choctaw Purchase, and which were put
on board a boat that left Jackson for said Purchase during the spring of 1833, I now give the following brief
statement.

" Virgil A. Stewart lived in this county two years
and better previous to his leaving here for the Choctaw
Purchase, in the State of Mississippi, during which time
he lived a bachelor, or kept a house of his own, until he
sold off his property for moving in the fall of 1832, at
which time I rented the farm which he had occupied,

and moved to his house, and he boarded with me the remainder of the time he stayed in this county. He was well provided with house furniture, farming utensils, and a numerous quantity of fine tools of almost every description that is used. These things he carried with him when he moved to the Choctaw Purchase, in the spring of 1833. He had a quantity of queensware, knives and forks, spoons of various sizes, casters, cruets, and all the necessary furniture for table use; a general supply of tinware, necessary for the use of a family; a quantity of valuable bed-clothing of various kinds; a considerable number of books; a quantity of paints; and such metals and materials as are used in making cotton-gins. In addition to the above, Mr. Stewart had a general supply of medicines and drugs, such as a family might need in case of sickness, &c. In short, I will say he was well provided for both comfort and convenience, having every thing that a family necessarily needs, even down to needles, thread, silk, thimbles, shears, scissors, and a variety of buttons, which he kept in his trunk for his own convenience. He had remnants of domestic and imported cloth, and packages wrapped in paper, the contents of which I did not know.

" Mr. Stewart's goods were in a separate apartment of the house while he boarded with me, but I frequently saw them when he used them, or when I wanted to borrow any thing from him, and I frequently had his property left in my care before it was carried to the boat in the spring of 1833. The above statements are due to Mr. Stewart and the public.

" Given under my hand and seal, this 7th day of October, 1835.

[Sealed.]   "HEZEKIAH ASKEW."

" *State of Tennessee, Madison County.* '

" Personally appeared before me, Harbut Nuisom, an acting justice in and for said county, Hezekiah Askew, a citizen of said county, who, being sworn in due form of law, did depose and say that the above certificate relative to the goods and property of Virgil A. Stewart is just and true.

" Sworn to and subscribed before me, this 7th day of October, 1835.

" HARBUT NUISOM, *Justice of the Peace.*"

Owing to the infamous slanders of Clanton and his clan, we have been compelled to introduce evidence on matters that are beneath the notice of a gentleman. We will here dispense with Clanton and his guilty train for the present, and turn our attention to the approaching trial of Murrell.

The trial of Murrell came on, and the courthouse was crowded to overflowing with the deeply anxious spectators, who thronged to hear the mysterious tale of Murrell's daring feats unravelled before the jury that were to decide this important case. The witness, Mr. Stewart, was called ; he appeared before the court and waiting congregation, and was sworn. He then commenced his evidence by giving a narrative of his adventure, and developing all the circumstances and occurrences which led to the introduction and acquaintance between Murrell and himself, frequently giving the subject of their conversation, and the language of the prisoner as he expressed himself in the company of the witness; and including all those feats of villany denominated by the prisoner the feats of the elder brother, together with the

H 2

manner in which the prisoner made himself known to
the witness, as being the elder brother himself. He
gave the occurrences and subjects of conversation connected with the confessions of the prisoner, both before and after he made himself known as the elder
brother, and the wonderful hero of the feats which he
had related.

The witness commenced his testimony in the afternoon, and was stopped at dark : the next morning he
resumed his place before the court, and finished his
evidence. He was many hours engaged in making
his disclosures, and was then cross-examined by the
prisoner's counsel on the evidence he had given the
preceding day. His answers were clear and satisfactory to all but the prisoner and his friends. The
friends of the prisoner, having been revealed before
his arrest, were afraid to appear in court, lest they
should be known and apprehended. This misfortune
of Murrell's disarmed him; for, in any other case, he
could have proved any thing he wished by his own
clan : now, their names were on a list given to the
witness by Murrell himself, and they dared not venture forward to his assistance.

Failing to destroy the evidence of Mr. Stewart,
Murrell's friends next endeavoured to prove that he
was interested in the conviction of the prisoner, and
that Parson Henning had hired him to detect him.
Accordingly they induced a man by the name of Reuben M'Vey, who was an enemy to Mr. Stewart, to
come into court and swear that Mr. Stewart had told
him the fact ; but, like all other liars, he was caught
in his own net; his story had so many contradictions

in it, that it was of no force.   Mr. Stewart was prepared to prove that M'Vey had sworn to a lie ; but the
prosecuting counsel deemed it unnecessary, as the evidence was its own refutation.   So far from being
hired to undergo the danger of this adventure, Mr.
Stewart would not even receive a handsome suit of
clothes which Parson Henning wished to purchase for
him, as a remuneration for his time and labour in pursuit of the negroes.

The malignant hatred which induced M'Vey to ruin
himself in trying to do Mr. Stewart an injury, arose
from the simple fact that the latter gentleman had refused to associate with M'Vey, not regarding him as a
gentleman.

Mr. Stewart's evidence was supported by gentlemen
of the greatest respectability that the country afforded.

John A. Murrell was found guilty of negro-stealing,
and sentenced to the penitentiary for ten years, at hard
labour.

Thus ended the trial and conviction of the great
" Western Land-Pirate," who reduced villany to a system, and steeled his heart against all the human family.

During the pleadings a Mr. Brown, one of Murrell's lawyers, bore on the feelings of Mr. Stewart in
an unwarrantable and dishonourable manner, for which
Mr. Stewart was determined to give him a Stansberry
reproof as soon as he could meet him in the street; but
he was prevented by his friends, who were old men,
and whose advice and request he felt himself bound
to respect.

The following is an extract from a letter written by
Mr. Stewart to a friend, that was afterward published,

5*

in which he answers Mr. Brown in a spirited manner.
And we would further remark, that the same sentiments are very applicable to many of his envious,
jealous, and bitter persecutors at the present time,
whom we could name, and who are ambitious of fame
and public favour ; but do not deem them of sufficient
importance to receive a passing notice, or to be designated by the finger of scorn.

"I feel the truest pleasure in seeing and knowing
that my friends and the community resent the dishonourable treatment I received from Mr. Brown in
his sophistical pleadings. The assumed privilege of
abusing and calumniating credible witnesses, as practised by gentlemen of the bar, is calculated seriously to
retard the operation of law and justice ; and, were all
men of my opinion on this subject, it would be relin-
quished by them in all cases sustained by conclusive
evidence.

"Let me lay before you a few of the unfair propositions, or rather syllogisms, in the syllabus of his pleadings.

"He declared I had acted with deception, and practised a falsehood on John A. Murrell, in procuring his
confidence by representing myself as a horse-hunter
and a villain; and contended that he who will act a
falsehood or practise a deception, will—for it is but the
next step—swear to it : and therefore my testimony
was undeserving of credit, and should not be listened to
or respected.

"He represented me as the friend of Murrell, and declared that a man who would betray the confidence of
a friend was a villain :—I had betrayed the confidence
of my friend, ergo, I was a villain.

"To this unfair mode of reasoning, I thus reply to

Mr. Brown :—When I took measures to secure the conviction of John A. Murrell, I was not proceeding against
a friend, but an enemy ; an enemy not only to me, but
to every honest man in the community : whose outrages
were insufferable, and whose systematic plans evaded
every effort to bring him to justice.   Thus the dignity of
our laws and institutions, which were established for the
protection of our lives, liberty, and property, lay insulted and trampled under the feet of that daring incendiary and his piratical legion, who gloried in the havoc
they were making of our property, and the dissensions
they produced in the social bands of society ; for to
both these ends were their purposes directed.   In my
proceedings against this formidable banditti, I considered myself justified in imitating measures which have
been taken by the greatest patriots and generals of our
country, whose opinions and acts we are bound to respect.

" As to the deceptions I practised on John A. Murrell
in obtaining his confidence and disclosures, I refer you
to the following in justification of my course.

" Recollect the deception practised by General Washington, at the time Major Andre, the British spy, was
captured, in trying to get Arnold the traitor back into his
possession ; and recollect Washington's reasonings on
that subject.   Sir, they will sustain me, and cover Mr.
Brown with shame and confusion.   And again I refer
you to the deception of Colonel Washington, practised
at Clermont.   See his stratagem in mounting the trunk
of a pine-tree on wagon-wheels, so as to resemble a
fieldpiece, which caused the garrison to surrender, and
has ever been considered a gallant act of Col. Washington.   But, because I dissembled the outward bearing
of a villain for the purpose of learning the conduct of
many villains, and ridding the community of a craft de-

structive to the peace and happiness of all civil and
honest society, Mr. Brown is not willing that I should
ever wear any other character than the infamous one
I represented to John A. Murrell, and he professed to
see no virtuous motives in my conduct which propelled
me to action. No, sir, as there was no large fee, or
other selfish consideration, to influence my actions, it
was a mysterious matter with him, because his own
narrow soul is too small to render the same services :—
and for that very reason, all such men as Milton Brown
have no right to express their contracted views of me
and my conduct; and, should they express them, they
are entitled to no credit. I consider him, and all such
men, nothing more than the organ through which the
venom of a detestable and piratical clan of villains was
vented towards me, whose machinations and calumny
were ignobly piled on my character by Mr. Brown, like
another ignominious hireling in iniquity.

"And what makes his skepticism and abuse the more
disgusting to good feeling and sense, they were unsupported by even the shadow of evidence, and must have
emanated from a desire to please a train of piratical villains, whose only purpose of life is the destruction of
all the social ties of society, and the prostration and
perversion of our national institutions, that have hitherto been the pride and boast of all freemen, and the safe
guardians of our lives and property.

"Were not my evidence and veracity supported by
as good citizens as our country can boast of ? Why,
then, the volley of abuse, sarcasm, and filth, that was
spawned and belched forth on my character by that son
of vanity ? Is it criminal to stand up in the defence of
our country, our wives, our children, our mothers, our
sisters, and all the tender and sacred ties of humanity
and justice ? If so, then I am a criminal, and deserve

all the slander and abuse I have received at his hands ;
and I am then willing to concede the right to the professional lawyer to shake hands with the vilest slan-
derer and defamer of character, and claim him as an
equal in crime and detraction ; but, until then, Milton
Brown is a disgrace to the high bearing and dignity of
the profession of the law. It is the duty of the lawyer
to see that his client is legally dealt with : but he has
no right to abuse a witness merely to please a villain
and his friends. Sir, you will please indulge me in a
few syllogistic remarks in answer to Mr. Brown.

" Any attorney at law, who will lie and misrepresent
evidence for the sake of indulging in abuse and slander on the character of a witness, is a base, corrupt
scoundrel, and should not be respected by any man.
Milton Brown lied and misrepresented my evidence for
the sake of indulging in abuse and slander on my character when a witness : therefore Milton Brown is a
base, corrupt scoundrel, and should not be respected by
any man."

Mr. Brown has since very justly experienced the
weight of Mr. Stewart's argument against him, in a
political point of view, and he could not have been
touched on a more sensitive part, as he is as ambitious as corrupt. Mr. S. can never forgive Brown for
the base and unmanly treatment he received at his
hands in Murrell's trial ; nor is it to be wondered at,
when we reflect on the motives that governed his actions on that occasion. Mr. Brown thought, as Mr.
S. had left Madison county, and was residing at a distance, any undue liberties he might indulge in with
his character would soon be forgotten, as he had no
relations or family influence in the country to breed

H 3

opposition against him; and that any laurels he might
gain in a professional point of view, by using the
means of lying, misrepresentation, sarcasm, abuse,
and a sacrifice of all honour and principle, would only
be considered smart, as it was practised on a strange
young man, who was destitute of family influence to
hold him in check. When we take this view of the
subject, who can blame Mr. Stewart's resentment?
But Mr. Brown was not apprized of Mr. S.'s popularity in that country, or he would have been more
cautious.

We will now offer the statements of General Bradford, of Jackson, Tennessee, who was the prosecuting
counsel on the part of the state.

"Jackson, Tennessee, October 10*th,* 1835.
" Mr. Virgil A. Stewart :—

" Sir—At your request, and in justice to you and
other persons concerned in the trial and conviction of
John A. Murrell, late of Madison county, Tennessee, for
the crime of negro-stealing, I deem it my duty to make
the following statement.

" At the July term of the Circuit Court of said county, I endicted the said John A. Murrell for the crime
above described, at which time he was tried, convicted,
and sentenced to be confined in the penitentiary for ten
years; I have prosecuted the pleas of the state for
many years, during all which time I have never known
any prisoner to have a fairer or more impartial trial than
Murrell had on this occasion. He was defended by several counsel, and that, too, with zeal and ability; and
they were allowed by the court every latitude usual in
such cases; and the jury who passed upon his case

stand as high for honesty and intelligence as any men in the county.

"In relation to yourself I have to say, that Murrell was convicted mainly upon your testimony, the facts of which were lengthy and complicated : that you underwent a most rigid cross-examination, and I have no hesitation in saying that I never heard any man sustain himself better. Your character was attacked directly in the defence, yet your veracity was sustained by some of our most worthy citizens, among whom were Colonel Thomas Loftin, of this county (Madison), and Alexander Patton, Esq., of this place. Indeed, the ample testimony borne to your good character was highly creditable. Until the trial of Murrell, you were to me an entire stranger; still the impression made upon me by you was favourable, and, as an officer of the government, I was satisfied at the time that he was rightfully and legally convicted of the crime of negro-stealing, on your evidence, and I have yet no reason to doubt it; and, moreover, the verdict of the jury, as I believe, met with the general sanction of those who witnessed the trial.

"Given under my hand, at Jackson, the date above.

"ALEXANDER B. BRADFORD,

"*Solicitor General of the* 14*th District in* ⎫
the State of Tennessee." ⎭

Sentiments of the citizens of Madison County, Tennessee.

"*State of Tennessee, Madison County.*

"We, the undersigned, citizens of said state and county, feeling sensibly the obligation we are under to Mr. Virgil A. Stewart, for the many dangers he has encountered in ferreting out the land pirate John A. Murrell, and bringing him to justice, present the amount annexed to our names as a donation, and token of our gratitude, for the important and dangerous services rendered by Mr. Stewart in capturing said pirate, believing, as we do, that he is entitled to it for the loss of time and expenses which were necessarily incurred by Mr. Stewart for the public good; and we mean further by this subscription and declaration of sentiments to manifest to the world our approbation and applause of the course pursued by Mr. Stewart, and not only appreciate his courage, but discountenance the odium which has been attempted at his character, in pursuing so disagreeable a course for the good of the community:—and we further consider that he deserves to be protected and upheld by society in the course he has pursued.

" William Armour, Allen Deberry, A. Patton, B. W. Burrow, M. Chalmers, Labon Dodson, M. Deberry, M. Cartmel, B. W. Perry, Samuel Givens, F. C. Edwards, E. H. Childers, Samuel Hays, J. H. Rawlings, Mills Durdin, Thomas Campbell, R. H. Lake, Hazael Hewett, H. R. Lacy, John Sanford, Zebulon Jackson, G. Slayton, Jacob Hill, William Taylor, C. T. Harris, James Voss, H. S. Ross, Gabriel Anderson, John Garison, D. L. McDonald, Alfred Sharp, S. Sypret, George Hicks, John Harrison, John Burrow, F. McKenzie, E. McKnight, A. Hutchens, G. Snider, John T. Porter, Philip Werlick, Mathias Boon, Thomas H. Shores."

" I, Mathias Deberry, do hereby certify, that I am and have been the sheriff of the county aforesaid for a number of years, and that I am personally acquainted with all the persons whose names appear to the above declaration of sentiments, and take pleasure in testifying, to all whom it may concern, that they are of the most honourable and respectable class of citizens of our state; and that the above declaration of sentiments towards Mr. Stewart has been subscribed to by all of the like character who have had an opportunity presented, and that the above subscription was unsolicited on the part of Mr. Stewart.

"Given under my hand at Jackson, the 29th day of September, A. D. 1834.

"MATHIAS DEBERRY, *Sheriff*."

CHAPTER XI.

IMMEDIATELY after the trial had closed, and Murrell's conviction was sealed, Mr. Stewart determined to prosecute his design, and, if possible, complete his publication. Accordingly, he commenced arranging his papers for this purpose, but still kept his design as much as possible to himself. It was generally believed at this time that Mr. Stewart intended to publish some facts relative to this affair; yet, even his own intimate friends were ignorant of the extent of Murrell's power, or the nefarious nature of his designs; he therefore deemed it unnecessary to endeavour to convince them, until he should bring all the circumstances in the case to bear together.

Mr. Stewart was now placed in an extremely trying situation. He had long since learned that his safety depended entirely upon his own judicious management and exertions, and consequently, although he communicated his design of setting forth to the world a detailed history of this whole affair to a few of his most intimate friends, yet still he determined to follow the course which prudence and the demands of his own personal safety suggested, and keep his designs for the present as secret as possible. It was peculiarly

1

mortifying to his feelings to meet with much incredulity from even those in whose faith and integrity
he reposed the most entire confidence ; and, if even
those who best knew him were unwilling to give cre-
dence to a limited and partial account, what was he to
expect from an unbelieving populace, when the facts
should appear before them in their true colours ? However, Mr. Stewart was not to be deterred by the incredulity of even his best friends from publishing the hazardous, but deeply important details, which he felt it
his duty to the community to disclose.

It will readily be perceived that the situation in
which these circumstances placed Mr. Stewart at
this time was not the most enviable ; possessing the
knowledge of facts of a nature the most vitally important to the whole country, but of a character so fear-
fully wild and aggravated that the very mention of them
seemed an imputation upon the good sense of those to
whom they were related, and that, too, when they
were but told in their most simple and mitigated form.

Notwithstanding the conviction of Murrell, and the
facts which had been adduced upon his trial, still
those which yet remained untold, and remained alone
in the knowledge of Mr. Stewart, and, to a trifling extent, with those friends to whom he had communicated
them, were of a character so unprecedented that he
had hardly any reason to hope they would find a
believing ear in the whole community. But, with a
magnanimity and generous sacrifice of self to the good
of his fellow-citizens, did this determined and perse-
vering man steadily proceed in his undertaking, and
determined, in the face of all opposition, with almost

equal danger in the publication as he had encountered in the means of obtaining this valuable information, to lay before the public a true and impartial statement of the facts, and patiently await until time should bring to light circumstances in corroboration of his story.

Such now was the state of Mr. Stewart's affairs. He still continued to reside in Madison county, Tennessee, from the period of Murrell's trial and conviction, in the month of July, up to the twenty-eighth of September, during which time he steadily continued his purpose of arranging and writing out his notes for publication, embracing the greater portion of the facts which he intended to make known to the world ; during which time the emissaries of the Murrell gang were not unemployed in striving to devise means to deter him from his undertaking. Private agents of the clan were sent to him in the guise of friends, to represent to him the dangerous position in which he would place himself by publishing such disclosures to the world ; while others endeavoured in another way to frustrate his design, and hinted, in the most artful and insinuating manner, the possibility that such a clan might be willing to advance a large amount of money to ensure his secrecy. In this manner did the beings who had enlisted in this dangerous gang endeavour to ascertain whether Mr. Stewart might not be vulnerable to bribery ; but all their insinuations failed. The generous and noble-minded man, who had already perilled his life, and willingly sacrificed his safety, for the good of his country and his fellow-citizens, was not capable of being seduced, by the hope even of a large reward, to withhold their operations and designs from those whose dearest interests were only to be preserved by the suppression of this dangerous and desperate gang.

On the twenty-eighth of September Mr. Stewart left the house of his old and valued friend, Col. Loftin, and took up his departure for Lexington, Kentucky, and towards evening reached the house of Mr. Deberry, the then acting sheriff of Madison county, with whom he remained till the next morning, and on the twenty-ninth again proceeded upon his journey by the way of Perry county, where he wished to meet with a gentleman who had written him concerning a tract of land in the State of Mississippi which he wished to purchase of Mr. Stewart.   There was another reason, however, why Mr. Stewart wished to travel by a circuitous route, and avoid those roads which were most frequented, which was, that he might avoid observation as much as possible upon his journey, and at the same time evade being intercepted on the way by any of the prowling emissaries of that formidable and dangerous gang, to whom he had rendered himself peculiarly obnoxious by his generous devotion to the interests of his country, by throwing open to the gaze of the world the picture of their iniquity.

The circumstances in which Mr. Stewart was placed naturally made him distrustful, and his mind was continually on the alert.   Under this state of feeling he had kept his intention of making the journey a profound secret, and to all inquiries as to when he intended to leave that part of the country he made the most circumspect replies.

On the night of the 29th, Mr. Stewart put up at a country house on the road, where he imagined that he

should be most likely to pass the night without observation, and quietly prosecute his journey next morning, after having enjoyed the grateful refreshment of a
quiet night's rest ; but he had not long been here before his anticipations were dissipated by the sudden
arrival of four men, who immediately made known
their intentions of passing the night at the house.
From these men Mr. Stewart failed not to receive a
most scrutinizing glance. They scanned his person
with the most critical eye, and endeavoured by the
most inquisitive interrogatories to learn every thing
connected with his intended course ; as to what part
of the country he intended journeying ; and by what
roads he should most probably travel ; whether he intended crossing the Tennessee river ; and, if so, by
what ferry ; and what direction he would then take.
These and many other such questions were put to
him by the strangers : and, although there was nothing in them more than might naturally be expected
from travellers journeying through the same country,
and anticipating enjoyment from each other's society,
still, to the naturally acute and peculiarly sensitive
mind of Mr. Stewart, they seemed to convey an omin-
ous import. He had been long enough among men
of desperate character to know that they could at
pleasure assume the guise of friendship, the better to
hide under its blandishments the evil designs which
they meditated ; and knowing, too, as he did, the peculiar relation in which he had placed himself in regard to a gang of desperadoes, whose nefarious designs were too well understood by him to give him
any promise of mercy if he should chance to fall into

16*

their hands. Ever on the alert, and naturally suspicious of every stranger, he determined to know no man by his appearance and pretensions, let them be never so alluring ; and, acting in the present case under these feelings, he studied every precaution to give to their inquiries the most evasive answers, and, at the same time, if possible, preserve the appearance and manners of one entirely ignorant of their designs. By his answers he led them to suppose that he had business in the neighbourhood which would detain him several days ; but, in an unguarded moment, he unthinkingly inquired of the host, in their hearing, which was the nearest road to Patton's Ferry, and what distance it was hence ; and it was not until circumstances afterward brought it to his remembrance, that his mind reflected upon the unsuspecting inquiry which he had made, and which was sufficient at once to frustrate all his previous carefulness in returning evasive answers to the interrogatories of the strangers. But so it often chances, that in the very moment of our self-assumed security, we are most apt to lay ourselves open to the very snares which our most artful and ingenious endeavours had been exerted to conceal.

By daybreak the next morning the four strangers left the house where they had lodged over night ; and Mr. Stewart, after having remained to breakfast with the host and his family, departed upon the same road, and continued his journey that day to the house of Mr. Gilbert, where he was detained until the morning of the 2d of October, when he again proceeded upon his journey.

Mr. Stewart had determined to cross the Tennessee river at Patton's Ferry, and pursue his journey through Columbia, in Murray county, and from thence to Lexington, Kentucky, by the way of Nashville, hoping thereby to be able to elude the pursuit of any who might have observed his motions with an evil design. The wild and desolate region of country extending along the road between Jackson and Patton's Ferry, seemed calculated to excite the most unpleasant emotions in the mind of a solitary traveller, and seemed fraught with dark forebodings to a mind so feelingly alive to every gloomy sensation as that of Mr. Stewart. The feelings which this dreary prospect created induced Mr. Stewart to place himself in readiness for any emergency that might chance to occur, and accordingly he withdrew his pistol from his portmanteau, where he had hitherto carried it, and, after carefully examining it, placed it in his side pocket.

Mr. Stewart had, until now, placed more reliance in the hope of eluding danger and observation, than in the event of a physical resistance when such danger might be at hand. Having taken these precautions, he continued his journey solitarily through this desolate and inhospitable region, and throughout the morning met with scarce an object to relieve his mind from the deep gloom that seemed to hang like an incubus upon him ; and in this state of feeling he journeyed along until it had reached the hour of four in the afternoon, by which time he had arrived at within some eight or ten miles of the ferry, when he was suddenly startled by the appearance of three men fully armed, who had been concealed behind trees by the roadside.

Mr. Stewart was for a moment startled by this sudden attack; but, instantly recovering his self-possession, he placed himself in an attitude of defence. The assassin on his right ordered him to dismount; but, notwithstanding the overpowering numbers and strength of his enemies, he summoned to his aid all his fortitude, and manfully refused to obey the summons; but his situation was truly hazardous, and, in all probability, one who had seen less of the buffets and hardships of life would have yielded a pliant and passive obedience to the stern mandate of a gang of desperadoes, armed at all points with the glittering weapons of death.

In the countenance of one of the villains Mr. Stewart imagined that he recognised the features of one of the four men who had lodged at the same house with him on the night of the twenty-ninth of September, but the other two he had no recollection of ever having seen before. He saw depicted in the countenances of all the appearance of determined vengeance and slaughter; and, as the fearful weapons of destruction were clashing and gleaming around him, he felt that each moment was destined to be his last. He saw himself within the very jaws of death; but the grim monster did not unman him of his firmness and determined resolution. He was determined to sell his life as dearly as possible, and either die defending the sacred gift which he had received from his Creator, or escape, if not immediate death, at least the premeditated tortures which he knew they had in store for him, and which he knew they would inflict with no sparing hand.

Mr. Stewart was armed with no other weapons than the small pistol, which he had haply taken the precaution about two hours before to remove from his portmanteau to a more convenient situation in case of need, and a heavy dagger, which he carried in his bosom. The assassin on his right stood within about two rods of Mr. Stewart, and was armed with a large fowling-piece, and his companion on the left held in his hands a long rifle ; the third member of this banditti placed himself back against a tree, immediately before Mr. Stewart's horse, armed with a heavy-barrel pistol ; his assailants thus disposed, one on the front and the two others on either side, stood in form of a triangle into which Mr. Stewart had entered.

The assassin on the right appeared to be the chief of the party : he continued drawing closer and closer to him, several times ordering him to dismount ; when within about six or eight paces of Mr. Stewart he stopped, and, with a determined tone, demanded whether he intended to dismount from his horse or not ; to which inquiry he received as determined an answer in the negative ; at which the fellow levelled his piece, but Mr. Stewart, being remarkably expert in the use of the pistol, drew it and fired in the villain's face before he had time to suspect such an event. The ball entered his forehead, and he dropped, apparently lifeless ; and, as he fell, his piece went off, but without effect ; for the charge passed harmlessly under the belly of the horse, and lodged in the ground a few yards distant. Mr. Stewart's situation now grew every moment more and more desperate ; the monster on his left levelled his rifle and fired, but without effect ; thus

leaving him for the moment to contend with but one
armed assailant; this was the man who had taken his
position in front, who, seeing that Mr. Stewart attempted to draw no other pistol after he had discharged the first, considered him then unarmed; and, to
make sure of his prize, he, coward like, advanced
within a few paces of Mr. Stewart, who, in the moment of his extremest danger, had yielded up nothing
of that courage and presence of mind so essential to
one placed in desperate circumstances : with a peculiar dexterity and an unerring aim, he flung the empty
pistol, which had already been effectual in prostrating
one of his assailants, with all his force in the face of
his companion, and struck him over his eye.   He was
so stunned by this unexpected blow that he was entirely thrown off his guard, and his pistol snapped and
fell harmless from his hand.

Mr. Stewart having then almost miraculously escaped so far unharmed, drew his dagger and rushed
his horse upon this assassin, for the purpose of plun-
ging it into his bosom ; but, while in the act of bending
forward to inflict the wound, he received a severe
blow across his breast from the heavy rifle in the
hands of the villain on the left.   This blow stunned
him for a moment, but, summoning all his physical as
well as mental strength and energy, he raised himself
in his saddle to turn upon his third assailant, when he
received a heavy blow upon the back of his head
and neck, which seemed to vibrate throughout his
whole frame, and which displaced him from his saddle and threw him across the horse's neck.   He discovered that he was badly wounded from the last

blow he had received, and made an effort to escape by flight; and, so soon as he could regain his saddle, he put spurs to his horse, and endeavoured to escape beyond the reach of his enemies. As soon as he had recovered from the excitement occasioned by this affray, he hastened the speed of his horse, and directed his course through a thick wood, the more effectually to avoid the chance of observation in case of pursuit; for he imagined that he might have to encounter other parties of this same desperate gang by continuing on the road; and consequently, not even in this perturbed state of mind, did Mr. Stewart forget the natural firmness of his character, for he still, even in the precipitancy of his flight, kept all his fortitude at his command; but, just at the moment of his turning from the road to enter the wood, the report of another gun sounded in his ear. This report, however, he judged was made by the horse-pistol belonging to the assassin whom he had stunned by the blow from his own pistol. Mr. Stewart had raised his left hand as a support to the back of his neck, which had been severely bruised by the blow from the stock of the rifle, and when in this position he received a buckshot in his arm, but which, however, did him no material injury.

Mr. Stewart now directed his course down a vale that extended on his right, and continued his flight through this unfrequented wood until he imagined that he had left his assailants something like three miles behind him. The immediate appearance of danger now no longer staring him in the face, he began to grow quite sick, and concluded that, in this condition, exhausted and wounded as he was, he should not be able to continue his flight much farther ; but he did not know how near his pursuers might be to him ; he however became more and more faint, and at last was forced to seek for a place where he might lie down unobserved from the surrounding country. He directed his course up a little bayou, along which he travelled to a spot that appeared entirely secluded and hidden by the thick foliage of the neighbouring hills, and dismounted in a grove of thick underbrush, and tied his horse where he would be most secure from observation : he took his portmanteau and blanket from the horse, and bent his steps some distance from him ; he thought that, should they pursue him and find his horse, they should not so easily discover him.

Mr. Stewart now lay down in great agony, and his feelings carried him almost to the brink of despair. He had long since looked upon his life as sacrificed to a generous emotion and warmth of soul ; yet still he determined to dispose of it as dearly as possible.

He now kept his mind continually on the alert, and kept a constant watch until the sun sank down in the west, and nature betook herself to repose. The shades of evening now began to gather round, and the stillness of the night seemed to add to the deep gloom of his feelings. Now and then the rustling of the dry leaves, as they dropped from their parent branch, broke upon the ear ; and occasionally a slight puff of air would breathe over the scene.

His feelings now grew wild and desolate ; he frequently found himself crawling through the brush and

thicket as if under the influence of a horrible dream ;
and in this frightful manner did he pass the whole
night of the 2d of October. Towards daybreak he
got a moment's rest, but awoke in almost indescribable pain ; his neck was much swollen, and he had
a considerable fever; his wounded arm was very stiff
and sore, and his whole frame was racked with misery; his mental excitement added still more to his
dreadful feelings ; his mind continually dwelt upon
his forlorn and almost hopeless condition, and the
danger that might still await him.

To attempt to find a house in that part of the country might prove fatal, for he knew not in what manner
the emissaries of that desperate gang might lie in wait
for him ; but, even should he chance to fall into the
hands of an honest man, he knew that he was likely
to be tracked out and discovered before he could sufficiently recover from his wounds, and at least would
be likely to be intercepted upon his departure from the
house. To attempt to continue his journey to Lexington, Kentucky, he now considered almost certain
death ; and to attempt to return to Madison county
seemed to him to threaten a like result. Although
Mr. Stewart had many excellent friends in this part of
the country, he could not now avail himself of their
services, for they could afford him but little aid, even
should they be made acquainted with his real situation. He was also well aware that he had many
deadly enemies, who exerted a mighty influence in
Madison county ; danger and death seemed to
stare him in the face on every side ; and, even should
he now be fortunate enough to escape from their

I   17

hands, he felt well assured that he could never remain in that part of the country after the disclosure
of the horrible transactions which as yet remained a
secret in his own bosom, and of the names of those
beings who conducted the machinery of this extensive
plan of operations.

Thus, as it were, proclaimed an outlaw, and hunted
down by those whose enmity was almost certain destruction, he came to the conclusion that it was his
duty to leave America. His mind being fixed, he directed his course across the country towards Columbus,
in the State of Mississippi, and intended to go from
thence to Mobile, and from there to some part of Europe, for a few years. This resolution being formed,
he aroused himself to the greatest exertions for putting it in execution.

It was late in the afternoon when Mr. Stewart bade
adieu to the desolate region which had served him for
a couch and place of concealment during the night :
he however first examined his horse, to see whether he
had not received injury in the rencounter, but happily
he found him free from all harm. Covered with blood,
and exhausted with faintness, and want of rest, and
food, Mr. Stewart mounted and began a retreat from
his hiding-place ; he set out in a southerly direction,
and determined to prosecute his journey through the
night. He was almost famished for want of water,
and he also wished to cleanse himself from the blood
that covered him before he should meet with any person from whom he should be liable to attract observation. After about an hour's travel he found water,
when he allayed his thirst, and cleansed his gar-

ments and person from the blood which covered them; he changed his dress and strove to divest himself of every thing that bore any mark of the affray; and, after as much as possible hiding every vestige of the encounter, he resumed his journey; he passed a farmhouse before dark, but studiously avoided coming in contact with any of its inmates. He met with several roads during the night, but not one of them appeared to run in the direction that he wished.

He continued his solitary journey through the woods and unfrequented paths until near midnight, when he met with a serious obstacle. A creek lay exactly before his course, which, in the night, he could not discern a fording-place to cross.

He now dismounted and relieved his horse from his burden, and, tying him by the head and leg, allowed him to go in quest of whatever he could find to satisfy the demands of hunger, which by this time had doubtless become most acute; for Mr. Stewart could not bear to tie him up for a second night, to fast again until he should arrive at some place of safety. Mr. S. again prepared his couch, and, stretching himself upon his blanket, attempted to get an hour's repose. The weather was not very cold, but was quite damp, and in his weak and exposed condition he took a violent cold from this exposure; this, added to his sufferings, produced a state of mind bordering on delirium.

On the morning of the fourth, he found his horse not far from the place where he had turned him loose the evening before, saddled him, and again proceeded upon his journey. Mr. Stewart, as well as his horse, was now almost exhausted from fatigue and

I 2

want of food, and he determined to stop at the next
house, be it at whatever hazard it might.   Mr. Stewart continued his ride until he came to a settlement-
road, and, about eight in the morning, stopped at a
farmer's house by the roadside, and immediately made
inquiries whether he could feed his horse, and procure something for his own breakfast.   The host
made a frivolous excuse at not being able to accommodate him, and Mr. Stewart then made inquiry if he
could tell him the road to Purdyville ; but, instead of
giving him the desired information, he answered all
his interrogations with other questions.

Mr. Stewart then told him that he was hungry, and
anxious to arrive at some place where he might stop
and obtain breakfast, and would be glad if he would
direct him without further equivocation.   The man
pointed out to him the way to the main road.   Mr.
Stewart thought it the most prudent plan to assume
another name, and change as much as possible his appearance.   He however required almost the whole
stock of his clothing from his portmanteau to meet the
demands of his present delicate situation.

Between eleven and twelve he arrived at a house
on the public road, which road was, in fact, but little
more than a distinguishable foot-path, where he procured refreshment for both himself and horse ; and, being extremely worn down by fatigue and exposure,
Mr. Stewart sought relief in a few hours' repose.

Mr. Stewart eluded all inquiries from his host by
observing a reserved demeanour, and alleging for his
conduct the ill health under which he was labouring.
Had he deemed it prudent, he would gladly have re-

mained at his house until he should have recovered from the effects of his wounds, and become in a condition better adapted to the fatigues and exposures incidental to a long journey through so wild and inhospitable a portion of the country; but, in case he remained, he would be forced to make known the circumstances of his rencounter, and consequently the development of his name and business would naturally follow, in which case he could promise himself but little hope of safety.

Under his present peculiar circumstances, Mr. Stewart thought it the most prudent plan to bear his situation as long as he could support himself upon his horse, and at least avoid an exposure of his real name and business until he should leave this part of the country far behind him. Mr. Stewart left this house, and proceeded upon the direct road to the Chickasaw nation; but was compelled to stop travelling before night from excess of misery. His fever grew worse and worse, and this, added to the pain arising from his wounds, made him almost delirious. He stopped at a house that day and procured food; but what passed during the remainder of the day he could not remember. The next house at which he stopped was at a Chickasaw settlement; but of the time that had elapsed since he left his previous stopping-place, he could form no idea, nor of the country over which he had travelled.

The old Indian with whom he lodged was very attentive and kind to him, and Mr. Stewart remained at this place until his fever had somewhat abated, when his extreme anxiety, and the loneliness of his situation,

17*

urged him to make another effort to continue his journey.

A port on the Tombigbee river, called Cotton-gin, was the point to which, under the direction of the Indian, he now directed his course; he spent one night at this town without attracting any peculiar observation, or being questioned as to his name and business. Having somewhat recruited himself by a good night's rest, he again set out next morning on the road to Columbus ; but, to his extreme disappointment, there was no boat running on the river at that time. At this place, as at Cotton-gin, he succeeded in keeping himself free from particular observation.

Mr. Stewart had the gratification, however, next morning, to learn from the keeper of the hotel where he stopped, that there was a party of ladies and gentlemen who were then crossing the ferry on their way to the river counties, and he immediately resolved to join the party, and travel in their company to some port on the Mississippi river, and then down to New-Orleans. Accordingly he hastened his movements as much as possible, and came up with the party just as they were setting out from the opposite side of the river. Mr. Stewart did not wish to make any new acquaintances, but merely to be able to travel along with this party, for the purpose of being less likely to attract observation on the road ; and at the same time be relieved from the fear of an attack while performing the remainder of his journey.

His retiring and unobtrusive manner saved him from any particular notice from the party with whom he was travelling. Towards evening they began to divide off in different squads, and seek for lodgings at the various cabins along the road, as they could not all find accommodations at the same house.

The first day after Mr. Stewart left Columbus, he stopped at a house where he met with some highly respectable citizens of Tennessee, who were travelling down towards the Mississippi river; he made the acquaintance of Captain Watson and his son, of Williams county, and travelled with them the next day. These gentlemen were the only acquaintances that he had made since he left the house of Mr. Gilbert, in Perry county, and this was the only place where he had ventured to make known his real name for the distance of more than two hundred and fifty miles. But he was destined to enjoy his new friends but a short time. The extremely distressing state of his wounds now brought him almost to the verge of despair; he found it to be impossible to ride faster than a walk, and gradually fell behind the rest of the party; a burning fever pervaded his whole frame, and he suffered under the most torturing pains; all of which, however, he endeavoured to smother as much as possible; but he was now again left alone; his situation would not allow him to keep up with the party, and he was obliged to travel again with no other companion than his own distressing sensations of both body and mind; he continued his ride for a few hours in this way, but, growing fainter and fainter, could no longer support himself, and fell from his horse senseless in the road.

In this deplorable situation Mr. Stewart remained for some time, when a wagoner passed by, who, had it not been daylight, would undoubtedly have run over his body; but fortunately he acted towards him the part of the good Samaritan, and rendered him all the assistance in his power. He removed him from his exposed situation to the roadside, caught his horse and tied him, so that he could have him at hand when he should be able to remount. Some time after this Mr. Stewart made a great exertion, and succeeded in remounting his horse, and again setting out on his journey. He had not rode far before he met very unexpectedly with a friend, whom the reader will hereafter know by the name of Walton.

This gentleman was travelling on his way from the Chickasaw nation to Memphis, Tennessee, and was in great haste to arrive there; but, meeting with his friend in his present wretched situation, he turned and accompanied him to the nearest house, and remained with him till the next day; when, being extremely anxious to proceed, he was forced to leave him and pursue his journey. Mr. Stewart informed him of his intention to leave the country for some length of time. He delivered to him his papers, and deposited two thousand dollars in his hands for the purpose of defraying the expense of their publication, which his friend promised to superintend. He advised Mr. Stewart to go further on, to the house of Mr. James Moore, who lived some miles ahead, in Madison county, as soon as he had sufficiently recovered, and promised to meet him at Natchez as soon as his affairs would admit.

His friend then bade him farewell, and left him in a state of mind much improved. He now felt that his

disclosures would be published without doubt, whether
he lived or not. The second day after his departure,
Mr. Stewart arrived at the house of Mr. Moore, where
he was treated with the utmost kindness and attention
until he was sufficiently recovered to prosecute his
journey. This was the first landlord to whom he had
made known his name since his departure from Madison county, with the exception of Mr. Gilbert, whom
he had called to see in Perry county. But Mr. Moore,
by his own kind attentions, as well as from the recom-
mendations of his friend, proved himself worthy of all
confidence, and to him Mr. Stewart made known the
relation of his whole affairs, as will be seen from the
following certificate of Mr. Moore on that subject.

" *State of Mississippi, Madison County.*

"I do hereby certify, to all whom it may concern,
that Virgil A. Stewart lay sick at my house, in this
county, in the latter part of October, 1834. At that
time he was on his way to Natchez from Columbus,
where he informed me that he contemplated taking a
passage on some boat for New-Orleans, and then making his way to some part of Europe, probably to
France. While sick, he informed me who he was, and
of his having put his papers into the hands of a friend
to be made public ; but that he had been hunted and
sought after with such avidity by a numerous band
of villains, that he felt it to be his duty to leave the
country until such time as the people would be sufficiently aroused to a sense of the extent and designs of
the banditti, and the danger to which he himself was
exposed in consequence of his adventure in exposing
the same. He then informed me of his having started
from Madison county, Tennessee, with the intention of

going to Lexington, Kentucky; and of his rencounter with three assassins near Tennessee river, which was the cause of his having turned his course through this country, to evade pursuit and assassination from the band of villains whom his adventure and trip with Murrell to Arkansas had exposed, and which they were trying to prevent being published.

" This statement is freely made, for the satisfaction of all, and in justice to Mr. Stewart.

" Given under my hand and seal, this 27th day of December, 1835.

[Sealed.] "JAMES MOORE."

The kind attentions of Mr. Moore soon enabled Mr. Stewart to again undertake the prosecution of his journey ; and his own anxiety urged him to set forward as soon as possible.

Mr. Stewart's mind was so entirely occupied with his own situation, and his troubles took such deep root, as almost entirely to eradicate all other reflections. He neglected taking note of the date, but thinks it was near the latter end of the month of October when he set forward from Mr. Moore's, bound for the city of Natchez.

He again thought proper to assume a feigned name, and passed through Clinton, Raymond, and Port Gibson without meeting with any circumstances worthy of note. About three miles from Port Gibson Mr. Stewart fell in with a young gentleman, and in his company continued during the remainder of his journey to Natchez.

Mr. Stewart found himself peculiarly happy in his new companion, for he esteemed him most highly for a combination of excellent qualities, rarely united in a young man : he possessed a mild and amiable disposition, agreeable manners, and, withal, was very intelligent ; free to converse, yet too modest to be troublesome and inquisitive. The society of this young man had a most salutary influence upon the feelings of Mr. Stewart. They arrived together at Natchez, and stopped at the same house, and during the whole time of their journey neither one of them inquired the name of the other.

While Mr. Stewart remained waiting at this place for letters from his friend, Mr. Walton, he took the opportunity of exploring that portion of the town known by the title of " *Natchez under the hill.*" It presented an awful sink of crime and pollution.* This scene so disgusted him, that he took the earliest opportunity of quitting the town ; for he could not feel himself safe in the vicinity of such a dissolute place, in his unhappy situation. After leaving a letter for his friend, he left Natchez for St. Francisville.

At the latter place, where he remained for a few days, he occupied most of his time in writing out the notes which he wished to place in the hands of Mr. Walton, and in writing to some of his friends. On the 10th of November Mr. Walton arrived at St. Francisville, and Mr. Stewart started in his company for New-Orleans ; but his health was so bad that his friend persuaded him to alter his determination, and they turned for the north, up the river.

Mr. Stewart's health now rapidly declined ; and,

* This has since become an interesting and decent portion of the city.

growing weaker and weaker from his wounds, and constant exposure and anxiety, he was obliged to lay by at Cincinnati, and remain there till the ensuing spring. During his stay at this place Mr. Walton prepared his publication for the press ; and, although he had been too unwell himself to give it that supervision which was necessary, still he was not willing to delay it any longer, it having been already put off much longer than he desired.

The pamphlet was finished in the latter part of February, 1835 ; Mr. Stewart sent it by mail to all the principal military, as well as civil officers of any note in the country. By the first of March he recovered his health sufficiently to travel, and visited New-Orleans, and saw that his pamphlet was distributed throughout the whole of the valley of the Mississippi. Mr. Stewart procured a suit of disguise, in which he equipped himself, and set out upon this expedition, which was at the same time arduous and hazardous. He took every opportunity of distributing his pamphlet wherever he went, and would frequently, after dark, secretly leave it in public places, where it would be most likely to fall into the hands of those for whom he had intended it.

In this way he was compelled to travel from one place to another, in disguise, for the purpose of self-preservation ; and, at the time, he knew of but one single individual in the whole western region in whom he could place entire confidence.

CHAPTER XII.

AFTER Mr. Stewart's "Western Land Pirate" was published and generally distributed throughout the Mississippi valley, it excited great curiosity, and was, as Mr. S. had expected, the subject of much speculation. "Such deeds of horror had surely never found an actor among Christians in the nineteenth century!" was the opinion of many. "It is all fiction!" said others. "It is a catchpenny affair!" would cry a third; notwithstanding he had, perhaps, found the book on his counter, and knew not how it came there. During this suspense of public opinion, the friends of Murrell and his clan, who had been exposed and held up to public odium, lost no time in endeavouring to discredit the publication and slander its author. Matthew Clanton and Col. Jarrot, the reputed friends of Murrell, united all their powers for the destruction of Mr. Stewart's character; and as drowning men, struggling for the last gleam of hope, they entered the field, bearing the arms of slander and perjury. At their heels were found murderers, thieves, and refugees, brandishing their envenomed weapons of destruction. The dark mantle of infamy was just closing in on them for ever. After rallying all the forces of vice and corruption, they resolved to make one united and vigorous effort in a desperate cause. From such a combination what but slander and detraction could be expected?

18

They sallied forth with an abusive and malicious
pamphlet, impeaching the honour of Mr. Stewart; and,
as that pamphlet may have obtained some circulation,
it may not be amiss to give it here a passing notice,
though by no means in its details : for, like its authors,
it is far too filthy to be handled with impunity; and
with them, save this slight interruption, it may repose
for ever in its couch of corruption.

The reader has before been informed, that when
Mr. Stewart last left the Choctaw Purchase, he made
George N. Saunders his agent, and that he had formed
a good opinion of him, and that Saunders had also professed to be a great friend to Mr. Stewart ; but that
there was something about him that prevented Mr.
Stewart from making a confidant of him, even in his
greatest distress. While standing amid the thickening
storm of danger and destruction, in a thousand frightful shapes, an hour that tries the soul and nerve of
man, George N. Saunders had been introduced to
Mr. Stewart by Clanton, a few months before he left
the Purchase. He is an elderly man, venerable and
amiable in his appearance and demeanour, but a devil
and villain at heart. He too was combined with the
conspirators for the destruction of Mr. Stewart ; while
making the greatest outward show of friendship and
respect, his demon soul rankled within, and, like that
of the midnight assassin, thirsted for blood. He is the
man that now comes forward and swears to a volley
of lies for Clanton and his motley companions in guilt
and iniquity. As the venerable George N. Saunders
is his main witness, we will here show the reader and
the world who George N. Saunders is.

" Covington, Aug. 20, 1835.

" The undersigned, citizens of Tipton county, Tennessee, having seen a communication in the Pittsburg (Mississippi) Bulletin, of Matthew Clanton, in which he relies on the certificate of Geo. N. Saunders to prove certain charges against Virgil A. Stewart, tending to destroy his character, do hereby certify, that we were well acquainted with Geo. N. Saunders during his residence in this county, and from our knowledge of him and his general character, we would not believe him upon oath in a court of justice. We know nothing of either Clanton or Stewart; but are unwilling to see the character of any human being destroyed by the testimony of so unworthy an individual as we know Geo. N. Saunders to be. We further certify, that so far as we know any thing of the circumstances related by Stewart in the ' Land Pirate,' they are true as set forth.

" D. A. DUNHAM,	W. BRANCH,
P. BRINGLE,	M. CALMES,
J. T. COLLIER,	R. I. MITCHELL,
G. D. SEARCY,	AND. GREER,
G. M. PENN,	SAM'L. GLASS,
N. HARTSFIELD,	SAM'L. HOLLIDAY,
J. A. GREEN,	S. A. HOLMES."

" *State of Tennessee, Tipton County.*

" I, Robert W. Sanford, clerk of the court of pleas and quarter sessions for said county, having been requested by sundry citizens of this county, do hereby cheerfully certify, that the gentlemen whose signatures appear to the foregoing certificate or statement are honourable and respectable citizens of Tipton county, whose veracity has not been questioned in any way within my knowledge.

" Given under my hand at office in Covington, this 27th day of August, 1835.

" R. W. SANFORD."

"*State of Tennessee, Tipton County.*

"I, Jacob Tipton, chairman of the court of pleas and quarter sessions, do certify, that R. W. Sanford is clerk of our said court, and that due faith and credit should be given to all his acts, both private and public.

"Given under my hand and seal, this 27th day of August, 1835.

[Sealed.]   "J. TIPTON, J. P., *Chairman.*"

"I, Jacob Tipton, chairman, as aforesaid, and clerk of the circuit court, do further certify, that I am acquainted with Geo. N. Saunders, formerly of this county, now of Mississippi; and that he is not worth the notice of any man, much less the public; and that he did, in a transaction with me, tear his name from a note of hand that he had given, and swore he never executed such a paper, which he afterward admitted and paid, rather than be endicted.

"Given under my hand, this 27th Aug., 1835.

"J. TIPTON.

"N. B.—For the truth of the above statement, I refer to Robt. G. Green, Esq., now residing at Lexington, Mississippi.   J. T.

"A true copy.

"*Test*, R. SCURRY, ROBT. G. BOON, PHILIP B. GLENN."

Next we see a certificate signed by a number of persons, speaking very disrespectfully of Mr. Stewart, and telling the public that Matthew Clanton had been honoured with the title of probate judge by the people of a new county in the Choctaw Purchase, and therefore he must be a gentleman: but let us reflect how an Indian country is first settled. Is it not by Tom, Dick, and Harry? Who is to be probate judge? Tom, Dick, or Harry; and sometimes Tom, Dick, or

Harry is a gentleman, and sometimes a villain, as Matthew Clanton has proved himself to be. But to the subject. Many of the names annexed to this certificate are those of refugees and men of no character, and many others had never seen Mr. Stewart, and therefore could know nothing about him. All who signed the first part of the certificate are perjured, and will swear falsely whenever it is to their advantage to do so. We offer the following evidence to sustain the truth of our assertions.

" *State of Mississippi, Holmes County.*

" The undersigned, citizens of the county and state above written, do hereby certify, that we were at Pontetoc, in the Chickasaw Purchase, on the 25th of 'September, 1835, and saw William G. Crawley introduced to Virgil A. Stewart at that place ; and we afterward heard the said Crawley acknowledge that he had never seen Mr. Stewart before that time. We were present when Mr. Stewart called on the said Crawley for his authority for signing a libellous and slanderous publication against his character, and we heard the said Crawley deny ever subscribing his name to any document derogating from the character of Virgil A. Stewart. He asserted that he had only signed a document giving Matthew Clanton a good character. He also stated that he had been acquainted with Matthew Clanton for six months at least.

" Given under our hands and seals, this 23d day of October, 1835.

[Sealed.]   " WILLIAM McALLISTER, ALLEN COLLINS."

" *State of Mississippi, Holmes County.*

" I do hereby certify, to all whom it may concern, that at the time Virgil A. Stewart left Yallabusha coun-

18*

ty, in this state, in May, 1834, he called at my store in
the county of Yallabusha, and settled a small bill which
I had against him.   Said Virgil A. Stewart then and
there informed me that he contemplated leaving that
county on the day following.   He also declared the
same facts openly in the presence of all in the house.
I do therefore feel it my duty to say to the world that
he did not leave Yallabusha county clandestinely, but
openly and aboveboard.

"Given under my hand and seal, this 18th day of
September, 1835.

[Sealed.]   "A. C. CHISHOLM."

*Declaration of the Sentiments of the Citizens of Carroll
County, Mississippi.*

"At a public meeting of a part of the citizens of Carroll county, Mississippi, on the 1st day of August, 1835,
at Smith's Mill, on motion of Robert M. Spicer, Doctor John Wright was called to the chair, and William
Blanks appointed secretary.   The object of the meeting being briefly explained by the chairman, the following resolutions were read and respectfully submitted :

"*Resolved*, That the undersigned, citizens of said
county, view with indignation the sentiments advanced
by Matthew Clanton, in his reply to the 'Western
Land Pirate,' on pages 15 and 37, in reference to the
manner in which he would esteem those who avowed
themselves the friends of Virgil A. Stewart.

"*Resolved*, That we look upon his (Clanton's) vindi-
cation of the charge alleged against him by Virgil A.
Stewart as entirely inadequate in its present form to
wipe away the stain on his character ; and, until further and stronger evidence is produced, we are not prepared to admit his innocence ; and take this method of
announcing to him and the public that we are the friends
of Virgil A. Stewart.

" *Resolved*, That the secretary furnish the editors of the Grenada Bulletin and Vicksburg Register with copies of our proceedings for publication.

" *Resolved*, That we adjourn, to meet again in Carrollton on Saturday next, the 8th August.

" All which resolutions were unanimously adopted, and subscribed by the following persons, viz. :—Titus Howard, James Blanks, Silas O Neal, Joel Smith, Thos. H. Wright, John Ward, John W. Smith, Patrick Riley, David A. Ren, Edward G. Howard, Stark H. Roach, James T. House, R. R. Williams, L. C. Maclin, Robert M. Spicer, Berry Green, John P. Rozier, Henry A. Roach, Edmond O'Neal, Clark Cobb, James Oldham, William S. Crowson, John Blanks, Byrd Matlock, Edwd. Moore, Richard S. Blanks, John Jackson, A. M'Millan, Charles P. Taylor, Peterson Pason, Bardin O'Neal, John B. Kerr, William Clark, David Cobb, Michael Magraw, William H. Beck, Branson Lattrem, John A. Howard, James Blanks, jr., S. S. Ward, R. S. Kerr, Wiley Rozier, S. B. Piers.

> " JOHN WRIGHT, *Chairman.*

" WILLIAM BLANKS, *Secretary.*"

> " *Carrollton, August 8th,* 1835.

" Met according to adjournment. By request, William G. Kendall read the above resolutions, when they were adopted and subscribed by the following persons, viz. :—William G. Kendall, Samuel Clay, John Clark, Matthew Little, William M. Thompson, John G. Russell, John R. Foy, John S. Crittenden, Reuben Henry, J. Cooper, J. Boyd, John E. Green, Jonah Ashley, Burrell Jones, G. W. Green, W. N. Miller, E. Elkin, Greenwood Leflore, Joseph Drake, John L. Irvin, Joseph Nelson, J. G. Russell, jr., Enoch Lattum, Derram Daverson, Richard Hester, Thomas Rhodes, Jas. Mathews, Thos.

Mathews, John S. Robertson, James M'Manaway, Morgan Smith, James Forbus, N. A. Barnett, Thomas M. Colman, D. Brown, John Brown, William G. Herring, John Mathews, W. P. Patton, John Robinson, R. H. Hawthorn, Daniel Fullinton."

Next we notice a certificate signed by several persons, stating that they saw a letter written by Mr. Stewart to Clanton, in which he acknowledged his guilt and dishonour. This is so absurd in itself, we deem it unnecessary to offer any proof; but for the special benefit of those certificate-makers, we will here give an extract from a letter written by Mr. Stewart to George N. Saunders, before he knew he was his enemy; and, as it was published by Clanton and Saunders for some purpose, we know not what, it will hardly be disputed. We have another object in calling the attention of the reader to this extract. It will be seen from this document that Mr. Stewart had never revealed himself to Saunders as to the evidence he had against Clanton and his future movements. It is as follows :—

*　　*　　*　　*　　*　　*

"I am very anxious to hear from you. Please write to me as soon as possible. I have the pleasure to inform you that I am sustained by the best citizens of the country, and that I have every assurance of the strongest protection. It would be as much as a man's life is worth to interfere with me in any way. The time is past that villains can do me any harm except in secret; plans and schemes will lie against me no longer. Mr. Saunders, recollect what I told you, about the last conversation we had together: you know that I said Clanton's feelings would bleed some day; but you did not understand what was then meant; but, sir, the four winds of heaven can now explain it. I have lived to see it, and can now die contented; not that I glory in Clanton's reproach (for you know that I loved him once), but that the high prerogative of heaven rules over vice and corruption, and makes them cower and yield submission to its wishes."

*   *   *   *   *   *

What would any rational man infer from the above declaration? Mr. Stewart was then speaking of Clanton as he felt, but never expected to see it in print. The reader and the public must draw their own conclusions.

There is a certain Mr. A. C. Bane, of Clanton memory, who has been calumniating Mr. Stewart by means of abusive and slanderous letters, in which he has endeavoured to produce the impression on the mind of the public that Mr. Stewart was an accomplice of Murrell's in villany. We now offer the following evidence to prove the baseness of his accusation.

"*Jackson, Tennessee, 30th September,* 1835.

"Whereas divers insinuations have been put in circulation, involving the character of Virgil A. Stewart, the author of the 'Western Land Pirate,' one of which is intended to produce the impression that said Stewart was associated with John A. Murrell in his thefts and robberies; I hereby certify, to all whom it may concern, that I was, at the time of Murrell's arrest for the crime of which he was convicted, and for which he was sentenced to our state prison, where he is now prisoner, on the evidence of said Stewart, as detailed in the 'Western Land Pirate,' the sheriff of Madison county in Tennessee; and that, previous to Murrell's conviction, after his arrest, he was a prisoner in my custody at least twenty days, fourteen of which he was kept in my office, near my dwelling-house, in the country, our jail being out of repair. The prisoner excited great curiosity, and many visited him during the time, as well strangers as citizens of our county; and the subject of the route with Stewart was one of the most common topics of conversation, of which he always conversed freely, and always admitted that he had never known Virgil A. Stewart; and always, when it was involved, candidly confessed that fact, and very frequently, when conversing freely on the subject, called and designated Stewart by the name of Hues; and on his way to the penitentiary, after conviction, he frequently spoke of Stewart, calling him Hues. It was also proved in court, that Stewart was presented to Murrell immediately after his arrest by way of interrogatory, and that Murrell then called him Hues. I have no hesitancy in saying that it has been as strongly proved, that John A. Murrell and Virgil A. Stewart were as completely strangers personally, except what Stewart probably was impressed with from the infamous character of Murrell, from circulating reports, as any two citizens who had lived as near. John A. Murrell was in the close custody of myself when present, and, when absent, of my son, Absalom Deberry, Mr. Richd. Turner, Mr. Henry B. Stewart, Mr. L. W. Stewart, and Maj. Charles R. Haskill, all or any of whom will cheerfully subscribe the foregoing, should it be necessary, as well as divers other respectable citizens who conversed with Murrell on the subject, and were as firmly convinced of the fact that Murrell and Stewart were strangers, as myself or the guard. There was found in the possession of John A. Murrell a form of affidavits for persons of the names of Dorks, Loyd, and Tucker. It was taken from him at Florence after he was retaken; it appeared to be a letter of instruction how to dispose of Stewart for passing counterfeit bills, but was not directed to any per-

son. This paper he admitted to have been written by
himself; said it was done before he broke jail at Browns-
ville, and afterward he carelessly kept it about his person, not expecting to have occasion to use it.

"The foregoing statement is made for the use and
benefit of the community, to make such disposition of
it as may be thought proper, it being what I thought the
public, and particularly Virgil A. Stewart, is justly entitled to.

"M. DEBERRY."

We would also refer the reader to the evidence of
the guard who arrested Murrell, on page 122 of this
work.

It appears that Clanton has endeavoured to excite
prejudice against Mr. Stewart by means of letter-wri-
ting and false accusation. We will here convict him
of a base falsehood, and an effort at slander, from his
own productions.

The following is a letter of Clanton's, in which he
accuses Mr. Stewart of forgery:—

"*Yallabusha County, Miss., Sept. 25th*, 1835.
"MESSRS ARTHUR, FULTON, & CO., }
"*Natchez, Miss.* }
"GENTLEMEN:—I have in my possession two letters,
written by Virgil A. Stewart to George N. Saunders,
of this county, directing him to forward his goods, &c. to
your address, to be forwarded by you to some point on
Red river, where he stated he designed settling. The object of this is to learn from you two facts in reference
to him. First, at what point on Red river were you directed by him to forward his things? and, secondly,
at what time was he first in Natchez, and requested
you to take the agency of his things? I have a letter

written on the 1st day of November, 1834, at St. Francisville, Louisiana, to George N. Saunders, requesting him to forward the things to you. It must therefore have been before that that he saw you. His fight near Patton's Ferry took place, according to his statement, some time in October, 1834. The certificate of Matthias Deberry, sheriff of Madison county, Tennessee, is dated the 29th day of September, 1834 [see 'Land Pirate,' page 80], at which time he was at Jackson, Tennessee.

"I presume you have already learned that no such fight ever took place, and that his certificates are forgeries. I hope, gentlemen, you will answer this instantly, and oblige

"Your obedient servant,
"MATTHEW CLANTON.

"P. S.—Direct your answer to Pittsburg, Yallabusha county, Mississippi."

We will now give Clanton's inquiries to the Georgians respecting Mr. Stewart, and the genuineness of his certificates of character from that state, with their reply to the same.

[*From the Natchez Daily Courier.*]

Jefferson, Jackson Co., Ga., Sept. 10th, 1835.

MR. WM. P. MELLEN:—

DEAR SIR,—You will understand, by reading the enclosed, the object we have in view by sending it to you for publication. It would be an act of justice to Mr. Stewart, and a satisfaction to the community in which he resides, to know that he was a man in good standing in this country.

Yours truly,   S. RIPLEY.

Jefferson, Jackson Co., Ga., Sept. 9th, 1835.

MR. EDITOR—The following letter was received at this place by mail a day or two since.

COPY.

" *Yallabusha County, Miss., August* 11, 1835.

"MR. SYLVANUS RIPLEY, Jackson Co., Ga.

" In a pamphlet recently published by Virgil A. Stewart, entitled ' The Western Land Pirate,' is the following certificate :

" ' *State of Georgia, Jackson County.*

" ' The undersigned, citizens of said state and county, do hereby certify, that we have been acquainted with Virgil A. Stewart, formerly of this county, now of Madison county, State of Tennessee, for a number of years (and some of us from his infancy), and that he has always supported a respectable and honourable character ;—and we take pleasure in recommending him to the confidence of the citizens of whatever county he may visit, assuring them that we entertain no fears of his ever committing any act derogatory to his character as an American citizen, or in the least calculated to forfeit the confidence to which he is herein recommended.

" ' Given under our hands, this 15th February, 1833.

" ' W. E. Jones, LL. D., Geo. R. Grant, M. D., M. Witt, LL. D., John Appleby, James D. Smith, E. C. Shackelford, Wm. Cowan, Esq., L. A. R. Lowry, Jno. M'Elhanon, Wm. N. Wood, Jno. Lindsay, W. H. Jones, Jackson Bell, A. C. Bacon, Wm. Niblock, Charles Witt, John Park, Maj., Samuel Barnet, Col., Jno. Shackelford, James Orr, G. Mitchell, LL. D., David Witt, Esq., H. Hemphill, George F. Adams, L. W. Shackelford, A. J. Brown, Esq., Green R. Duke, W. C. Davis, Jno. Carmichael, Charles Bacon, Samuel Watson, Wm. Morgan, J. Cunningham, M. D., Lewis Chandler, Wm. D. Martin, Esq., G. M. Lester, Wm. Park, J. W. Glen, Esq., James Nabus, Geo. Shaw, Maj.'

" ' *Georgia, Jackson County.*

" ' I, Sylvanus Ripley, clerk of the superior and inferior courts for the county aforesaid, do hereby certify, that I am acquainted with Mr. Stewart, the person named in the above recommendation, and believe him to be of good moral character ;—and also with the persons whose names are signed to the same—as professionally connected—who are entitled to the same '

" ' Given under my hand and seal of office, the 27th day of February, 1835.

" ' SYLVANUS RIPLEY, *Clerk.*

K 19

" '*Georgia, Jackson County.*

" 'I, Edward Anderson, one of the judges and chairmen of the inferior court for the county aforesaid, do hereby certify, that Sylvanus Ripley, who gave the above certificate, is the clerk of said courts ;—and I further certify, that I am well acquainted with Virgil A. Stewart, and heartily accord with the sentiments expressed by the above respectable citizens of this county.

" '   EDWARD ADAMS, *Judge and Chairman.*"

" The object of this communication is to inquire what you know of this certificate ? Was such a one ever given to Virgil A. Stewart ? What was his standing among you ? I make these inquiries because his pamphlet has created considerable excitement among the people of this country, and he is believed by many of us to be an impostor and villain. Please let me hear from you without delay. Direct your letter to Pittsburg, Yallabusha county, Mississippi.

" Yours very respectfully,
" MATTHEW CLANTON."

" From the foregoing we regret to learn that doubts are entertained by some of your citizens in regard to the genuineness of the certificate it contains—and also of the integrity of the individual (Mr. Stewart) to whom it was given. As an act of justice to Mr. Stewart, and in order that his character may be duly estimated by the citizens among whom he now resides, we repeat to you, and through you to the public (if you will do us the favour to give publicity to our statements), that we have known Virgil A. Stewart intimately for a long time— he having been principally brought up among us—and that his character for honesty, probity, and integrity, so long as we knew him, would not suffer by a comparison with that of any other individual with whom we are or have been acquainted. And we whose names appear to the foregoing certificate further certify, that said certificate was made and assigned by us—and that it contains but a feeble expression of the estimation in which we hold the character of the individual to whom it was given : and finally, we would state, that we-have no doubt the above-stated sentiments in regard to Mr. Stewart would, upon application, receive the united concurrence of all his acquaintances in this part of the country.

" Jno. H. Pendergrass, W. H. Jones, George Shaw, Samuel Watson, W. B. Winters, Charles Bacon, Edward Adams, A. J. Brown, Benj. S. Adams, H. Webb, Middleton Witt, William Cowan, Jackson Bell, Sylvanus Ripley, John Appleby."

It appears from the above documents that Clanton made his inquiry to the Georgians on the 11th of August, and, after receiving the above reply, we find him writing to Arthur, Fulton, & Co., on the 25th of September, charging Mr. Stewart with forgery. What dependance is to be put in the assertions of such an unblushing villain? Would he not swear away the life of Mr. Stewart? Do we not see his latter accusation against Mr. S. made in the very teeth of light and knowledge? We leave the reader and the world to determine his merits, and shall only add, that he and his associates in crime may revel in all the infamy of their profession, and heap abuse on abuse, without giving offence or attracting notice in future.

K 2

PROCEEDINGS AT LIVINGSTON.

AFTER the exposition and discomfiture of the clan
and their designs, a fragment of its more daring members conspired to carry out the plans of their chieftain on the 4th of July, instead of the 25th of December, and thus anticipated the vigilance of the community ; but, being deprived of the management of their
arch demon, who had successfully directed the clan and
conspiracy over thirteen states, for eight years, without miscarriage, their plans were unsuccessfully managed, which exposed them to the fury of an injured
and incensed community, as will be seen from the following history of Madison county, Mississippi.

*Proceedings of the citizens of Madison county, in the
State of Mississippi, at Livingston, in July, 1835,
in relation to the Trial and Punishment of several individuals, implicated in a contemplated Insurrection
of the Slaves in that state, as reported by the Committee of Safety.*

ADDRESS OF THE COMMITTEE.

THE Committee of Livingston have caused to be laid
before their fellow-citizens and the public the grounds
upon which an imperious necessity, as they conceived,
and still firmly believe, compelled them to act, and cause
the lives of a number of their fellow-beings to be taken.
No one need be informed that the principle of self-
19*

defence is the first law of nature, derived from our Creator as essential to the preservation of life.

When, too, it is recollected, that all we hold most dear in this world was involved in the common danger, and calling for every manly energy in its defence, the odds will be found very great between the cold reasoning of statesmen and lawyers, and the vituperations of fanatics at a distance. But imminent and pressing as was the danger, the organization of a committee, chosen by the unanimous consent of their fellow-citizens, assembled on the occasion, and invested by them (however unclothed with the forms of law) with the fearful power of life and death, was the result. This may, nevertheless, be considered salutary, not only as providing against and checking the impending danger, but as wresting and restraining those wild sallies of passion, and not unfrequently of private revenge, which mark the devastating career of an excited and enraged people. The awful responsibility which thus, by the unsolicited suffrages of their fellow-citizens, devolved upon the committee, called for the most patient exercise and calm deliberation of their judgments, not only to break the force of the coming storm, but to shield the innocent from being confounded with the guilty— no very easy task in times of great public excitement, and when the people are driven, from the urgency of the occasion, to resort to natural law for safety. If the committee have in any instance erred, in consigning the innocent to death, of which they remain yet to be convinced, it has not been produced by precipitation on their part—for due deliberation and an earnest desire to find out the truth, rather than the guilt of the accused, have been attested by the length of time devoted to the examination of each case. To those acquainted with the circumstances and condition of the surrounding country and population at the time, an apology for the strong measures adopted by the citizens, and by the committee, under the authority confided to them, would be unnecessary; it may not be to those at a distance.

The question may arise among the latter, why was not the civil authority appealed to? and which, the committee are free to declare, is always greatly to be preferred, when its powers are competent to restrain the evil. The civil authority was inadequate to this end in

Madison county; for there is no jail in that county sufficient to contain more than six or eight prisoners, and even those very insecurely; and, whenever prisoners would have been despatched to any other county, a guard would have been required, which would have left many families defenceless; and it was unknown at what moment this protection might be required; besides, immediate example, and its consequent terror, without hope from the law's delay or evasion, seemed, as in truth it was, indispensable to safety.

Already had many of the slaves marked out the victims of their lust or revenge; and no time to convince them of the fatal attempts of their rash enterprise was to be lost. If they had been permitted to commence it, though a failure must have eventually taken place, horrid would their momentary triumph have been. That the plot was headed by a daring band of villanous white men, there now remains no doubt, and the desperate evil required a prompt and efficient remedy, to the extent of the one resorted to by the citizens of Madison county, and carried into effect by the committee.

PROCEEDINGS.

About the middle of the month of June, 1835, a rumour was afloat through Madison county that an insurrection of the slaves was meditated; no authentic information, however, having been obtained how or where the report originated, most of the citizens were disposed to treat it as unfounded, and consequently took no steps to ascertain its truth or falsehood, until within a few days previous to the fourth of July.

After ascertaining that the report had emanated from a lady residing at Beatie's Bluff, in this county, about nine miles from Livingston, a number of gentlemen waited upon her, for the purpose of learning upon what grounds or suspicions she had given publicity to it. The lady, in compliance with their request, informed them that she was induced to believe an insurrection of the negroes was in contemplation, from the following circumstances, and parts of conversation she had overheard among her house-girls.

She remarked, her suspicions were first awakened by noticing in her house-servants a disposition to be insolent and disobedient; occasionally they would use insulting and contemptuous language in her hearing respecting her, and their general deportment towards her was very unusual, and very different from such as she had been accustomed to receive from them before; and that she was satisfied something mysterious was going on, from seeing her girls often in secret conversation when they ought to have been engaged at their business.   She forthwith determined to scrutinize their conduct more closely, and, if possible, to ascertain the subject of their conversation; and in a few days she heard the girls in conversation, and, among other similar remarks, she heard one of them say, " she wished to God it was all over and done with; that she was tired of waiting on the *white folks*, and wanted to be her own mistress the balance of her days, and clean up her own house."   Soon after, she again heard the same girl engaged in secret conversation with a negro man belonging to a neighbour.   From the low tone in which the conversation was carried on, she was unable to hear it all, but gleaned the following remarks: The girl remarked, "Is it not a pity to kill such * * * *?"   The man replied " that it was, but it must be done, and that it would be doing a great favour, as it would go to heaven, and escape the troubles of this world."

The lady communicated to her son in the evening what she had heard that morning, who told the girl she had been overheard in conversation that morning, and that she *must* tell it.   She, thinking all of it was overheard, without hesitation or punishment, confessed what it was.   She related the same in substance, but more fully; and the above remark of the girl in full was, "Is it not a pity to kill such a pretty little creature as this?" having reference to a child she then held in her arms. And, in addition to the above, she said that the negro man had informed her that there was to be a rising of the black people soon, and that they intended killing all the whites.   And, in conclusion, the lady remarked, that from these hints she had given publicity to the report.

To make assurance doubly sure, and to try and see if something more specific could not be obtained, the girls were examined by the gentlemen, and their statements corresponded in every particular with the above communication of the lady. The report of the gentlemen of course was, that they had good reason to believe that an insurrection of the negroes was contemplated by them, and warned their fellow-citizens to be on their guard, and requested them to organize patrols, a matter which had been entirely neglected heretofore, and to appoint committees of vigilance throughout the county.

This report awakened the people in a measure from their lethargy. Meetings were held in different parts of the county for the purpose of taking into consideration the state of affairs.

On the 27th of June, at a large and respectable meeting of the citizens, held at Livingston, Colonel H. D. Runnels in the chair, resolutions were adopted, appointing patrols and committees of investigation, who were requested to report the result of their inquiries and discoveries at an adjourned meeting, to be held at Livingston on the 30th June.

On the 30th June, pursuant to adjournment, the citizens again met at Livingston; Dr. M. D. Mitchell was called to the chair, when Mr. William P. Johnson, a planter near Livingston, made a report of his investigation on his own plantation. He informed the meeting that he had instructed his driver, a negro man, in whom he had confidence, to examine all the negroes on his place, and see if they knew any thing of the conspiracy. He said, in compliance with his request, the driver had examined all the negroes on his place, and had learned from an old negro, who was in the habit of hauling water from Livingston, that there was to be (using his own language) "a rising of the blacks soon, but did not know when; that he had learned it from a negro man belonging to Ruel Blake, who lived in Livingston." The driver, he said, asked him for powder and shot, pretending to him he wanted it to shoot the white people when the rising should take place: he, the old negro man, told him he had none, but that he would get him some; that Blake's boy, Peter, told him he intended to break open the store of Wm. M. Ryce, and steal some kegs of powder: afterward ascertained that Blake's boy had assisted in unloading wagons at the store, and that he had asked what was in the kegs when he was carrying them in.

K 3

Mr. Johnson had the old negro brought to town and
put into the hands of the committee of investigation for
Livingston, whom he instructed to use him as they might
deem proper. The negro man was asked to confess
what he had told the driver of Mr. Johnson the evening
previous. He denied positively ever having any conversation with the driver; and the committee, finding they
could get nothing out of him by persuasion, ordered
him to be whipped until he would tell what the conversation was, they not being informed of its nature.

After receiving a most severe chastisement, he came
out and confessed all he knew respecting the contemplated insurrection, and confirmed in every particular
the statement of the driver, but could not tell what particular day was fixed upon for the insurrection. He
said Blake's Peter told him he would let him know in
a few days. Johnson's negro implicated no white
men, but said a negro man belonging to Capt. Thomas
Hudnold was engaged in the conspiracy.*

Blake's boy was forthwith taken into custody and
put under examination, but refused to confess any thing

* This negro was implicated by Johnson's negro man. The citizens attempted to take him, but he, suspecting something was not
right, moved off when the gentlemen entered the field where he
was at work. He was run by *track-dogs* some two hours without
being taken, making his escape by taking to water. He remained in
the woods until the excitement had partially subsided. By the
laudable exertions of his master, he was decoyed into Livingston,
where he was taken. He was reputed a desperate and daring villain, and had been a terror to the neighbourhood for some years.
There was evidence sufficient obtained, during the examination of
the other criminals, against him, to satisfy the committee he was
guilty, and it was agreed upon, when he should be taken, to hang
him. However, nothing was said about the determination of the
committee. In the meantime the committee of safety had adjourned
when he was taken. The citizens seemed determined he should be
hanged, and consequently organized a committee, composed of some
of the members of the first committee and other freeholders, who
condemned him to be hanged; and, in pursuance of the sentence,
he was executed in Livingston. Under the gallows he acknowledged his *guilt*, and said that R. Blake told him of the insurrection
in the first of the spring, when Blake and he were in a swamp getting out gin-timber. He said it alarmed him when Blake told him
of it, which Blake noticed, and told him to say nothing about it,
and he would give him $5, which he did; at last he consented to
join in the conspiracy; Blake told him he *must* kill his master *first*,
which he promised to do. Blake told him he was to be one of the
captains of the negroes, &c.

respecting the conspiracy—having been informed, previous to his examination, that a conspiracy of the negroes to rebel against their masters was on foot, and that they wished to know if he had any knowledge of it. He was severely whipped by order of the committee, but refused to confess any thing—alleging, all the time, that if they wanted to know what his master had told him, they might whip on until they killed him ; that he had promised him that he never would divulge it. After obtaining all they could from the two old negroes, the committee had them remanded into custody for further examination.

These developments being circulated through the country, seemed to convince the people that a conspiracy was on foot, which had the effect of creating considerable alarm, from not knowing when it would be attempted.

It was the general impression at this time that it would be attempted on the night of the 4th of July, being a day always given to them as a holyday, when they are permitted to assemble together from the different plantations, and enjoy themselves in uninterrupted feasting and festivity.

The boy who was overheard in conversation at Beatie's Bluff having run off, and the negro man of Mr. Johnson having implicated no white men as accomplices, the general impression was, that the conspiracy was confined to the negroes of a few plantations, and principally within the knowledge of *negro preachers* (generally considered to be the greatest scoundrels among negroes), who were supposed to be the originators of it, as has been the case in all negro conspiracies heretofore detected in the slave-holding states.   Of course there could be but little system or concert in their plans.

It was agreed upon, by common consent of the citizens assembled in the various meetings, that when the ringleaders in the conspiracy should be detected, to make examples of them immediately by hanging, which would strike terror among the rest, and by that means crush all hopes of their freedom.

The citizens in the neighbourhood of Beatie's Bluff were not idle. During the investigations at Livingston, to which they were mainly indebted for the detection of the conspirators, and the discovery of their sanguinary and diabolical designs, they had, by their indefatigable exertions, succeeded in detecting the negro ringleaders, from whom they obtained confessions of their plans, and of some of their white accomplices.

After two days of patient and scrutinizing examination of the negroes implicated at Beatie's Bluff, their guilt was fully established, not only by their own confessions, but by other facts and circumstances, which could not leave a doubt on the mind. Each negro was examined separate and apart from the rest, neither knowing that another was suspected or in custody; each acknowledging his own guilt, and implicating all the others; every one implicating the same *white men,* and the whole of their statements coinciding precisely with each other.

After ascertaining so fully the guilt of these negroes, and the time for the consummation of the design being at hand, the situation of the country being such as to render consummation so easy, the whole community, and the owners of the negroes in particular, demanded the immediate execution of the guilty, and they were accordingly hung on the 2d of July. In order that the facts relative to the proceedings at Beatie's Bluff may be fully understood, and inasmuch as a full knowledge of them will go to explain and justify the course pursued by the committee at Livingston, which was subsequently organized, it is deemed necessary here to insert at large a statement procured from a gentleman near Beatie's Bluff, who was cognizant of the whole transaction.

Mr. Mabry's Letter.

MR. SHACKELFORD :—

DEAR SIR,—I now attempt to comply with your request, in giving you what information came to my knowledge during the late investigations had before the citizens in the vicinity of Beatie's Bluff, in regard to the late contemplated insurrection in Madison county. I had been absent from the county until the Sunday before the 4th of July; when I arrived at home, I learned that there was some apprehension that

the slaves of the vicinity intended an insurrection—
that Madam Latham had overheard a conversation between one or two of her house-girls and one of Mr.
Landfair's men, in which she distinctly understood the
man to say that the negroes were going to rise and kill
all the whites; and, when being asked by one of the
girls what they would do with such a child as she then
held in her arms (having one of her mistress's grand-
children in her arms), he replied, that they intended to
put them to death, as it would be doing them a service, as they would go to heaven, and be rid of much
trouble in this world, &c. On the first day of July we
had a small meeting at the bluff, when I was requested
to examine the two girls. They both said, in unqualified
terms, that the boy above alluded to had informed them
that the negroes intended rising and slaying all the
whites. Mr. James Lee, who resides near the bluff,
a very close observer of men, both white and black,
had his suspicions aroused from what he had seen and
heard, and was consequently on the alert both day and
night. He had overheard conversations which confirmed him in his suspicions, and this was of great service to the committee in the investigations; among
the slaves he had heard two of Capt. Sansberry's boys,
Joe, and Weaver (a preacher). There was a motion
made that a committee of three be appointed to arrest
Joe and examine him; whereupon Capt. Beatie, James
M. Smith, and myself were appointed, and immediately
proceeded to the plantation of Capt. Sansberry, who
promptly delivered up Joe for examination. This man
Joe is a blacksmith, and works for the public. I had
sent one of my men to the shop twice some short time
before this. This man of mine, Sam, I consider a great
scoundrel; and I felt confident that, if Joe knew any
thing of the intended insurrection, Sam was also in the
scrape. This I communicated to Capt. Beatie and Mr.
James M. Smith, before we commenced the examination
of Joe. The first question we put to Joe was this: Do
you know who we are? Joe replied that he knew
Capt. Beatie and Mr. Smith, but that he did not know
me. I immediately insisted that he did know me, and
continued to look him full in the face for some minutes, until he began to tremble. When I saw this, I
asked him if he knew Sam, and when he saw him last?

20

Joe replied that he knew Sam, and had seen him twice not long since at his shop. I then told him that our business with him was to know the conversation that passed between himself and Sam at their last interview. He declared that nothing had passed between himself and Sam but what was usual when fellow-servants meet. We then called for a rope, and tied his hands, and told him that we were in possession of some of their conversation, and that he should tell the whole of it; after some time he agreed that, if we would not punish him, he would tell all that he could recollect. He said he knew what we wanted, and would tell the whole, but that he himself had nothing to do with the business. He said that *Sam* had told him that the negroes were going to rise and kill all the whites on the 4th, and that they had a number of white men at their head: some of them he knew by name, others he only knew when he saw them. He mentioned the following white men as actively engaged in the business : Ruel Blake, Drs. Cotton and Saunders, and many more, but could not call their names ; and that he had seen several others. He also gave the names of several slaves as ringleaders in the business, who were understood to be captains under those white men. He said that one belonging to his master, by the name of Weaver, and one belonging to Mr. Riley, by the name of Russell (*a preacher also*), and my old carpenter, Sam, were of the list of captains. Joe stated that the insurrection was to commence the 4th of July ; that the slaves of each plantation were to commence with axes, hoes, &c., and to massacre all the whites at home, and were then to make their way to Beatie's Bluff, where they were to break into the storehouses, and get all the arms and ammunition that were in that place, and then proceed to Livingston, where they would obtain re-enforcements from the different plantations ; and from thence they were to go to Vernon and sack that place, recruiting as they went ; and from there they were to proceed to Clinton; and by the time they took the last-mentioned place, they calculated they would be strong enough to bear down any and every opposition that could be brought against them from there to Natchez ; and that, after killing all the citizens of that place, and plundering the banks,

&c., they were to retire to a place called the *Devil's Punch Bowl*—here they were to make a stand, and that no force that could be brought could injure them, &c. While Joe was going of with his confession, Capt. Sansberry, and his overseer, Mr. Ellis, brought up old Weaver : he would not confess any thing; said that Joe had told lies of him, and that he did not know any thing about the matter at all. He was put under the lash, Mr. Lee being present, who had overheard his conversation with Mr. Riley's boy Russell, in which he heard them pledge themselves to each other that they would never confess any thing, either of themselves or any others; and although he frequently repeated these words to Weaver, yet he would not confess. Joe was set at liberty, and Weaver remained in confinement. We then went to Mr. Riley's and took up Russell : all was mystery with him; he knew nothing, nor could he conceive what we were punishing him for; we now concluded that we would hand him over for safe keeping to Mr. Ellis, who took charge of him, and just as he arrived at home with him Mr. Lee rode up, and told Russell that he had overheard Weaver and himself in conversation, at a certain place and time, and that he should tell him what had passed between them. Mr. Lee at this time struck him twice; Russell asked him to wait, and he would tell him all about the business; he then went on to make a full statement of all that he knew. His statement was, in all particulars, precisely like the one made by Joe. Next day we again met at the bluff; a number of slaves were brought in; among the rest, one belonging to Mr. Saunders, by the name of Jim, a very sensible, fine-looking fellow. I was appointed to examine him; he would not, for some time, make any confession; but at length agreed that, if I would not punish him any more, he would make a full confession, and proceeded so to do. His statement was very much like that of Joe's; implicating, however, more white men by name than Joe had done, and some more slaves. There was a man present on the ground by the name of Dunavan, whom he pointed out as deeply implicated; he also pointed out a man by the name of Moss, and his sons, as being very friendly to the slaves; said that to him they could sell all they could lay their hands on; that he always furnished them with whiskey; and, also, that these bad white men, while in the neighbourhood, always made Moss's house their home; but that he did not know whether he, Moss, intended to take any part with them in the intended insurrection. Jim further stated, that it was their intention to slay all the whites, except some of the most beautiful women, whom they intended to keep as wives; said that these white men had told them that they might do so, and that he had already picked out one for himself; and that he and his wife had already had a quarrel in consequence of his having told her his intention. Jim gave the names of Blake, Cotton, Saunders, and Dunavan, as deeply engaged in the business.

Bachus, a boy belonging to Mr. Legget, confirmed all that Jim had stated, and added one more white man's name to Jim's list. The name given by Bachus I understood to be *Sliver*, a *pedler;* and that *Sliver* was making up money to buy arms, &c.; and that he, *Bachus*, had given him six dollars for that purpose, and had not seen him from that time. This man we could never get hold of. After getting through with these examinations, Jim, Bachus, Weaver, Russell, and Sam, were all put to death by hanging. And being sent for to-day to take my seat on the committee organized and appointed at Livingston, I do not know any thing more that transpired at Beatie's Bluff, except this,—one of Mr. Landfair's boys who was implicated made his escape, and when he was brought back to the bluff the people met and hung him. I was present at this hanging.

The above is all that I now recollect that took place at the bluff while I was present.

Very respectfully, your obedient servant,

JESSE MABRY.

September 20, 1835.

The news of the execution of the negroes at Beatie's Bluff, and of their horrid and sanguinary intentions, as developed by their confessions in the preceding report, being quickly circulated through the county, had the effect of arousing the citizens from their inaction, and of dispelling the illusion, and warning them of the awful reality of their precarious situation. They were now apprized, for the first time, when the conspirators would attempt to consummate their unholy work. They ascertained that they were not to contend alone with a few daring and desperate negroes, and such of their deluded race as they might enlist in their daring and bloody enterprise, but that these negroes were instigated and encouraged by some of the most wicked and abandoned *white men* in the country ; highway robbers, murderers, and abolitionists, who were to supply them with arms and ammunition, and lead them on to the work of massacre and carnage, conflagration and blood.

In order that the proceedings of the people of Madison county at this critical and trying emergency may be the better understood and justified, the situation of the county should be here fully explained.

The county is settled principally in large plantations, and on many of them there is no white man but an overseer, most of the large planters being absent at the north ; and on a number only the families of the absent—being at least 50 negroes to one white man in the neighbourhood of Livingston and Beatie's Bluff, where the scene of desolation was to commence. Having no arms for their defence but their fowling-pieces ; no organized militia in the county ; what would the ordinary array of arms avail, opposed to the stealthy marauder of the night—the demon of the firebrand and the dagger—and no place of security as a retreat for their families ? The only prospect before them was certain destruction, should they fail to arrest the progress of the impending danger. Intense excitement was pervading the whole community at this time, and was increasing every hour.

The following white men, Cotton and Saunders, were arrested and in custody ; and this, too, before the disclosures of the negroes at Beatie's Bluff were known ; the arrest being made upon circumstances of suspicion and facts, indicating in a very strong degree their agency and participation in the plans then hastening to their full development and consummation. And when the disclosures made at Beatie's Bluff, as above unfolded, were fully made known at Livingston, there seemed to be left no alternative but to adopt the most efficient and decisive measures.

The question became general—what should they do with the persons implicated? Should they hand them over to the civil authority? This would seem, under ordinary circumstances, to be the proper course. But, should that be the course, it was well known that much of the testimony which established their guilt beyond all doubt, would, under the *forms* of the law, be excluded; and, if admissible, that the witnesses were then no more. If, from our peculiar situation, the laws were incompetent to reach their case—should such acts go unpunished? Besides, from what had been seen and witnessed the day before, it was universally believed, and, doubtless, such would have been the fact, that these persons would be *forcibly* taken, even from the custody of the law, and made to suffer the penalty due to their crimes. Should they even be committed for trial, there was much reason to apprehend that they would be rescued by their confederates in guilt—if not by *perjury*, at least by breaking jail. They had an example of the dreadful excitement on the evening of the 2d July, at Livingston. Immediately after the execution of the negroes at Beatie's Bluff was made known at Livingston, it created a most alarming excitement. The two old negro men who were in custody of the committee of examination at Livingston were demanded by the citizens; and, previous to a vote of condemnation, and a full examination, they were forcibly taken by an infuriated people from the custody of those who intended to award them a fair trial, and immediately hung.

The time was near at hand when the intentions of the conspirators would inevitably be carried into effect, if some prompt and efficient means should not be adopted by the citizens to strike terror among their accomplices, and to bring the guilty to a summary and exemplary punishment. It was not believed that the execution of a few negroes, unknown and obscure, would have the effect of frightening their *white* associates from an attempt to perpetrate their horrid designs; which *association* was fully established by the confessions of the accused and other circumstances.

There was no time to be lost; and, for the purpose of effecting their object, to arrest the progress of the impending danger, to extend to the parties implicated something like a *trial*, if not *formal*, at least *substantial*, and to save them from the inevitable fate of a speedy and condign punishment, the citizens circulated a call for a general assemblage of the community on the day following, at Livingston, which call was obeyed ; and, at an early hour the next day, July 3d, there collected a vast concourse of people from the adjoining neighbourhoods.

This meeting, thus speedily assembled (for it was full by 9 A. M.), was composed of at least one hundred and sixty respectable citizens of Madison and Hinds counties, whose names are appended to the resolutions, who, then and there, acting under the influence of the law of self-preservation, which is *paramount to all law*, chose from among the assemblage thirteen of their fellow-citizens, who were immediately organized, and styled a " Committee of Safety ;"– to whom they determined to commit what is emphatically and properly called the *supreme law*, the *safety* of the people, or *salus populi est suprema lex*, and then pledged themselves to carry into effect any order which the committee might make ; which committee were invested by the citizens with the authority of punishing all persons found guilty by them of aiding and exciting the negroes to insurrection, as they might deem necessary for the safety of the community ; all of which will more fully appear by the subjoined resolutions, adopted at the meeting which organized the committee.

Dr. M. D. Mitchell being called to the chair, on motion of Dr. Joseph J. Pugh, the following resolutions were unanimously adopted :—

Resolved, That a standing committee be by this meeting organized ; that the said standing committee shall consist of thirteen freeholders ; that the committee shall have a regular secretary and chairman ; that they do meet every day at 9 o'clock, A. M., and sit until 4 o'clock, P. M. ; that the committee shall have power to appoint the captain of any patrol company ; to bring before them any person or persons, either white or black, and try in a summary manner any person brought before them, with the power to hang or whip, being always governed by the *laws* of the *land* so far only as they shall be applicable to the case in question, otherwise to act as in their discretion shall seem best for the benefit of the country, and for the protection of its citizens.

Resolved, That Hardin D. Runnels, Thomas Hudnold, sen., Israel Spencer, Sack P. Gee, M. D. Mitchell, Nelson L. Taylor, Robert Hodge, sen., John Simmons, James Grafton, Charles Smith, D. W. Haley, Jesse Mabry, and William Wade, be chosen and appointed by this meeting as a committee of safety.

Resolved, That the said committee have power to appoint any person to fill any vacancy that may occur in their body by death, resignation, or otherwise; and further, the said committee shall have power to call a meeting of all the citizens of this county, when in their discretion they may deem it necessary; and that the said committee be clothed with all the power heretofore assumed by *this meeting*.

Resolved, That nine members of said committee constitute a quorum, with power to discharge all the duties assigned said committee.

Resolved, That said committee have power to appoint their own chairman and secretary; that it be the duty of the secretary of said committee to keep a record of all the proceedings of said committee, and also to procure from the secretary of this meeting all its proceedings, and to preserve the same.

Resolved, That we whose names are hereto affixed, do hereby pledge ourselves to sustain said committee against all *personal* and *pecuniary* liability which may result from the discharge of the duties hereby assigned them. And further, that we will in like manner sustain all persons in the discharge of the duties which may be from time to time assigned them by said committee; and that we are not responsible for any acts done by persons acting without the orders of said committee.

John N. Legrand, Irvin C. Wadlington, A. W. Robinson, T. C. Griffing, John G. Andrews, John C. Smith, Thomas Coleman, Thos. Hudnold, jr., Garret Goodloe, John Lowe, Ira Harris, H. H. Schrock, Jos. T. Pugh, Wm. M. Royce, Sol. S. Mitchell, T. P. Jones, Charles B. Green, Thos. Shackelford, Hiram Perkins, John G. Ott, John A. Gilbreath, Jno. R. Grigsby, Albert G. Bennett, Jona. Coleman, Jose W. Camp, C. S. Brown, Samuel Barrow, Alfred Perry, Wm. Pack, Abner Sholan, John Steady, S. W. Ewing, L. Estill, R. S. Hodge, William S. Rayner, Geo. D. M'Lean, Wm. G. Doyle, Henry G. Pipkin, Halcut Alford, Charles L. Starr, Jeff. E. Gagdon, S. B. Thompson, W. M. Bole, A. S. Leppingwell, James P. Wyatt, Thos. Collins, Robert Clark, N. S. White, Littleton W. House, W. D. F. Harrison, M. Dulaney, Wm. Wells, George W. Coffee, Daniel Mann, Robert M. M'Gregor, John T. Long, Elijah Boddie, L. W. Wesley, Wm. Simmons, Albert Hendrick, W. B. Hendrick, Benj. Pulliam, Wm. H. Atkinson, Willis B. Wade, Robert T. Cecill, W. E. Harrold, Guilford Griffin, James T. Wilson, Edwd. Cheatham, Joseph A. Fort, John A. Cotten, Ramsey M. Cox, R. S. Hunter, Reuben I. Gee, Duncan York, H. M. Merreth, D. P. Austin, Stephen M. Old, James G. Goodhue, James S. Wood, John Fletcher, Harry Latham, Gane. Logan, Thos. Saunders, G. P. Wadlington, Jas. M. Smith, A. M. Goodloe, Pierson Reading, sen., Geo. Dixon, Jona. Van Cleare, Edwin R. Isler, S. C. M'Gilvary, Nathan B. Pequin, Jno. S. Cock, Eleazer Kilpatrick, Geo. Trotter, Benj. W. Trotter, Jas. F. Beazley, Jas. D. Hester, Edward Wills, Saml. B. Simmons, L. B. Trotter, Jas. Patterson, Dempsey Taylor, Wm. Barrow, William Frith, Andrew C. Steger, Edwin Perry, Thos. Atwood, Robert G. Anderson, William Bennett, Saml. Moseley, Harrison Gill, Jos. L. Holland, Thornton Sandridge, Hugh M'Elroy, Geo. W. Amos, N. Webb, Edwin Bass, James R. Jones, Wade H. Mills, D. W. Saxon, John W. Lindsey, G. Flint, N. W. Bush, B. Wells, T. J. Catching, G. W. Walsting, B. Strother, H. Hayneau, Wm. H. Steger, Isaac Rhodes, John Bisco, Henry Hines, Joseph Clark, Gadi Gibson, M. N. Gasy, Wm. Gartley, John H. Rollins, S. D. Shackelford, Samuel D. Livingston, James Avery, William B. Ross, William Wildy, T. B. Daugherty, Osmun Claiborne, Alexander Allen.

M. D. MITCHELL, *Chairman.*

WILLIAM ROYCE, *Secretary.*

With the organization of the committee, all disposition to continue the scene of the previous evening ceased. The community then seemed to be relieved from the intensity of their concern about the state of things, and hailed and regarded the organization of the committee (really a committee of safety) as a relief from their fearful and unsettled condition.

All were determined to support the committee; some

formed themselves into guards, and dispersed in search
of offenders; others waited on the committee to re-
ceive their orders. Previous to taking up any case, the committee organized themselves, and elected Dr. M. D. Mitchell chair-
man, and William M. Royce secretary. After being
organized, they adopted rules to govern them in their
examination of offenders; which rules they adhered to
during the continuance of their authority. They determined to take no cognizance of any crime which
was not directly connected with the contemplated insurrection; to examine *all* witnesses under oath; to
punish no man without strong circumstantial evidence,
in addition to the dying confessions of those previously
executed, or such other evidence as should seem con-
vincing to *all* of the guilt of the accused; to give the
accused every opportunity that the nature of the case
would admit of, to prove their good character, or any
thing that would go to establish their innocence; and,
in fact, to give them all the privileges allowed to criminals in courts of justice in similar cases, partly to permit them to explain doubtful points by their own voluntary statements.

At 10 o'clock, A. M., on the 3d, the committee commenced their labours with the examination of the case
of Joshua Cotton.

Trial of Joshua Cotton.

This man had been in the State of Mississippi about
twelve months; was a native of some one of the New-
England states, but last from the western district of
Tennessee. On his arrival in this state, he settled at
the Old Indian Agency, in Hinds county, where he
married soon after. From the agency he moved to
Livingston, in Madison county, where he set up shop,
and hoisted a sign as "Steam Doctor."

William Saunders, at the meeting of the citizens held
at Livingston, on the 30th June, stated that Cotton was
in the habit of trading with negroes; would buy any
thing they would steal and bring to him; that he believed Cotton had stolen John Slater's negroes, in connexion with Boyd—(afterward ascertained Boyd had
stolen them).

This disclosure, and other evidence of his bad char-

acter being generally known, led to his arrest on the
1st of July. But Saunders having left town, and no
evidence being offered at his examination sufficient to
justify the citizens in detaining him, he was by their
order discharged.* Immediately after his dismission he
returned to the house of his father-in-law, whither he
had removed with his family a *few days* prior to the
discovery of the insurrection. Saunders, in the meantime, was making off, as he said, for Texas. He informed a gentleman on his way to Vicksburg, that a
discovery of a conspiracy of negroes was made in Madison county, and disclosed to him all their plans, as
subsequently developed, in the course of the investigations of the committee at Livingston, and said that
Cotton *wanted him to join them, but he would not.* He
likewise stated that it was the intention of the conspirators, should *some* one of the *clan* fail to rob one of
the partners of the commission house of Ewing, Mad-
dux, & Co., who was then on his way from New-Orleans to Livingston, to rob their house at Livingston.
This part of their plan was to be attended to by Cotton
and Blake. The gentleman, believing Saunders to be
one of the conspirators, had him arrested and delivered
into the hands of the Livingston guard, who were in
search of him, and he was brought back to Livingston
on the 2d of July.

On the strength of Saunders's confessions Cotton
was again arrested, and he brought back to Livingston
on the same evening.

Immediately after the organization of the committee,
he was brought before them for trial.

Doctor William Saunders, under oath, confirmed his
statements made before the meeting on the 30th June;

---

* He was not liked by the citizens of Livingston, with whom he
had no social intercourse. In his business transactions he had been
detected in many low tricks, and attempts to swindle. It was in
evidence before the committee, that he had left Memphis, Tennessee
(soon after the conviction of the celebrated Murrell), with a wife and
child, who were *never afterward heard of.* As an evidence of his
want of feeling and affection for his second wife, Saunders stated to
the committee that he, Cotton, had made a proposition to him to
take Cotton's second wife to Red river, in Arkansas, and there leave
her, with the promise that Cotton would meet her as soon as he
should settle his affairs in this country; at the same time informing
Saunders that his object was to abandon her.

and that Cotton, and Boyd (who was supposed to be
Cotton's brother), and some others, had been extensively engaged in negro-stealing; and that Cotton had
contracted to purchase from a gentleman in the neighbourhood of Livingston a number of Spanish horses,
but that he never completed the purchase; but always
claimed them as his, and turned them loose in the
country, as a pretext for hunting them, that he might
have opportunities to converse with the negroes, and,
by that means, seduce them from their allegiance to
their owners, by instilling rebellious notions among
them; and to form plans, and to make converts to his
propositions, which he could not do by being a steam-
doctor.

It was in evidence before the committee, in confirma-
tion of Saunders's statement, that he was repeatedly
seen skulking around the plantations in the neighbourhoods of Livingston, Vernon, and Beatie's Bluff: if asked
what he was doing, his answer was, "hunting horses."

A boy, after the execution of the negroes at Beatie's
Bluff, was arrested in that neighbourhood on suspicion
of being connected with the conspirators; although not
knowing what the negroes had confessed, he acknowledged he knew something about the contemplated insurrection, and that he obtained his information from a
white man in the neighbourhood of Beatie's Bluff. One
day, while hunting horses in a prairie, the man, he said,
told him he was hunting horses likewise, and soon began
to question him respecting his master; if he was a bad
man? whether they, the negroes, were whipped much?
and asked how he would like to be free? and told him
his plan for liberating the negroes, &c. (as will be seen
hereafter, as developed in the course of the trial); said
he *took* a drink of brandy with him, and made him *drink
first;* he said he lived in Livingston, and that he must
come and see him, and then he would tell him when the
insurrection was to commence; he said he did not know
his name, but thought he would know him if he could
see him. This conversation took place about the last
of May. The negro was brought to Livingston, ten
miles from his home, on the morning of the 3d of July,
for the purpose of finding out who the man was he had
conversed with, if he should be in custody. Cotton, at
the time the negro man was brought in town, was in

custody, but not chained. The negro man was introduced into a room where some six or seven men were
chained, and requested to point him out; he looked at
them all, and said the man was not among them; Cotton then being in the crowd, the company were requested to form a circle, in order that he might see all
in the room. When he saw Cotton, he boldly pointed
him out, and exclaimed, "That is the man who talked
with me in the prairie." Cotton looked thunderstruck,
and came near fainting on hearing the annunciation of
the boy. The boy made the same statement to the
committee in the presence of Cotton, which he did not
deny.

The statement at length of Saunders, to the gentlemen previously noticed, was in evidence before the
committee. That there was to have been an insurrection of the negroes on the night of the fourth of July,
and that certain white men intended to head them.
Cotton was considered one of the chief men, in connexion with Ruel Blake; and that operations were to be
commenced first at Beatie's Bluff; and that Cotton intended to remain at Livingston, to attend to that place,
and to secure the arms, ammunition, and money in both
places, and then commence the work of murder, pillage,
and fire; and from thence they were to go to Vernon,
rob that town, and murder its inhabitants, and so on to
Clinton and Jackson—arms being deposited at or near
the Old Agency for their use in taking the latter place,
robbing the bank, &c. Such were the declarations of
Saunders before his arrest, which he neither could nor
did deny before the committee on the third of July, but
confirmed them by saying Cotton told him all when
he requested him to join the clan; which statement of
Saunders was made in the presence of Cotton.

On the 4th of July the confessions of the negroes
hung at Beatie's Bluff were in evidence before the committee, as it was seen in the preceding report of the
proceedings at Beatie's Bluff. Cotton was said to be
one of the ringleaders in exciting them to insurrection.

After having much other corroborating testimony,
the committee had Cotton removed from the committee-room, in order that they might deliberate on his
case.

Immediately after leaving the room, he exclaimed to

L 21

the guard, " It's all over with me !" All I wish is, that
the committee will have me decently buried, and not
suffer me to hang long after I am dead. " Great God !"
was the exclamation of the by-standers—" Cotton, you
do not know that you will be convicted ?" He replied,
despondingly, " that the testimony was so strong against
him that they must convict him—that they *could* not
avoid it." Some said, " He must be a very guilty man
to condemn himself; and, if he was guilty, he had
better tell the truth; that it would be some atone-
ment for his guilt to tell them who were his accomplices," there being a number of white men in custody at the time, in Livingston and elsewhere in the
county. Cotton replied to their request by saying, " If
the committee would pledge themselves not to have
him hung immediately, he would come out and tell them
all he knew about the conspiracy." The request of
Cotton was communicated to the committee, who in
answer said, through their chairman, " That they would
not pledge themselves to extend any favour to him
whatever; that they were satisfied as to his guilt, and
that he might confess or not." In answer to the reply
of the committee, Cotton sent word to them, " If they
would hear what he had to say, he would make a confession ;" and accordingly he made the following confession, which he signed and swore to.

Cotton's Confession.

I acknowledge my guilt, and I was one of the principal men in bringing about the conspiracy. I am one
of the Murrell clan, a member of what we called the
grand council. I counselled with them twice; once
near Columbus, this spring,* and another time on an
island in the Mississippi river. Our object in undertaking to excite the negroes to rebellion, was not for the
purpose of liberating them, but for plunder. I was trying to carry into effect the plan of Murrell as laid down
in Stewart's pamphlet.† Blake's boy, Peter, had his
duty assigned him, which was, to let such negroes into
the secret as he could trust, generally the most daring
scoundrels; the negroes on most all the large planta-

* He was absent from Livingston about three weeks in March;
no person ever knew where he went to.
† See ante, p. 53—60.

tions knew of it; and, from the exposure of our plans in said pamphlet, we expected the citizens would be on their guard at the time mentioned, being the 25th of December next; and we determined to take them by surprise, and try it on the night of the 4th of July, and it would have been tried to-night (and perhaps may yet), but for the detection of our plans.

All the names I now recollect who are deeply concerned, are Andrew Boyd, Albe Dean, William Saunders, two Rawsons, of Hinds county, who have a list of all the names of the men belonging to the Murrell clan in this state, being about one hundred and fifty; and the names of all who are connected with me in this conspiracy, being fifty-one. John and William Earl, near Vicksburg, in Warren county, Ruel Blake, of Madison county. I have heard Blake say he would make his negroes help, and he was equal in command with me. Lunsford Barnes, of this county; James Leach, near Woodville, Wilkinson county; Thomas Anderson, below Clinton, in Hinds county; John Rogers, near Benton, Yazoo county; Lee Smith, of Hinds county, and John Ivy, in Vernon.* There are arms and ammunition deposited in Hinds county, near Raymond.

July 4, 1835.   JOSHUA COTTON.

The committee, after receiving his confession, condemned him to be hanged in an hour after sentence, in order that the news of his execution might be circulated extensively before night, thinking it would frighten his accomplices from the undertaking.

After his condemnation, he made publicly some additional disclosures, which unfortunately were not re-

---

* This man, whose name has been associated with so much villany, and so often mentioned in the preceding work, was implicated by Cotton as an accomplice of his in the late contemplated insurrection of the negroes in Madison, was in the neighbourhood of Livingston at the time of the discovery of the conspiracy. Having been released, as will be seen in the disclosures of the Earles, by their perjury, he was seen in a swamp near Livingston by a gentleman, who communicated the information to the citizens then assembled in Livingston, where they soon started him with track-dogs, and pursued him until it became so dark that the dogs could not be followed any longer; in the morning they resumed the chase; but, unfortunately, he escaped from the dogs by getting on to a horse he found in the woods, and has never been heard of since; having left a large family dependant upon charity for subsistence.

2

duced to writing. Under the gallows he acknowledged his guilt, and the justness of his sentence, and remarked, "it was nothing more than he deserved;" and likewise invoked the vengeance of his God, if every word he had written was not true; and said that all those he had implicated were as actively engaged in the conspiracy as he was. And, lastly, in answer to some person who asked him "if he really thought there would be any danger that night?" he said "he did, if they should not hear he was hung." His last words were, "Take care of yourselves to-night and to-morrow night;" and swung off.

Trial, &c., of William Saunders.

This man was a native of Sumner county, Tenn.; he emigrated to this state last fall, and commenced overseeing in Madison county, near Livingston, but did not remain at it long: his deportment was such as to induce his employer to discharge him. After his discharge, becoming acquainted with Cotton, he joined him in the practice as a steam-doctor, in Hinds county. His conduct in Hinds attracted the notice of the gentleman with whom he boarded; he would often be out all night, and never could give satisfactory explanations for so doing; always giving some equivocal answer. The gentleman afterward ascertained that while at his house, and without any reasons therefor, he was often seen not only in remote parts of Hinds, but also in Madison and Yazoo counties. While in Hinds his conduct was of such equivocal character that the gentleman with whom he boarded ordered him to leave his house; and his reasons for so doing were explained to the committee, which went to show that Saunders was a fit instrument for such an enterprise. After his departure from Hinds, he was seen lurking about in the neighbourhood of Livingston, where he was on the 30th of June. From his intimacy with Cotton, and his character being none of the best in the estimation of the citizens of Livingston, they were induced to take him up, and see if he could give any account of himself. At the meeting, as has been seen, he made some disclosures, and was discharged. By divulging his knowledge of the conspiracy, as previously noticed in Cotton's trial, he was arrested and brought back to Livingston, where, on the 3d of July, he was put on trial before the committee.

The close connexion existing between this man and Cotton, rendered it necessary to examine witnesses in the presence of both ; and, in most all cases, the evidence applied to each.

In addition to the above circumstances, it was in evidence before the committee that he had been a convict in the penitentiary of Tennessee for stealing ; likewise abundant proof of his general bad character was in evidence before the committee, which it is unnecessary to notice, as his own confessions went to confirm it.

Albe Dean, under oath, said Saunders was one of the promoters of the insurrection.

The confessions of the negroes hung at Beatie's Bluff were before the committee, in which his name was mentioned by all four of the negroes, in connexion with Cotton's, in the manner as set forth in the preceding report of the proceedings at Beatie's Bluff, not knowing what each had confessed, &c. The committee were satisfied, from his intimacy with Cotton, that he must have been one of the *clan*. It was a question with the committee how he could be cognizant of the plans of the conspirators without being one of them. He said, Cotton had informed him of the conspiracy and his intentions when he requested him to join the clan ; and that, when Cotton made the proposition to him, he positively refused, and attempted to dissuade Cotton from the attempt ; and henceforth determined to cease all intercourse with Cotton, which determination he had adhered to. It was proved satisfactorily to the committee, that Saunders was on very intimate terms with Cotton, and that they were seen in secret together in Livingston but a few days before the developments at Beatie's Bluff. Saunders was asked why he did not reveal what he knew of the conspiracy when first arrested ! He made no satisfactory excuse for refusing.

In addition to the facts and circumstances in proof against Saunders before his conviction, Cotton stated that no one was privy to the designs of the conspirators but such as had consented fully to engage in them ; that Saunders had so consented, and was fully possessed of all their plans and designs, and had consented to co-operate with them.

Saunders, like all others, when conscious of guilt,

and desirous of preserving their lives by making disclosures, and fearful that by making them his life
would not be preserved, exclaimed, " Were I to disclose
all I know respecting the conspiracy, I would be shot
down in ten minutes after entering Livingston" (about
the time he was entering Livingston) ; leaving it to
the speculations of his hearers whether his fears were
of the citizens or of the spies of the *clan* who surrounded him.

There was other evidence before the committee of a
similar kind to the foregoing, together with concur-
rent circumstances.

The majority of the committee were of opinion that
Saunders was guilty, though they had not passed sentence on him, nor did they till Cotton came out and
confessed his own guilt, disclosing the name of Saunders as one of his accomplices, and a chief actor in
bringing about the conspiracy; which disclosure was
made to the committee in the presence of Saunders;
whereupon the committee, by a unanimous vote, found
him guilty, and sentenced him to be hanged; and, in
pursuance of the sentence, he was executed on the 4th,
with Cotton.

Thus, after all his treachery, he fell a victim to his
crimes.

Trial of Albe Dean.

This man was a native of Ashford, Connecticut,
whence he emigrated to Mississippi two years since.
His general character before the disclosure of the
conspiracy was not good; he was considered a lazy,
indolent man, having very few *pretensions* to honesty.
He had previously resided in the neighbourhood of
Livingston, where he pretended to make a living by
constructing washing-machines, until he became acquainted with Cotton, when he abandoned his business
and turned steam-doctor, and went into partnership
with Cotton, Saunders, & Co., and settled in Hinds
county. He was known to associate with negroes,
and would often come to the owners of runaways
and intercede with their masters to save them from a
whipping. It was in evidence before the committee
that he was seen prowling about the plantations in the
neighbourhoods of Vernon, Beatie's Bluff, and Living-

ston, ostensibly for the purpose of inquiring for runaway horses, which he did with great particularity—
sometimes inquiring for a black, bay, gray, or other
colour that suggested itself at the time. It was evident that horse-hunting was not his business, but that
he was reconnoitring the country, and seeking opportunities to converse with the negroes. He acknowledged that he was in the swamp near Livingston when
the notorious Boyd was *started* by the dogs. (See note
on page 243.)

Dean was arrested at the instigation of Saunders,
who said he was a great rascal, and one of the conspirators. He was brought to Livingston with Saunders, on the 2d of July. On Monday, the 6th of July,
he was placed on trial before the committee; but was
in presence of the committee during the trial of Saunders and Cotton, and heard the whole of the testimony
which went to implicate him. It was in evidence before the committee, that, when on his way to Livingston, he had asked a witness, among other things, if
some of Mr. W. P. Perkin's negroes were not engaged
in the conspiracy; and particularly if Hudnold's Ned (a
noted villain, whom he, Dean, had often endeavoured to
screen from a whipping) was not concerned. He also
inquired if Mr. Wm. Johnson's, Ruel Blake's, and some
other gentlemen's negroes were not accused. He
was not aware, at the time, that the very negroes about
whom his inquiries were made had not only been suspected, but some of them actually hung; and, when informed Blake's negro had been hung, he asked if he had
made any disclosures about him. He was identified as
one of their white accomplices by *negroes* accused.

And, lastly, he was accused by Dr. Cotton, who
said, "Dean was one of his accomplices, and deeply engaged in the conspiracy, as a member of the
Murrell *clan*." After a cool and deliberate investigation
of his case, he was, by a unanimous vote of the committee, found guilty of aiding and exciting the negroes
to insurrection, and sentenced to be hanged.

In pursuance of the sentence, he was executed on
the 8th of July, with Donovan, and died in dogged
silence, neither acknowledging his guilt nor asserting
his innocence.

This man requested that his name should not be

given to the public, as his father was a public man, and it might lacerate the feelings of a venerated mother, who still survived. This request the committee and the writer would have scrupulously regarded, but that the name of this unfortunate man had already been made public by the *officious* and *gratuitous* information of some of the letter-writers, who have already given his name to the public.

Trial of A. L. Donovan, of Maysville, Ken.

After the trial of Dean, this young man was brought before the committee for examination, having been arrested on the evening of the 2d July, at Beatie's Bluff. His deportment, some weeks previous to his arrest, was very suspicious, from his intimacy with the negroes in the neighbourhood, being suspected at the time of trading with them, &c. His behaviour was so reprehensible as to compel the gentleman with whom he boarded to tell him, if he did not change his course he must leave his house, which he did a few days after, and went to the house of a man by the name of Moss, reputed a great scoundrel, whose name is mentioned in the report of the proceedings at Beatie's Bluff: there Donovan remained until his arrest. Donovan's conduct was so very extraordinary and suspicious after he commenced boarding with Moss, as to induce the citizens of the neighbourhood to watch his movements. He was repeatedly found in the negro cabins, enjoying himself in negro society. Some persons *requested* him to leave the place, but he refused, alleging as a reason that he had to take care of some old keel-boats (which were entirely useless), half sunk, in Big Black river.

After the plot of the conspirators was discovered, instead of using his exertions to ferret out the ringleaders, and to assist the citizens in their efforts of detection, he would be found sneaking about the negro quarters, seeking opportunities to converse with them ; and was caught at the house where the discovery of the conspiracy was made, engaged in earnest conversation with the girls who divulged the plot.

After arrests were made and examinations were going on, his conduct was such as no honest man would pursue ; he would introduce himself into any company of gentlemen he would see conversing; this in itself at

the time, was not noticed, as every one was desirous
of finding out something to direct him in his investigations; but he would then go off and engage in conversation with Moss and his sons-in-law, who he knew,
from their character, were suspected of being engaged
in promoting the insurrection.

Even after several negroes were taken on suspicion,
he still persisted in his attempts to converse with them,
and at one time actually undertook (while the citizens
were examining one) to release a negro who was tied,
which negro afterward implicated him. He was requested by the gentlemen who were examining the
negroes not to come about them; they were compelled
to take this step, from the fact that, when he was present, the negroes *would say nothing*, for the experiment
was frequently tried; but when they were apprized that
Donovan was not present, their disclosures were full,
complete, and corresponding ; the experiment was tried
several times with the same success.

When he found he could not be permitted to be present at the examination of the negroes, he evinced considerable uneasiness, and kept walking to and fro, in
view of the negroes under examination.   The cause of
his anxiety and alarm was soon explained; after his
removal the negroes commenced a full detail and ex-
pose of the whole conspiracy (being at the time one or
two hundred yards apart, and examined one at a time).

Among other white associates implicated by them,
Donovan was said to be one of their leaders, and deeply
concerned with them in the conspiracy.

After being implicated by a number of negroes at
Beatie's Bluff, the citizens thought proper to arrest him
and bring him to Livingston, where the committee then
organized was in session.

He was put on trial before the committee on the 7th
July, and, in addition to the testimony before adduced,
the following evidence was brought forward, which
proved his participation in the conspiracy :—

A negro man from Beatie's Bluff stated that Donovan
was one of the white men engaged in persuading him
to rebel with the rest, on the 4th of July, and that he
had often solicited him to join them; Donovan said
nothing was easier than for them to get their freedom;
that the negroes could kill all the white people; and, if

they should be pushed, that he would take them to a free state.

The confession of another negro man was in evidence before the committee, who pointed Donovan out at the time of the negro's examination, and said, "HE was to be one of their captains at Beatie's Bluff." It was also in evidence before the committee, that another boy, just before his execution, pointed Donovan out, when in a crowd, and said HE was one of the men who persuaded him to enter into the conspiracy, and had encouraged him to go on, and get as many negroes to join as possible: other negroes implicated him.

A young man of unimpeachable character testified to the committee, in the presence of Donovan, that he and Donovan were walking through the field of his employer about the 25th or 26th May, when Donovan remarked to him that he should hate to be an overseer very much. Witness asked him why? He answered, it was such cruel work to be whipping the *poor negroes*, as he was obliged to do. Witness told him he never whipped only when they deserved it, and that was not often. Donovan exclaimed—"My friend, you will not have use for this long," at the same time putting his hand on witness's whip. Witness was a little astonished, and asked him to explain himself. Donovan, by way of explanation, remarked, the reason why he would not have use for it long was, that the negroes would soon be all free in this state. Witness replied, he knew the owners were not going to set them free, and that he (Donovan) ought to know that they could not effect their liberty by force, as they had tried it two or three times, and always failed; and that he thought they were now contented to remain in slavery. Donovan replied warmly, in answer to his remarks, "*that they could obtain their liberty by force, and that they would do it, not by themselves, but with the aid of thousands of rich, smart white men, who were ready to head them, with money, arms, and ammunition for their use.*" And, before leaving the plantation, requested permission of witness to converse with the negroes, and to inform them of their rights, &c. Of course, after the expression of such sentiments as above set forth, his request was denied, and at the same time he received a little good advice, and a *threat* from witness that, if he was seen on the plantation again, he might expect a "*benefit*" from his negro whip; and, using witness's remark, Donovan cut out, and he had not seen him since until before the committee on his trial.

The committee were satisfied, from the evidence before them, that Donovan was an emissary of those deluded fanatics at the north—the ABOLITIONISTS. And, that while disseminating his incendiary doctrines among the negroes to create rebellion, he had found out that he was anticipated by a band of cut-throats and robbers, who were engaged in the same work, not wishing to liberate negroes, but to use them as instruments to assist them in *plunder*. Being of a dissolute and abandoned character, as will be seen by his wife's letter to him,* and ripe for every rash enterprise, he joined the

——"   * MAYSVILLE, 24th August, 1834.

MY DEAR ANGUS:—I once more take up my pen to inform you I received your letter of the 18th; you say you have not heard from me since you left here—for what reason I cannot tell—I have answered every letter since you left this place. You say you have little hopes of receiving an answer to this. Do you think that woman's heart is so hard, or that she could forget the one she once loved? No, she could not. Your conduct has grieved me more than you have any idea of, or I think you would not have done so. I feel thankful to hear that you have come to a full determination to break off from all bad habits, and to study yourself and try to become a useful member of society; this I have long prayed for; I hope now my prayer is answered in some degree. O, my dear Angus, pray to God that he may change your heart, and give you grace to put those good resolutions into practice. I cannot consent to come there and live until I am fully convinced that you will not return to your former ways, which I think time will prove. If you study geography and grammar (which I think will be the best thing you can do), Mr. Barnes will transfer his school to you. Then I shall have no objection to coming there to live; in the meantime, I shall expect you to lay up something to commence housekeeping with, for I fear you have not done it yet, though you have had a year to do it in, and I not received a cent from you since you left here; and now, before I close this letter, let me earnestly entreat you to be on your guard, and never give way to those evils you have so fully determined to forsake; for it is a great consolation for me to think of seeing you again, and once more enjoying your company. I have not said any thing concerning my health; I still have a weakness in my back and breast, which I fear I shall never get over; Mr. Gibson and family are well; your father's family are well also; I might say a good deal more, for there are a great many changes taken place since you left here, but I defer for the present. I want you to write often; and I subscribe myself yours, affectionately,

MARY A. S. DONOVAN.

ANGUS L. DONOVAN.

conspirators with the hope of receiving part of the spoils.
If there had been any doubt on the minds of the committee as to his connexion with the conspirators, he
would at least have been sentenced to be hanged for his
attempts at diffusing among the negroes rebellious notions.   On the 7th he was condemned to be hanged.

Accordingly, at twelve o'clock on the 8th of July he
offered up his life on the gallows, as an expiation for his
crimes.   He said, from the gallows, that the committee
did their duty in condemning him; that from the evidence they were compelled to do so.

Thus died an ABOLITIONIST, and let his blood be on the
heads of those who sent him here.

Trial of Ruel Blake.

After the trial and execution of Donovan and Dean,
the committee were engaged in the trials of some suspected individuals, who were all discharged; no evidence appearing against them to prove their connexion
with the conspiracy, until the arrival of Blake in Livingston.   Blake had resided in Madison county some
two or three years.   Although he had so long lived
among them, he could claim but few or none as friends.
He was of a cold, phlegmatic temperament, with a for-
bidding countenance; kept himself almost aloof from
white society, but was often seen among negroes.   His
character, as known to the citizens, was one of the darkest die.   He was noted for cold-blooded revenge, insatia-
ble avarice, and unnatural cruelty; had been detected in
several attempts to swindle his fellow-citizens, who,
if they exposed his rascality, were ever after the objects
of his deadly hatred.

From his own account, he had been a seafaring man
in his youth, having commenced at it when in Connecticut, his native state; and, from vague hints he would
occasionally drop, it was the general impression that
he had been a pirate.   He worked at his trade of gin-
wright, which he had learned after coming to this
county, up to the time of the discovery of the contemplated insurrection of the negroes in Madison, when he
had opportunities of becoming acquainted with the negroes on most of the large plantations in Madison; and
was, at the time of the discovery of the conspiracy,

working in the neighbourhood of Livingston. His old negro was implicated by Mr. Johnson's negro, as has been seen in the preceding part of this work, and taken up by the committee of examination of Livingston. Blake being in Livingston at the time, the committee requested him to examine his own negro. It will be recollected that this negro had refused to divulge any thing, and persisted in it. The committee, believing him to be guilty, requested Blake to whip him, and *make* him tell what he knew about the conspiracy.

Blake informed his negro, before he commenced whipping, what it was for, and *requested* him to tell all he knew about it. The boy refused, and Blake commenced whipping him, but in such a manner as to convince every one present that he did not wish to hurt him, occasionally striking a hard lick to keep up appearances. The citizens found that Blake would never get any thing out of him; believing his presence acted as a restraint on the boy, they politely requested Blake to withdraw from where his boy was, and let them try him. Blake withdrew a short distance, and kept walking to and fro, each turn getting closer to his boy, until the boy commenced talking, when he could stand it no longer, and rushed through the crowd to where his negro was, and swore, if he was touched another lick, they would have to whip him first. The gentleman who was whipping the negro drew his whip to strike Blake, and a rencounter ensued, which resulted in a knock down or so. The by-standers, from the best of motives, and to prevent more serious consequences, which would most certainly have resulted had they not got Blake away, dragged him off and told him to "run," or the gentleman he had grossly insulted "would kill him if he should see him." Blake, taking the hint, put off at full speed through Livingston; and, to frighten him, the boys, *et cetera*, raised a hue and cry, and ran him a few hundred yards.

Blake being a slave-holder, no one at that time supposed, or had the most distant idea, that he was connected with the conspiracy, but attributed his conduct to sympathy for his negro; and, in the confusion of the moment, the remark of Blake's negro was forgotten, or not viewed in the light it afterward was. It will be recollected the negro said, " Gentlemen, if you are whipping me to make me tell *what my master told me*, you may whip on till I die, for I promised him I never would tell:" and he never did.

After the developments at Beatie's Bluff, the citizens began to reflect about Blake's extraordinary conduct, and became satisfied something *more* than sympathy for his negro had influenced him to act as he had done on the 30th of June, when steps were immediately taken to arrest him, he having left Madison county on the morning of the 1st July, at the request of Capt. Thomas Hudnold, for whom he was at work, who, out of the kindest motives for Blake, and the gentleman he had insulted, provided Blake with a horse and money to go away on, and instructed him to stay away until the excitement should subside; Blake promising him, when he returned, to make the necessary apologies. It must be recollected that he was provided with the horse and money before it was *known* or *suspected* any white men were engaged in the conspiracy.

Blake, in the meantime, went from Livingston to Vicksburg, and thence to Natchez, where he remained a few days, and returned to Vicksburg, where he was passing himself off as an Indiana boatman at the time he was taken—five hundred dollars reward having been offered for him.

He arrived in Livingston on the 8th of July, under a strong escort, intimations being obtained that an attempt would be made by the *clan* to rescue him.

His appearance in Livingston created a most alarming excitement; and, but for the committee's being in session, in all probability he would have been forcibly taken from the guard, and immediately executed. After arriving, he was immediately put on his trial before the committee, when the following evidence was adduced in connexion with the above circumstances:—

It was in evidence before the committee that he had engaged his own negroes to rebel on the night of the 4th of July, and that he had promised to assist them. In corroboration of the above, his own negroes testified that he told them there was to be an insurrection of the negroes on the night of the 4th of July.

The confessions of the negroes hung at Beatie's Bluff were in evidence before the committee, all of whom, and in manner as set forth in the report of the proceedings at Beatie's Bluff, implicated him; likewise testimony of negroes from the bluff was in evidence.

The confession of Dr. Cotton was in evidence before the committee, who swore, it will be recollected, that Blake was deeply concerned, and one of the chief men in the conspiracy; and that he had heard Blake say he would assist his own *negroes* on the night of the 4th of July, &c.; which statement was confirmed as above by Blake's own negroes. Every disclosure which was made was replete with testimony against him.

After hearing all the evidence, every opportunity was given him to produce counteracting testimony, which he failed to do. There being no doubt on the minds of the committee, he was, by a unanimous vote, condemned to be hanged. He appeared to be conscious that he would be hanged; and, just before leaving the committee-room, he requested the committee to give him time to settle his affairs.

On the 10th of July, in the presence of an immense concourse of people, he was executed. He privately commended the verdict of the committee, and said they could not have done otherwise than condemn him from the evidence before them, and publicly, under the gallows, made the same declaration.

He protested in his innocence to the last, and said that his life was sworn away.

Trial of Lee Smith.

This man was a resident of Hinds county, originally from Tennessee. His character previous to his arrest had been reputed good. He was said, by Cotton, to be one of his accomplices in the conspiracy.

It was in evidence before the committee, that at the time the guard was approaching the house where he was, he manifested a disposition to get at his gun, which was in the yard near him, he being engaged at the time in cleaning another. He was told, if he attempted to defend himself he would be shot down. He was so alarmed as to faint; he had pistols and some guns, and a large quantity of ammunition; he asked if he was charged by Cotton as being connected with the conspiracy. This arrest was made before he could have been apprized of Cotton's confession, it not being known out of Livingston at that time (6th of July).

He was asked if he was acquainted with Cotton, and answered that he had seen him but twice—which was false, for it was proved satisfactorily that he was intimate with Cotton, and that he was one of the firm of Cotton, Saunders, & Co., in the steam practice. From the multiplicity of evidence introduced to establish his good character, and the circumstances in addition to the confession of Cotton not being sufficiently strong, the committee thought they could not punish him, but determined on *requesting* him to leave the state in as short a time as was convenient; which request he has complied with. After his discharge he was taken by some of the citizens of Hinds county (where he lived) and Lynched.

Trial of William Benson.

This man was a native of New-York, from the neighbourhood of Albany. He worked as a day-labourer in Madison. Had been working for Ruel Blake. After Blake's flight he remained in the neighbourhood till Cotton was hanged, when he made an attempt to escape from the county, but was taken by the guard, and brought to Livingston and tried.

His name was mentioned by negroes in some disclosures made at Vernon.

On his trial no other evidence was adduced in addition to the above, with the exception of the testimony of R. Blake's negro man, who said Benson asked him if it was not a hard case for the negroes to remain in slavery; and said that they ought to be free, which they might easily be, there being at least twenty negroes to one white man; and with *sticks* alone they might whip the whites.

These remarks were made in the presence of Ruel Blake, who said nothing against his talking in that manner.

He was considered by the committee a great fool, little above an idiot, and it was thought that the best way to dispose of him would be to *order* him off; which order he complied with.

Trial of Lunsford Barnes.

This young man was accused by Dr. Cotton of being an accomplice of his in the conspiracy. His character was always considered good, ever since he had lived in Madison county; was reputed to be a good, honest, hard-working boy; was very ignorant and uneducated. He was often seen in company with Cotton and Saunders, and others who were represented by Cotton to be of the Murrell clan. It was in evidence before the committee that he was very intimate with Cotton, and had agreed to go to Texas with him to sell stolen negroes. Other evidence was before the committee which did not add any thing to his good character. The committee, considering his youth, and not being fully satisfied that he was guilty, ordered him to leave the county, which he has done.

Trial of William and John Earle.

These two men were brought from Warren county to Madison, by several respectable citizens of that county, on the 18th of July. It will be recollected that their names were given by Cotton in his confession as his accomplices in the late conspiracy.

The citizens of Warren being apprized of the confession of Cotton, and believing the Earles to be rascals, from their course in relation to Boyd, who they afterward acknowledged had been released from the custody of the law by their swearing to lies, and proving an *alibi* before the examining court, determined to bring them to Livingston and have them tried. On their arrival in town they were placed in confinement to await their trial. The committee were not in session at the time of their arrival; and, before they met, William Earle, without any fear or compulsion, made the following disclosure before a justice of the peace:—

"My brother John told me there was going to be a rising of the negroes; and Boyd said to me, about the 12th of June, We can live without work; that there was to be a rising of the negroes on the 4th of July, and Cotton and Saunders were to be captains; that he was to go to Natchez with his company. Boyd and Saunders told me the same one day, and said that men by the names of Lofton and Donley were engaging negroes to enter into the conspiracy. Boyd wanted me to gather as many negroes as I could, and meet him near the Big Black. Samuels, William Donley, and Lofton, said George Rawsin would join them; Lofton was to be captain in the Yazoo swamp. All of us were sworn to stick to our own company; Lofton administered the oath, and took it himself. We all calculated to take Madison county ; and by that time we expected to have force to visit the large plantations in the river counties, and, by the time we arrived at Natchez, we could take any place. We held out the idea to the negroes that they should be free ; but we intended they should work *for us.* Spies were to go ahead on all occasions. My brother John and Boyd were riding about three weeks, trying to get out as many negroes as they could. Brother and I were summoned on Boyd's trial before the examining court, to prove his character, &c. ; we were sworn to stick to our party ; we thought Boyd would have sworn the same for us that we did for him ; we swore to lies."

He gave the *sign* of the party, &c.

After making this disclosure he was remanded to custody, and that night committed suicide, by hanging himself to the round of a ladder which was in the room, with his handkerchief.

When his brother John heard of the death of William Earle, he evinced great delight, and said he was glad he had hung himself; that his brother had made *him* a rascal, and, if both had been released, he thought William would certainly have killed him for something he had divulged.

On the 18th July John Earle was brought before the committee for examination, when he made the following disclosure on oath:—

" I have known Andrew Boyd since last fall. Mrs. Boyd told me that Boyd was a bad man ; that he stole negroes and gave them free papers. Lofton first told me about the insurrection of the negroes, and that they were to *rise* on the 4th of July. I heard of the 'Domestic Lodge' in March last from Lofton, who showed me the sign of the lodge, and *wanted* me to join it. I knew *Dr. Wm. Saunders, Albe Dean, Dr. Cotton, A. Boyd, Ruel Blake, Scrugs,* near Old Agency, and *John McKnight,* all of whom were members of the 'Domestic Lodge,' and were engaged in the conspiracy ; they were to have arms and ammunition at the Old Agency in Hinds county, in Yazoo Swamp, near Vernon, and at Baton Rouge, La."

He was asked why he did not tell that? Answered that he was afraid he would be killed by the clan, because they had threatened his life if he divulged any thing.

The arms they intended distributing among the negroes, and Boyd and Lofton told him the insurrection was to commence in Madison county, and so on to Natchez, &c.

"My brother, I think, belonged to the 'Domestic Lodge,' because he told me he would shoot me or any one else who would divulge any thing, or come after Boyd, who was then suspected of having stolen Slater's negroes. My brother told me to keep my mouth shut about Boyd and Lofton, and not to keep company with Wm. Slater, who lost five negroes Boyd had stolen from him; Lofton told me that Cotton told him, that men of influence would join in the conspiracy; Jas. S. Ewing was the man Boyd was to rob on his way from New-Orleans;* Boyd wanted me to join them; Lofton and Boyd informed me some of Capt. Hudnold's negroes intended joining them, &c.; William Donley, who lived in Yazoo, is one of the clan."

He had made a disclosure voluntarily, before his brother William made any; for which he was afraid his brother would kill him if they were released.

After hearing all the testimony in his case, a great deal of which is not shown, the committee came to the conclusion he was *guilty*, but would take no further steps in relation to him until they could hear from Warren. A copy of his disclosures, and the proceedings in his case, were forwarded to the gentlemen who brought the Earles to Madison. In a few days a guard was sent from the "Committee of Safety" at Vicksburg, requesting the committee of Livingston to deliver him into their hands, which request was complied with.

With this case the committee adjourned sine die.

———

EXECUTIVE DEPARTMENT, *Jackson, July* 8, 1835.

GENTLEMEN :—I regret extremely that, in consequence of my absence, you were not furnished the arms desired by you for the protection of the citizens of Madison

* Told so by Cotton.

county.   It is true that the arms had been distributed among the people of this vicinity, who, like yourselves, were much alarmed from the apprehension of a general insurrection among the slaves, against which nothing but the vigilance of the people can protect us.   But if, in your opinion, the insurrectionary movements are not sufficiently quelled to secure the safety of the people of your county, I will cause a portion of the arms at this place to be forwarded to you, and, if required, you will please send for them.   I have employed the bearer of this communication to carry it directly to you.

Gentlemen: with a sincere hope that by your vigilance you may be enabled to protect yourselves against all danger from a deep-laid conspiracy for the destruction of yourselves and families,

I am, very respectfully, your obedient servant,

H. G. RUNNELS.

Messrs. M. D. Mitchell, Chairman, James Grafton, John Simmons, W. Wade, Sack P. Gee, Israel Spencer, Thos. Hudnold, Charles Smith, Jesse Mabry, Robt. Hodge, H. D. Runnels, and Nelson L. Taylor.

⁎ The letter to the governor eliciting the above cannot be found.

———

Livingston, July 9, 1835.

To his Excellency H. G. RUNNELS :—

SIR,—We have the honour of acknowledging the receipt of your excellency's letter, by the hand of Samuel Thornhill, Esq.; in reply to which we would observe, that on the return of our messenger from Jackson, we despatched another to Vicksburg, for the purpose of procuring arms for defending ourselves, which we so much stood in need of; should we be unsuccessful in *this*, we shall without delay send for those you have the goodness to offer.   In the investigation of all the cases that have come before us, we have found that deep-laid plans have been prepared for the destruction of the whites, and the overthrow of all our liberties.   Having full confidence in your patriotism, we shall, sir, ever look to you as the source of aid and counsel, with the pledge for ourselves and country

that we will never forsake her in the hour of danger, nor permit her rights to be infringed by a lawless club.
We have the honour to be,
Sir, your excellency's ob'dt serv'ts.
[Signed by the committee.]
H. W. ROYCE, *Secretary.*

Beatie's Bluff, 7th July, 1835.
To DR. MITCHELL and the members of the committee at Livingston.

GENTLEMEN :—I am not anxious to spread unnecessary alarm, but would suggest to your body the propriety of making such arrangements as to have all of the roads strictly guarded; for, from all the discoveries that we are able to make, we have spies upon our proceedings every night, and you should name to the people the propriety of guarding the roads in every direction by two or three discreet persons in a company, to proceed in the most private manner possible.
Respectfully yours, and your acts are mine, in every sense of the word,
HERVEY LATHAM.
We all concur in the above :—W. M. Riley, Wm. E. Haruld, J. L. Pennington, A. Legget, D. D. Lavidfair, J. H. Grember, Samuel A. Matthews, Samuel K. Sorsby, Jas. Lee, Wm. T. Graves, S. A. Ratliff, Wm. Hester, Hugh Somers, Henry Amsden, jr., Keightley Saunders.

I hereby certify that the manuscript of Alonzo Phelps, which I have in my possession, to the amount of between sixty and seventy pages, contains a statement of a plan for exciting an insurrection among the slaves of the south. He mentions, in his rude and coarse phraseology, his inclination to break forth from the prison in which he was confined, for the purpose of bringing about an insurrection among the slaves. He discusses the expediency of the measure very freely; but finally relinquishes the project, from considerations of humanity. He, in another portion of the manuscript, acknowledges having a large number of associates, whose names he cautiously concealed from the public, and

from me likewise. These facts, connected with the circumstance of his being recorded in Stewart's pamphlet as one of the Murrell clan, induce me to feel additional confidence in the developments made by Stewart. The manuscript of Phelps is in my possession, subject to be examined by the curious. I refrained from the publication of that part of the manuscript alluded to, solely on account of my believing it dangerous to publish it.   H. S. FOOT.
    April 15th, 1836.

GAMBLERS AT VICKSBURG

THE following history of the proceedings of the citizens of Vicksburg, in hanging five professional gamblers, on the 6th day of July, 1835, is given for the satisfaction of those who may wish to be correctly informed on that subject. It will be seen that the difficulty with the gamblers at that place was unconnected
with the insurrection, except the high state of excitement that pervaded the whole southern country at that
time, which had led the citizens to deal more rigorously with all offenders; and more especially those
of an abandoned and dissolute character, as all professional gamblers are. The exigency of the times had
determined the citizens of Vicksburg to purge their
city of all suspicious persons who might endanger the
public safety; and deeming the den of vipers that had
for many years infested the city under the vile yet
plausible appellation of sporting gentlemen, highly
dangerous to the welfare of the city at so critical a
time; believing them fit subjects for the rashest enterprise that might present itself, as they are a class of
beings wholly disconnected with all the social ties of
society and the better principles of man—wholly un-
restrained by any moral compunction, from the perpe-
tration of any act that their avarice or revenge might
suggest, the citizens resolved that all professional

gamblers should leave the city; and they were the
more determined to put their resolve into execution,
inasmuch as the revengeful spirit of the whole fraternity was imbittered against them and the place, as
will be seen from the following history of that extraordinary occurrence, as reported by the citizens and
those who were eyewitnesses of the circumstances.

"Our city has for some days past been the theatre
of the most novel and startling scenes that we have
ever witnessed. While we regret that the necessity
for such scenes should have existed, we are proud
of the public spirit and indignation against offenders
displayed by the citizens, and congratulate them on
having at length banished a class of individuals, whose
shameless vices and daring outrages have long poisoned
the springs of morality, and interrupted the relations of
society. For years past, professional gamblers, destitute of all sense of moral obligation—unconnected with
society by any of its ordinary ties, and intent only on
the gratification of their avarice—have made Vicksburg
their place of rendezvous—and, in the very bosom of
our society, boldly plotted their vile and lawless machinations. Here, as everywhere else, the laws of the
country were found wholly ineffectual for the punishment of these individuals; and, imboldened by impunity, their numbers and their crimes have daily continued
to multiply. Every species of transgression followed
in their train. They supported a large number of tip-
pling-houses, to which they would decoy the youthful
and unsuspecting, and, after stripping them of their pos-
sessions, send them forth into the world the ready and
desperate instruments of vice. Our streets were ever
resounding with the echoes of their drunken and ob-
scene mirth, and no citizen was secure from their villany. Frequently, in armed bodies, they have disturbed
the good order of public assemblages, insulted our citizens, and defied our civil authorities. Thus had they
continued to grow bolder in their wickedness, and more
formidable in their numbers, until Saturday, the 4th of
July (inst.), when our citizens had assembled together,
with the corps of Vicksburg volunteers, at a barbecue,

to celebrate the day by the usual festivities. After dinner, and during the delivery of the toasts, one of the officers attempted to enforce order and silence at the table, when one of these gamblers, whose name is Cabler, who had impudently thrust himself into the company, insulted the officer, and struck one of the citizens. Indignation immediately rose high, and it was only by the interference of the commandant that he was saved from instant punishment. He was, however, permitted to retire, and the company dispersed. The military corps proceeded to the public square of the city, and were there engaged in their exercises, when information was received that Cabler was coming up, armed, and resolved to kill one of the volunteers, who had been most active in expelling him from the table. Knowing his desperate character, two of the corps instantly stepped forward and arrested him. A loaded pistol and a large knife and dagger were found upon his person, all of which he had procured since he separated from the company. To liberate him would have been to devote several of the most respectable members of the company to his vengeance, and to proceed against him at law would have been mere mockery, inasmuch as, not having had the opportunity of consummating his design, no adequate punishment could be inflicted on him. Consequently, it was determined to take him into the woods and *Lynch* him—which is a mode of punishment provided for such as become obnoxious in a manner which the law cannot reach. He was immediately carried out under a guard, attended by a crowd of respectable citizens—tied to a tree—punished with stripes—tarred and feathered, and ordered to leave the city in forty-eight hours. In the meantime, one of his comrades, the Lucifer of his gang, had been endeavouring to rally and arm his confederates for the purpose of rescuing him—which, however, he failed to accomplish.

"Having thus aggravated the whole band of these desperadoes, and feeling no security against their vengeance, the citizens met at night in the courthouse, in a large number, and there passed the following resolutions :—

" *Resolved*, That a notice be given to all professional gamblers, that the citizens of Vicksburg are *resolved* to

M   23

exclude them from this place and its vicinity; and that twenty-four hours' notice be given them to leave the place.

" *Resolved*, That all persons permitting faro-dealing in their houses, be also notified that they will be prosecuted therefor.

" *Resolved*, That one hundred copies of the foregoing resolutions be printed and stuck up at the corners of the streets—and that this publication be deemed notice.

" On Sunday morning, one of these notices was posted at the corners of each square of the city. During that day (the 5th) a majority of the gang, terrified by the threats of the citizens, dispersed in different directions, without making any opposition. It was sincerely hoped that the remainder would follow their example, and thus prevent a bloody termination of the strife which had commenced. On the morning of the 6th, the military corps, followed by a file of several hundred citizens, marched to each suspected house, and sending in an examining committee, dragged out every faro-table and other gambling apparatus that could be found. At length they approached a house which was occupied by one of the most profligate of the gang, whose name was North, and in which it was understood that a garrison of armed men had been stationed. All hoped that these wretches would be intimidated by the superior numbers of their assailants, and surrender themselves at discretion, rather than attempt a desperate defence. The house being surrounded, the back door was burst open, when four or five shots were fired from the interior, one of which instantly killed Dr. Hugh S. Bodley, a citizen universally beloved and respected. The interior was so dark that the villains could not be seen; but several of the citizens, guided by the flash of their guns, returned their fire. A yell from one of the party announced that one of the shots had been effectual, and by this time a crowd of citizens, their indignation overcoming all other feelings,—burst open every door of the building, and dragged into the light those who had not been wounded.

" North, the ringleader, who had contrived this desperate plot, could not be found in the building, but was apprehended by a citizen, while attempting, in company with another, to make his escape at a place not far distant. Himself, with the rest of the prisoners, was then conducted in silence to the scaffold. One of them, not having been in the building before it was attacked, nor appearing to be concerned with the rest, except that he was the brother of one of them, was liberated. The remaining number of five, among whom was the individual who had been shot, but who still lived, were immediately executed in presence of the assembled multitude. All sympathy for the wretches was completely merged in detestation and horror of their crime. The whole procession then returned to the city, collected all the faro-tables into a pile, and burnt them. This being done, a troop of horsemen set out for a neighbouring house, the residence of J. Hord, the individual who had attempted to organize a force on the first day of this disturbance for the rescue of Cabler, who had since been threatening to fire the city. He had, however, made his escape on that day, and the next morning crossed the Big Black, at Baldwin's Ferry, in a state of indescribable consternation. We lament his escape, as his whole course of life for the last three years has exhibited the most shameless profligacy, and been a continual series of transgressions against the laws of God and man.

"The names of the individuals who perished were as follow: North, Hullams, Dutch Bill, Smith, and Mc-Call.

"Their bodies were cut down on the morning after execution, and buried in a ditch.

"It is not expected that this act will pass without censure from those who had not an opportunity of knowing and feeling the dire necessity out of which it originated. The laws, however severe in their provision, have never been sufficient to correct a vice which must be established by positive proof, and cannot, like others, be shown from circumstantial testimony. It is practised, too, by individuals, whose whole study is to violate the law in such a manner as to evade its punishment, and who never are in want of secret confederates to swear them out of their difficulties, whose oaths cannot be impeached for any specific cause. We had borne with their enormities until to suffer them any longer would not only have proved us to be destitute of every manly sentiment, but would also have implicated us in the guilt of accessaries to their crimes. Society may be compared to the elements, which, although 'order is their first law,' can sometimes be purified only by a storm. Whatever, therefore, sickly sensibility or mawkish philanthropy may say against the course pursued by us, we hope that our citizens will not relax the code of punishment which they have enacted against this infamous and baleful class of society—and we invite Natchez, Jackson, Columbus, Warrenton, and all our sister towns throughout the state, in the name of our insulted laws, of offended virtue, and of slaughtered innocence, to aid us in exterminating this deep-rooted vice from our land. The revolution has been conducted here by the most respectable citizens, heads of families, members of all classes, professions, and pursuits. None have been heard to utter a syllable of censure against either the act or the manner in which it was performed.

"An Anti-Gambling Society has been formed, the members of which have pledged their lives, fortunes, and sacred honours for the suppression of gambling, and the punishment and expulsion of gamblers."

Startling as the above may seem to foreigners, it will ever reflect honour on the insulted citizens of Vicksburg, among those who best know how to appreciate the motives by which they were actuated. Their city now stands redeemed and ventilated from all the vices and influence of gambling and assignation houses ; two of the greatest curses that ever corrupted the morals of any community.

PUBLIC SENTIMENT.

Clinton, Miss., July 31*st*, 1835.

At a large and respectable meeting of the citizens of Clinton, Miss., called for the purpose of taking into consideration the laudable and adventurous conduct of Virgil A. Stewart, in the capture of the celebrated land pirate, John A. Murrell, of Tennessee ; J. B. Morgan was called to the chair, and E. D. Fenner appointed secretary.

The object of the meeting having been explained from the chair, on motion, a committee was appointed to draught a preamble and resolutions suited to the occasion ; and the following gentlemen nominated, viz., H. S. Foote, Thos. Harney, and G. W. Thatcher.

After retiring for a short time, the committee returned and reported the following preamble and resolutions, which were unanimously adopted, viz. :—

Whereas the citizens of Clinton have understood that Mr. Virgil A. Stewart has just arrived in this town, and are desirous of manifesting that respect for him which they consider him to deserve, by reason of his having been instrumental in bringing to condign punishment the notorious villain John A. Murrell, and

Whereas it is understood that the said Stewart positively declines receiving any pecuniary compensation for the services performed by him in bringing to light the most bloody plot ever designed against the lives and fortunes of any community ; therefore,

Be it resolved, That Mr. Stewart be invited to a public dinner, to be given him in this place at such time as he may designate, as a testimonial of the high respect of this people for his disinterested, patriotic, and perilous enterprise, undertaken, not for his own benefit, but for the general good.   It was furthermore

Resolved, That William M. Rives and E. D. Fenner be appointed a committee to present Mr. Stewart a copy
23*

of these resolutions, and request his compliance with the first resolution.

Resolved, That Mr. L. Lindsey, G. W. Thatcher, and T. Parsons, be appointed a committee of arrangements, to raise a subscription, provide for the dinner, &c.

Resolved, That the proceedings of this meeting be signed by the chairman and secretary, and published in the newspapers of this county.

J. B. MORGAN, *Chairman.*

E. D. FENNER, *Secretary.*

Clinton, August 1st, 1835.

To VIRGIL A. STEWART.

DEAR SIR,—The undersigned have been appointed a committee, in behalf of the citizens of Clinton, to present you a copy of a preamble and resolutions recently adopted at a public meeting convened in this place, and request that you will designate some day when it will suit your convenience to meet our fellow-citizens at the festive board. With earnest wishes for your safety and happiness,

We remain yours, respectfully,

E. D. FENNER,
WM. RIVES.

Clinton, August 1st, 1835.

To Messrs. E. D. FENNER and WM. M. RIVES.

GENTLEMEN,—I herewith acknowledge the receipt of your polite invitation on the part of the citizens of Clinton. I am sorry that my business is such that I cannot designate a day when I can meet them at the festive board. I must therefore beg leave to decline the invitation, and assure the citizens of Clinton that I could not receive a richer reward for my services than the confidence and respect of my fellow-citizens.

In conclusion, I beg leave to express my high respect for your citizens, and my gratitude for the distinguished attentions shown me since my arrival in your city.

With high respect,

I am your friend and servant,

VIRGIL A. STEWART.

Canton, Miss., August 5th, 1835.

MR. VIRGIL A. STEWART :—

DEAR SIR,—At a meeting of the citizens of Canton, held this evening at the courthouse, S. D. Livingston, Esq., was appointed chairman, and Colonel Henry Phillips secretary; whereupon the following preamble and resolutions were unanimously adopted :—

Whereas Mr. Virgil A. Stewart has lately arrived in town—a gentleman who has recently placed the people of the southern and western states under great obligations to him. by his disclosure and detection of an infamous conspiracy, formed by an extensive and desperate banditti, directed against the fortunes and lives of our fellow-citizens—a conspiracy which, for its deliberate and extensive organization, and the important and destructive consequences attendant upon its ultimate aim, is perhaps unprecedented in the annals of crime ;—and whereas, believing that we can no better exhibit a sense of our obligations to Mr. Stewart than by extending to him the hospitalities of our town in a public manner—therefore,

Resolved, That Mr. Stewart be invited to partake of a public dinner to-morrow, at 1 o'clock, P. M., at the house of W. H. Bole, Esq., of this town.

Resolved, That T. J. Catching, T. C. Tupper, D. M. Fulton, C. I. Starr, Henry Phillips, S. D. Livingston, and Thomas Collins, be a committee to communicate the above invitation to Mr. Stewart, request his acceptance of the same, and make such other arrangements for the occasion as they may deem necessary.

We therefore beg you to accept the above testimonial of the gratitude of our fellow-citizens, and assurances of the high esteem of,

Dear sir, your obedient servants,
THOMAS J. CATCHING,
DAVID M. FULTON,
SAMUEL D. LIVINGSTON,
THOMAS COLLINS, Jr.,
CHARLES I. STARR,
HENRY PHILLIPS,
T. C. TUPPER.

New-Orleans, August 21st, 1835.

Mr. Virgil A. Stewart :—

Sir,—The " Louisiana Native American Association," a patriotic institution lately organized in this state, being apprehensive that your noble and unprecedented exertions for the welfare and happiness of your species are likely to prove abortive, by the almost total disappearance of your pamphlet in relation to the great western conspiracy, not a single copy being procurable in this city; and said association believing, further, that your pamphlet has been surreptitiously obtained by the secret emissaries of said conspiracy, in order to be effaced from public consideration and destroyed, they are desirous of reprinting an edition of one thousand copies, to be distributed throughout the State of Louisiana. Said association has therefore authorized me as their official agent, to address you, and to solicit your permission to reprint said pamphlet in this city at their expense, and to inquire of you on what conditions you will waive your copyright, so as to enable them to accomplish this important act, and, at the same time, to promote your laudable and patriotic intentions.

Entertaining, as the " Louisiana Native American Association" does, the most exalted estimate of your philanthropy, magnanimity, and disinterestedness, they trust you will not deny them this request.

An immediate reply will be received by said association as a special favour, in addition to the great obligations which they have already received at your hands, in common with the entire American family.

With personal considerations of the highest esteem and admiration, I remain, sir,

Your most obedient servant,
JAMES S. McFARLANE,
Corresponding Secretary of the Louisiana Native American Association.

———

Manchester, Miss., Sept. 8th, 1835.

To Mr. James S. McFarlane, *Corresponding Secretary of the Louisiana Native American Association, at New-Orleans.*

Dear Sir,—I have just received your complimentary and polite communication on the part of the honourable body you represent. Your association requests permission to publish one thousand copies of the "Western Land Pirate," for the benefit of your state. You have my entire approbation to publish five thousand copies, which I hope you will do as soon as possible.

In conclusion, I beg leave to express my gratitude and respect for the good opinion and friendship of your honourable association.

With high respect, I am
Your friend and servant,
VIRGIL A. STEWART.

THE END.

JUL 7 '76	DATE DUE		
FEB 9 '77			
FEB 8 '78			